D0921618

PROBLEMS AND
PERSPECTIVES IN ETHICS

PROBLEMS AND PERSPECTIVES IN ETHICS

by Thomas M. Garrett, S.J.

Associate Professor of Philosophy,
University of Scranton

SHEED AND WARD: NEW YORK

In Memory of My Mother
Who Never Needed the Help of Philosophers

ACKNOWLEDGMENTS

Like every book, this one owes a great deal to those people who challenged my ideas and forced me to rethink various aspects of my theory. In particular, I owe a debt to D. G. Fitzpatrick and Vincent Burns of Fairfield University, to Donald Wolf and John L. Thomas of the Cambridge Center for Social Studies, and to Robert Springer of Woodstock College. Though they may see the fruit of some of their suggestions, they will also realize that I have felt free to disagree with them on several important points. In one way or another, the book is different because of their comments.

Mrs. Gladys Sperber and Mrs. Evelyn Evanko labored valiantly over rough manuscript that often looked like a road map of the moon. In addition, they showed me many places in the manuscript where my powers of communication were more than usually feeble.

Finally, I wish to thank all the publishers mentioned in footnotes who have kindly granted their permission to use copyright materials.

CONTENTS

A PREFACE TO BE READ CAREFULLY   xiii

1/ THE TANGLE OF ETHICS   1
*Introduction—What Is Ethics?—Ethical Scepti-
cism—Ethics, Science, and Communication—
Taking a Stand—Ethical Systems—Some Alternative Positions—Basic Issues*

2/ MAN AND HIS KNOWLEDGE   15
*Introduction—Man in General—The Individ-
ual Human Being—The Paradoxes of Man—
Theological Concept of Man—Creature and
Creator—Matter and Spirit—Death and Immortality—Time and Eternity—Unique Individuals and the Common Human Nature—I
and We—Man's Knowledge—Ethical Judgments—Ethical Judgment and the Whole Man
—Relations with Other Systems—The Work To
Be Done*

3/ THE GOOD   41
*Introduction—The Problem—The Word Good
—The Functional Meaning of the Good—
Insights from Aristotle—Hierarchy or Relative
Position of Ends—Christian Influence—Intui-*

ix

*tion or Proof—The Means—Obstacles to
Knowledge of the Good—Some Conclusions
and Implications—Relationship to Other Theories—The Work To Be Done*

4/CHOICE AND DISCRIMINATION   61
*Introduction—Difficulties—The Problem of Re-
sponsibility—Some Necessary Refinements—
Other Factors—A Preliminary Summary—The
Hierarchy of Goods—The Necessary and the
Useful—Urgency of Needs—The Ethical and
the Unethical—The Ethical Good—Negative
Analysis of Acts—Relations to Other Systems
—The Task Ahead*

5/OBLIGATION AND FREEDOM   86
*Introduction—The Problem—Hypothetical Ob-
ligation and Objective Necessity—Absolute
Obligation and Objective Necessity—Defini-
tions—General Obligations—The Greater Good
—Use of Freedom and Creativity in the Ethical
Life—Obligation and Freedom—Implications
and Summary—Relation to Natural Law The-
ories—Relations to Other Systems—By Way of
Summary*

6/RIGHTS AND THE ETHICS OF POWER   106
*Introduction—The Existence of Natural Rights
—Types of Natural Rights—The Limits of
Rights—Problems of Application—Cultural
Factors—A Right to Equality—Rights and
Power—The Ethics of Defense—Power and the
Promotion of Rights—Power and Belief—Is
Power Ethically Neutral?—By Way of Con-
clusion*

7/ETHICS, INTELLECT, AND FREEDOM
OF CONSCIENCE   130
*Introduction—Childhood Training—Growth
and Ethics—Affectivity—The Control of Affec-*

tivity—By Way of Summary—The Adult and the Community—Enlarging Ethical Categories —The Need for Information—Is It Better To Be Ignorant?—Ignorance and Personal Responsibility—When in Doubt—Taking a Stand —Preparation for Ethical Knowledge—The Rights of Conscience—By Way of Summary

8/LOVE AND INTERPERSONAL RELATIONSHIPS   157
Introduction—Sartre: The Other as Enemy— Love and Love—Mutuality—Loving and Liking—Forms of Benevolence—Growth in Love —Benevolent Love and Interpersonal Relations —Selfishness and Love of Self—Paradox of Love—Is Man Obliged to Love Benevolently?— Love and the Ideal

9/THE EXPRESSION OF LOVE   180
The Problem—Emotion and the Expression of Love—Growth in Emotional Maturity—The Need for Understanding—The Problem of Love and Justice—Expression by Omission—Involvement in Evil—The Compartmentalized Conscience—Some Limits—Tactics and Pitfalls— The Subtlety of Love—Priorities in Loving

10/THE BODY AND LIFE IN TIME   200
Introduction—Method—The Value of Life— Suicide—Summary—The Lives of Others— Self-Defense—Capital Punishment—Remarks on War—Health and the Preservation of Life— By Way of Summary

11/THE DIMENSIONS AND MEANING OF SEX   222
Introduction—Methods and Limits—The Biological Dimension—The Personal and Interpersonal Dimensions—Marriage—The Promiscuous—Other Sexual Practices—The Social Dimension of Sex—Are There Exceptions?— Obligations of Society—The Religious Values

12/SOCIETY IN GENERAL   244
    Introduction—Need for the Group—Types of
    Groups—Needs and Purposes—The Common
    Good—Authority—The Limits of Authority—
    The Location of Authority—Multiple Sources
    of Authority—The Relationships of Societies—
    Authority and Unity—The Giant Task of Ethics

INDEX   **265**

A PREFACE TO BE READ CAREFULLY

This book cannot be understood without reference to its history and the particular purposes of the author. The preface, then, is not a formality but a part of the book which should be read.

Problems and Perspectives in Ethics is the result of my efforts to solve four sets of problems. The first set of problems involved the detection and criticism of my own implicit assumptions in teaching ethics. The second set grew out of my efforts to answer questions which my students had, as opposed to the ones I thought they should have. This meant answering the questions of people who wanted to evolve a personal ethic, rather than to study philosophy for its own sake. The third set of problems arose from the need to provide a workable framework for my writing and consulting work with businessmen and doctors. Finally, my counseling work with both students and adults presented me with yet another set of problems. In particular it made me see the necessity of developing an ethical theory which could be brought to bear on the growth problems of individuals.

In the process of teaching, writing, consulting, and counseling I became aware that many of my own assumptions were questionable from a purely philosophic point of view. In some cases these assumptions were theologically sound, but philosophically no more than reasonable. In other cases the assumptions involved questions of fact, and I discovered that the facts had changed. Unfortunately there are probably other questionable assumptions which I have not as yet detected. Hence many of my conclusions are put forth tentatively, as starting points rather than as finished products.

The questions of students, many of whom had no background in philosophy, were particularly challenging. They showed me that mere technical analysis could not answer the questions of those who were in the process of forming their ideals in a world where there were few fixed points. Above all, students made me see that ethics involved the commitment of the person, and not merely an intellectual assent. Because the young know that ethics involves their lives, they want more than a disinterested and scholarly catalogue of opinions with appropriate critical comments. For these reasons I have avoided many technical points, and have attempted at times to give the feel of a topic rather than a technical analysis.

My dealings with businessmen and professional groups convinced me that ethics will pay its way in the real world only if theory comes to grips with the facts that people experience. The effort to grapple with problems which were real, complex, and often new has forced me to modify theory. Frequently the experience of real problems has led me to the conclusion that at this stage no one really knows the answer. In short, the real world, as well as the questioning of my own assumptions, has caused me to be tentative where others seem more sure of themselves.

My counseling work made me see that many ethical problems arose from the fact that even adults had not made an effort to think out their ideals. I discovered that younger people were often confused about the nature of love and its expression, and in fact about the place of emotion in human life. As a result they often found themselves confused and unable to make decisions. For this reason I have tried to raise questions about these difficult areas even when I cannot answer them adequately.

The overall impact of my effort to face the four sets of problems has been the writing of a very limited book. It does not attempt to cover the entire field of general ethics. It does not try to solve all problems or summarize all opinions. The book aims to make the reader aware of some of the basic problems involved in developing a personal ethics. While it does supply one method of analysis, I do not pretend that this is the only method of analyzing ethical problems. The readings at the end of the chapters are, indeed, intended to introduce the reader to other approaches even though these may not agree with my own. Moreover, the questions at the end of each chapter are intended to challenge the reader to do his own thinking. For the most part, these questions are not answered in the text.

Undoubtedly this book is not academic enough for the professional, nor practical enough for the man of action. I am sure that some will attack me for moral scepticism, while others will criticize my tendency to look for quasi-absolutes. Others will not like my emphasis on reason, and some will surely object to the importance I assign to emotion and its control. Such criticisms will not discourage me. On the contrary, they will be proof that the book is, in some feeble way, grappling with the real world.

Although this book is an attempt to grapple with the real world, it is only one man's approach to reality. As a matter of fact, it hardly communicates even my own flawed vision of what is. At best it is an invitation to the reader to open his eyes and to engage in personal reflection. Since each human being has a unique vision of the world, the reader should not expect to agree with everything I say. If he does, he is not thinking and using his own experience to supplement and supplant my ideas of the way things are and ought to be.

One final note may help to eliminate some misunderstanding. This is a book in ethics. It is not moral theology. Indeed, I have made every effort to keep it from becoming a sort of disguised moral theology. At the same time, being a religious man, I accept the value of the work done by theologians. I believe, however, that the effort to develop a philosophic ethic is important. If nothing else, the philosophic effort shows us the need for a theology. Often the philosophic ethic raises new problems for the theologian and thus spurs on his work. Often, too, the purely philosophic ethic can help the theologian in his effort to obtain a deeper knowledge of the world around him.

1/ THE TANGLE OF ETHICS

Morality, ethics and law are frequent subjects of conversation even among those who know little about them. For this reason, if for no other, the words are often used vaguely and even interchangeably. At the very start, then, it is necessary to assign some precise meaning to these key terms which will be used constantly throughout this book. A mere definition of terms, however, will not set the stage for what follows. Ethics is an emotional term. It is associated with limits, values, and the inner life of man, so that its use has deep personal resonances. We must face this fact and look at some of the attitudes which can block an understanding not only of definitions but of the process of ethical reasoning itself. Only in this way can we lay the groundwork for some of the basic commitments which are involved in the study of ethics and of man himself.

WHAT IS ETHICS?

The word ethics has almost as many meanings as it has users. For some it is identified with what people of a given culture think is right and wrong. In this sense it is a descriptive part of sociology concerned with morals as understood in a given culture. Others

1

take ethics as an almost purely theoretical science which examines the notions of the good, right, and obligation. In this sense it is almost a branch of metaphysics. For yet others, ethics is a sort of accepted etiquette in a given area of life, a code of good behavior, but without any ultimate basis in reality. In this sense there is an ethics even among thieves of a certain caliber. At the other extreme, ethics is identified with the moral teaching of the great religions. There are even cynical definitions which identify the ethical with what society will let you get away with. There are simplified approaches which identify ethics with the golden rule or with the injunction to take what you can from life.

Sometimes ethics is called moral philosophy or the science of morals. These are valid statements but subject to misunderstanding. The word moral and its opposite, immoral, are all too often identified with questions of sex or with the mores or code of a given society. In order to avoid confusion I prefer to use the term ethics, though it, too, is somewhat ambiguous.

Ethics is concerned in all the things mentioned above, but it is not identical with any of them. It is the *science* of the goodness and evil of human actions and human institutions insofar as this can be ascertained by reason. It is also the *art* of living one's life so as to realize in oneself and one's society the values discovered by the science. It is concerned with what people think is good or evil insofar as this can supply valuable clues. On the other hand, it does not accept even widespread opinion as an ultimate norm or measure, but sets out to test opinions both by analysis and by experience gathered from a large number of auxiliary sciences such as psychology and sociology.

Ethics is also involved in the theoretical definition of the good, rights, and obligations, since these have vast practical consequences. Indeed, these concepts are the principal concern of general ethics. The notions, however, are not developed for their own sake but for use in solving concrete problems in everyday life. Ethics, then, is vitally concerned with what is and with what ought to be, and not merely with a few abstractions. If the principles cannot be applied to the life of the individual, to his relations with others and with the society of which he is a part, they are useless for real ethics.

The practical orientation of ethics has led to the development of various fields of applied ethics. There are specialists in medical ethics, business ethics, political ethics, social ethics, and a dozen other fields. These experts are concerned with developing methods of applying general principles to particularly complex situations where a man needs to know both ethics and one or more specialized arts or sciences. For this reason, if for no other, ethics involves more than the simple precepts learned at a mother's knee or the basic values taught in Sunday school.

Because ethics works on the basis of unaided reason, it is distinguished from moral theology and the teachings of the great religions, though it is not necessarily at odds with them. The great religions use not only reason and ordinary human experience but data and precepts which have been divinely revealed. Moral theology, then, enjoys resources which are not available to unaided reason. Ethics is an incomplete science. It cannot pretend to give the final answer to all questions of right or wrong.

Although moral theology and ethics are distinct, they do influence one another in the real world. Directly or indirectly, the thinking and institutions of men in Europe and America have been shaped by both philosophy and the moral theologies of Christianity and Judaism. So far as we can see, theology rather than philosophy initiated ideas such as the dignity of the individual man, yet this concept is certainly of vital importance in several philosophic systems. On the other hand, philosophic notions of nature have influenced the formulation and even the content of some moral theologies. Such mutual borrowings are useful so long as we recognize them as borrowings.

Ethics must be distinguished not only from moral theology but from the law. Law is concerned with the minimum regulation necessary for the public order. Ordinarily and rightfully, law does not pretend to judge the rightness or wrongness of every human act or institution. Law may even tolerate evil lest greater harm come from trying to repress it. Ethics is concerned not only with the minimum public order but with the individual and his intimate relationships with others. Moreover, ethics criticizes law as it does custom and usage in an effort to make sure that legal institutions are in accord with more basic concepts of good and evil.

Everything said thus far points to the difficulty of ethics. Ethics involves a search for the ultimate justification of judgments about good and evil. At the same time it seeks to present the justification in such a way that both men and societies can make practical decisions about concrete situations. At one and the same time ethics must grapple with ultimates and with the complex world we live in. Because ethics looks for ultimates, it must question even received commandments. Because ethics is concerned with a changing and infinitely complicated world of men, its answers are always capable of further refinement. Ethics, then, is dynamic; a scientific quest and not merely a static body of knowledge.

ETHICAL SCEPTICISM

Many modern men will sneer at the idea of a science of good and evil because they do not believe there are any answers to the questions: What is evil? What is good? They ask who is to say what is right or wrong. Strangely enough, their questions are honest even though they are tinged with cynicism. Men want to know what is right and what is wrong even when they despair of an answer. They want to know how to solve their problems in a reasonable way. They want to give a direction to life, because without direction life becomes an agony of uncertainty about all important issues.

The ethical or moral sceptic deserves real sympathy and help, for he is a victim of the world in which he lives as well as of his own personal incapacity. The old ethical and moral landmarks have been wiped away in many areas of human life. The accepted slogans and behavior patterns that once governed existence in a simple society have been found inapplicable to modern days, for they often rested not on reason or revelation, but on a cultural adaptation to a world that no longer exists. In the face of this situation some are tempted to throw out all norms along with outmoded courting customs and family relationships. After all, if the bikini bathing suit does not turn an eye, where once it would have caused a riot, what norms can there be?

In a pluralist society, morals and ethics are debated heatedly in those areas which most involve human passion: sex, power, and property. Even the religious man, left without the support of his community and often without reasoned and reasonable instruction, starts to lean towards those opinions which let him do what he wants to do. Often, sound theological opinions are presented so poorly that religious faith itself is made to look ridiculous. When faith is weak, even the best theological exposition will not convince a man who demands mathematical certitude for moral precepts. Both pluralism and defective religious preaching have helped to cast many adrift on a sea of moral scepticism.

Some few see a return to sound theology as the solution to this problem. Unfortunately, faith is a gift, and it is hard to build a society and its educational system on the basis of a gift which God does not give to everyone at the same time. In addition, even moral theology must operate within some framework of reason and experience if it is to communicate the divine moral revelation to modern men. There is not only room for ethics as a science of reason but a real need for it. If nothing else, ethics may help to build some minimal world of common ethical discourse in which men of different faiths can meet and unite for necessary social action, whether through law or through other social institutions.

In the last analysis, ethical scepticism is due to the personal condition of individuals who have been led to doubt their own reason and their own worth. Some people object to strong opinions on principle. The society which exalts the freedom of the individual can also pressure him to conform in all sorts of unreasonable matters. The old grumble and the young revolt. In any event, there is an emotional anarchy which makes it difficult for the immature to reason on ethical questions. If a man is fearful and resentful and does not know what he is or where he is, he can hardly attack the deepest questions about the nature of right or wrong. He may be brilliant in answering some neutral question in physics or chemistry, but he will have little success in ethics.

Often, indeed, the young say "I think" when they really mean "I feel." What they feel, unfortunately, is frequently a compound of anxiety, desire, myths, and odd facts picked up from some sensational treatment of a serious topic. As a result, you will often find the young holding vigorous and strict opinions in the areas that do not directly affect them, and very lenient opinions in the areas that do. When forced to justify either position, or indeed any position, they are liable to end up with the "I think" reply. The conclusion must be that it is extremely difficult for the young to grapple with moral ideas, since they lack both experience and self-control. As a result idealistic youth, with all its noble aspirations, is the greatest victim of moral despair and scepticism.

ETHICS, SCIENCE, AND COMMUNICATION

The moral scepticism of both young and old is increased by cultural attitudes such as the following: (1) a demand for more certitude than man can have; (2) an exaggerated respect for the certitudes of the physical sciences; (3) a naive idea that the communicability of an idea is the test of its truth.

Although most men live much of their lives on the basis of mere prejudice, unfounded opinion, and low probabilities, they want *absolute certitude* in ethics. A man does not hesitate to marry a wife, buy a house, or choose a profession on the flimsiest basis or on no basis at all, but he hesitates about an ethical principle because he does not have the clear certitude of mathematics. The reason is simple. Ethical principles demand commitment and not merely nominal assent. They involve deep changes in one's life. They impose limits on one's desires and impulses.

In general, the conclusions of ethics are not absolutely certain, although some of its first principles are. They are, however, more certain, or at least more probable, than the whims of children or the so-called common sense of many unthinking adults. Even when a conclusion must be qualified as "the only reasonable position on the basis of our knowledge," it is still better than principles which are only expressions of "I feel." As men, we must do the best we can with what we have, even though we would like more assurance.

Most men would accept limited certitude except for the fact that they believe science offers complete certitude. If we can have real certitude in science, why can't we have it in ethics? There are several answers to this question. In the first place, even the physical sciences do not give absolute certitude. Their conclusions are tentative, ready for revision or even for scrapping. They are useful since they enable us to control reality a little better than we could if we lacked even a reasonable hypothesis based on the available evidence. The social sciences, such as psychology, history, sociology, and economics, are even more tentative when it comes to principles. The reason is clear. They, like ethics, must deal with a part of reality which includes man and the creations of his freedom. The facts of man's freedom and the contingency of practical affairs supply the second reason for the paucity of absolute certitudes in ethics. Because man is free in many areas, all sciences that deal with him are forced to qualify most statements so as to limit both their generality and firmness. For all this, the sciences of man are highly useful, since they at least enable us to reduce the area of doubt and to act on some reasoned basis.

The naive view that the communicability of an idea is a test of its truth is related to the scientific principle that conclusions must be verifiable by others before they can be accepted into the body of scientific knowledge. This is a good working principle, but it should not cause us to overlook several important points. Scientific principles and conclusions are not practically verifiable by everyone, but only by those who have spent years in preparing themselves for the work. The principle of verification indiscriminately applied could force men to disregard areas of reality which they see clearly but cannot put into words. A man knows his inner states but cannot really communicate them to anyone. A genius sees relationships which others will be blind to for hundreds of years. Finally, there are truths that can be communicated to the mature and intelligent but are so much nonsense to others.

This should surprise no one, for language is a feeble instrument when men do not want to listen. People tend to perceive what pleases them and to ignore what is unpleasant. Truths which threaten desires and whims are often rejected. The inability to communicate what you know, however, is no reflection on its truth. Indeed, if the truth is profound and demands commitment, it would be surprising if it were easily grasped by all men.

TAKING A STAND

In view of all this, the student of ethics should realize that he cannot study ethics without taking a stand. He will soon discover that he cannot communicate his own reasoned convictions to others unless they too can be made to take a stand. This should not be surprising, since ethics is a practical science and practical questions demand decisions.

The most basic stand must be taken with regard to the following question: Do I want to run my life on the basis of a consistent set of reasoned principles? If the answer is No, then the reader can put down this book here and now. Everything that follows will only be idle speculation; an interesting, but rather meaningless, analysis. At the same time, the man who wants to answer the basic question negatively should realize the consequences of his reply. A man without a reasoned and consistent approach to life and ethics is the plaything either of emotions or of social pressures. He may find that he has destroyed even the few limited things he values because he has not thought through their relationship to the real world. He may find that he has abandoned the control of his own life, since control is difficult without some frame of reference, no matter how incomplete.

The man who answers Yes should also realize the price he will pay. Reasoned opinions will set him off from many of his contemporaries. They will force him to face the unreasonableness of many drives within him. They will often force him to admit that he has been wrong in theory as well as in practice. An affirmative answer commits a man to hard work which does not yield all the neat certitudes he would like to have. The work is interesting, passionate even, but it is not easy. Finally, the answer Yes involves a commitment to choose between competing ideas of man, the world, and ethical systems.

ETHICAL SYSTEMS

The need to take a stand with regard to ethical systems developed by brilliant men and acknowledged philosophers imposes too great a strain on many people. At this point the weak take refuge in the purely rhetorical question, "Who am I to say?" But we may ask, "Who else is to say?" We cannot allow others to settle our lives and destinies no matter how brilliant they may be. Even God demands that we take a free stand on our own as a condition of salvation. To say nothing is the equivalent of saying a great deal. In the present case it means that life is meaningless or that the search for meaning is useless. It is to abdicate all really significant control over one's life.

Actually, the difficulties of taking a stand have been exaggerated in many instances. The basic issues which separate the systems of ethics often involve matters which are accessible to men of ordinary talent and little experience in formal philosophy. A person does not have to be a genius to decide whether or not pleasure is the sole good. A person who has experienced love can decide whether or not love is a real possibility. Anyone who can read is capable of judging the results of holding that might makes right.

As this book advances we will see that all ethical systems contain some truth and that no ethical system, including our own, is complete. We must sift opinions, take stands, and attempt to develop a personal and workable ethics. The necessity of taking a personal stand and developing a personal approach to ethics involves real problems. At first glance the personal element might seem to destroy the possibility of arriving at some accepted definitions and principles. Honesty forces us to admit that different men will take different stands. However, to the extent that the stand is reasoned and is taken by a man who lives in a group, I believe there will be

considerable convergence, so that common, if not universal, definitions and principles can emerge. This will not happen overnight,
but that is not to be expected of men who live and work in a world
subject to historical and cultural limitation. Furthermore, if the
commitments are humble and open-ended, we can hope that the
movement towards reasoned acceptance of common grounds may
proceed more rapidly than when men had rather narrow viewpoints.

SOME ALTERNATIVE POSITIONS

Although we will be meeting sets of alternatives throughout the
book, a few of the more basic choices should be faced at the very
start.

One of the most basic oppositions exists between the cognitivists
and the non-cognitivists. The cognitivist says that ethical statements tell us something about reality and its value. Ethical
statements are not purely subjective, though generally they do say
something about the speaker's attitude. When I say, "That is a
good horse," I am saying something about the horse and not
merely indicating my approval of the horse.

Although most men are almost spontaneously cognitivists, there
are thinkers who claim that ethical statements are in the final
analysis only descriptions of a subjective state. "That is a good
horse" does not say anything about the horse independent of my
approval. I may be able to give some reasons for my judgment,
such as the fact that the horse has a nice coat, but these reasons
are ultimately only expressions of my subjective state. Thinkers
who hold this position are called, unimaginatively, non-cognitivists.

Among the cognitivists, the biggest split is between the *naturalists* and what may be called *metaphysical transcendentalists*. The
naturalists are split into various groups, but all agree that the
justification and meaning of ethical statements is to be found in
some natural process in the world of time. This is to say that the
meaning of the world and of ethical statements is to be found
completely in the world we know directly. They disagree with the
metaphysical transcendentalists, who insist that the world is a

creature which cannot be explained without a creator. The transcendentalist sees the ultimate justification of ethical statements as possible only in terms of the ultimate meaning of the world, which is found outside the world itself. Ethics, then, must ultimately transcend the world.

Writers in ethics also disagree over the relationship between the world of intentions and the world of consequences. Although most men probably consider both the *why* and the *what* of a man's actions, a writer such as Kant wants an ethics which does not depend on the consequences of actions but only on the intention of the actor. On the other hand, the utilitarians look almost completely to the effects of an action in judging its goodness.

Today one of the most important splits is between those who claim that even in ethics we can make *valid universal statements* about what is good or evil for man, and those followers of *situation ethics* who claim that every situation is unique and that there are only particular judgments valid for the unique situation. The advocate of situation ethics does not generally deny that general statements are useful in a large number of situations. He insists, however, that there are no universal statements. For these thinkers the statement that murder is wrong means that murder is generally wrong; it does not tell me that murder is wrong in each and every situation. The people on either side of this line may be transcendentalists or naturalists, believers in God or atheists. The issue, however, cannot be avoided, for it would be silly to work up a science of universal statements which could not be used in making judgments about particular actions.

While differences about fundamental philosophic issues divide ethical systems, other differences can arise from the purpose of the system. Some writers present a *code ethics* designed to explain the minimum which even the mass of men ought to observe. Others develop an ethics of the ideal, a *wisdom ethics,* suitable only for the elite. Code morality, with its collection of precepts bearing on the minimum, can seem an empty sham to the ethically sensitive. A wisdom ethics, on the other hand, can appear so impossible of realization that few pay it serious attention.

BASIC ISSUES

As we proceed, other options will be presented. At this point, however, it should be noted that the basic issues in ethics are settled by the stand one takes with regard to the nature of man, of human knowledge, and ultimately of all reality. Disputes about whether or not a particular act is good or bad may hinge on the way one sees facts or perceives a given situation, but the differences between systems are based on the positions one accepts in philosophic anthropology, epistemology, and metaphysics. What one accepts in these philosophic disciplines determines what one accepts in ethics to such an extent that much of ethics is an explicitation and application of these basic philosophic positions. Indeed, any real basic disagreement ultimately has to face these issues. You cannot argue with a communist without facing the issue of materialism, nor with an existentialist without talking of natures, nor with a utilitarian without unearthing the underlying question of whether there is knowledge beyond the purely sentient. If these problems are dodged or glossed over, ethics can never have ultimate roots nor any real internal consistency.

It is necessary to take stands on basic issues, but it is also necessary to refuse false options. Because reality and humanity are rich in possibilities, there are few *either-ors*. Most often we face the choice between either, or, or, or. Indeed, many of the errors in philosophy are due to the fact that men ask the wrong question or ask the right question but phrase it badly. There are no right answers to questions which are phrased so as to eliminate the only right answer. For hundreds of years men fought over the problem of universals because they asked whether the universal was inside the mind or outside it. It took the genius of Saint Thomas to see that there was a third possibility: the idea was universal inside the mind as a way of existing, but the content of the idea was outside the mind, though it did not exist there in a universal manner in the concrete.

Since ethics does depend on the stand one takes in philosophic anthropology, epistemology, and metaphysics, it is only fair that the writer should state his own position, so that the reader will be able to decide whether it is worth his while to follow the rest of the author's treatment. This statement of position will be the task of the next chapter. Not everyone may want to agree with the positions presented. They should not, however, be rejected merely because they sound unfamiliar or do not correspond with the reader's present positions. Honesty demands that the position of another should be tested not only against a broad experience but also against the practical consequences of the opposing position. After all, ethics is a science with immense practical consequences.

If men do not have a common human nature, are the racists correct? If man does not have a spiritual side, are the communists in the right? If man is not free, does it make sense to speak of responsibility? If man cannot know any universals, are we lost in a wilderness where might is the only valid criterion of right? In short, a rejection of one position involves the acceptance of another, which ought to be tested for its congruence with reality and its consequences for the position we take in life.

POINTS FOR DISCUSSION

1. Catalogue and analyze the notions of ethics held by both acquaintances and public figures.
2. What are the practical consequences of various notions of ethics?
3. What are the main features of the moral theology taught by various churches?
4. Does "I think" always mean "I feel" in our culture? What is the significance of feeling?
5. What factors besides those listed in the text might lead to ethical scepticism?
6. Even if communicability is not the test of truth in ethics, why is it still important?
7. Discuss the consequences of the various alternate positions presented. Would the definition of ethics itself vary from system to system?

8. What are some of the moral attitudes in your culture or group which should be criticized by ethics?
9. List and discuss some of the false options that are being forced on modern man. For example: socialism versus capitalism; conformity versus nonconformity.
10. Why does one's position in ethics depend on one's epistemology, metaphysics, and philosophic anthropology?

READINGS

On the Nature of Ethics

William K. Frankena, *Ethics* (Englewood Cliffs, N.J.: Prentice-Hall, 1963), pp. 1–10.

Jacques Leclercq, *Christ and the Modern Conscience* (New York: Sheed & Ward, 1962), pp. 39–68.

William Lillie, *An Introduction to Ethics* (New York: Barnes & Noble, University Paperbacks, 1961), pp. 1–19.

On the History of Ethics

Luther J. Brinkley, *Contemporary Ethical Theories* (New York: Philosophical Library, 1961).

Jacques Maritain, *Moral Philosophy* (New York: Scribner's, 1964).

Henry Sidgwick, *Outlines of the History of Ethics* (Boston: Beacon Press, paperback edition, 1960).

William Curtis Swabey, *Ethical Theory from Hobbes to Kant* (New York: The Citadel Press, 1961).

Mary Warnock, *Ethics Since 1900* (London: Oxford University Press, 1960).

Anthologies

W. T. Jones, Frederick Sontag, Morton O. Beckner, and Robert J. Fogelin, *Approaches to Ethics* (New York: McGraw-Hill, 1962).

Religious Ethics

F. Ernest Johnson, *Patterns of Ethics in America Today* (New York: Collier Books, 1962).

2/ MAN
AND HIS KNOWLEDGE

INTRODUCTION

The foregoing chapter took certain implicit stands about man and his knowledge. It assumed that man can know good and evil and that he can rule his life in accord with his knowledge. In saying that man will have to take a stand, the existence of freedom is assumed. These assumptions will not be accepted by everyone. Even those who accept them do so only as part of a more complete idea of the nature of man, both as an individual and as a species. This more complete idea of man is, unfortunately, not perfectly clear. It contains mysterious and problematic elements. This is not surprising, since we are constantly learning more about man and his relation to the world around him.

In the present chapter we want to expand the concept of man which underlies the rest of this book. In particular, we want to point out those elements in the concept which are problematic. Unless the reader appreciates the difficulties in the area of philosophic anthropology, he will not understand the problem of developing ethical theory.

MAN IN GENERAL

The beings who make up what we call the human species exhibit a wide variety of characteristics. The individuals differ in size, shape, color, intelligence, language, culture, and attitude. Some are selfish, pleasure-seeking, power-hungry; others are tender, disciplined, altruistic. Despite these differences, we do form an idea of a species based on common characteristics. This idea is of the utmost importance in ethics. If a special color is part of the idea, we will tend to treat those of another color differently. If a man is a human being only if he is altruistic, we will have to exclude those who are selfish. If a being is a man only when he has shown signs of intelligence, then small children are not men.

In the present book we will not define the species in terms of characteristics such as color, attitude, or actual possession of intelligence. We will call the species the group composed of rational animals and the offspring of rational animals. The definition will apply not only to those who show signs of intelligence but to those who we have reason to believe have a capacity for intelligent human action. In this way we include those who have sprung from human parents even though they may not exhibit direct proof of intelligence. The inclusion of children who have not reached the age of reason is important, since later in this book we will be arguing about the rights even of unborn human beings. If we excluded not only children but lunatics and the seriously retarded, we would be depriving them of rights by the mere fact of definition.

The normal rational animal and the rational animal living in groups also exhibit other characteristics. While not every man is a tool maker, every group of men includes tool makers. While not every human being reproduces sexually, every group includes fathers and mothers. We may say that a man is a tool maker and reproduces sexually even though this statement is only true collectively and not distributively. Statements of this type are important since they indicate the existence of collective universals which appear to be necessary for survival and growth.

In all groups, the normal human being has certain characteristics, even though their definitions of the normal are not identical. The normal person uses speech and conceptualizes his experience. He controls his impulses so that his behavior is relatively predictable. Such a person has ideals and standards which he strives for even though he sometimes fails. The normal person is subject to conflicts, but on the whole he enjoys a relatively high degree of self-respect.[1]

Kluckhohn has pointed out that most groups even agree about certain goals and values.

. . . No society has ever approved suffering as a good thing in itself. As a means to an end (purification or self-discipline), yes; as punishment—as a means to the ends of society, yes. But for itself—no. No culture fails to put a negative valuation upon killing, indiscriminate lying, and stealing within the in-group. There are important variations, to be sure, in the conception of the extent of the in-group and in the limits of toleration of lying and stealing under certain conditions. But the core notion of the desirable and nondesirable is constant across all cultures. Nor need we dispute the universality of the conception that rape or any achievement of sexuality by violent means is disapproved. This is a fact of observation as much as the fact that different materials have different specific gravities.[2]

The statements we can make about normal men and groups of men, even though we cannot make them about each and every individual man, are important. They point to a normal way of living and to some underlying factors which lead men to at least a few common ways of coping with the environment. Almost spontaneously we judge that there is something wrong about the individual who does not follow the general pattern. Such judgments need to be examined carefully. After all, it may not be good for the group if each and every individual reproduces or makes tools.

Subgroups of men may often assume that their way of doing things is characteristic of all men or all groups. Americans, for example, assume that self-interest is a basic human characteristic. The studies of anthropologists and sociologists have made us aware that this is not necessarily so. Different cultures have different patterns of motivation as they have different ways of expressing the tendencies of men in general. Although such facts will make us hesitant about extending our statements concerning men in general, they should not cause us to overlook the standard ways of acting in given cultures. The fact that all people do not raise their children in the same way does not mean that a particular method of child rearing is unimportant. Indeed, the development of some predictability is necessary for social life and survival. As a result, accepted ways of doing things may make claims on individuals even when there is no intrinsic justification for the particular way.

By way of summary the following points should be noted. There are a fairly limited number of universal statements we can make about each and every man. We can, however, make a larger number of statements about normal adults in any culture. These statements are particularly important. A third set of statements apply to all groups of men, even though the statements cannot be made of each and every member of the group. We may also make statements about all normal men or about all groups in a given culture. While these statements are true only for the given culture, they nevertheless supply us with information necessary for determining the relationships of concrete individuals to concrete social situations.

In this book we use all these types of statements, since we are interested in helping men in a particular society. Some of these statements would have to be changed if we considered ethical problems in another culture. On the whole, however, we want to make statements that are valid for all men or most men; no matter what their cultural and social position may be.

THE INDIVIDUAL HUMAN BEING

The individual human being cannot be summed up in a few neat phrases. For the individual, the things that make him different from other men are almost as important as the characteristics he shares with others. The individual is a product not only of a biological process but of his own culture, and especially of his own free choices. Heredity, culture, and choice have either opened up or closed concrete sets of possibilities. Things that are impossible for men in general may be possible for a concrete individual. An Einstein, for example, was capable of much more than the generality of men. At the same time, we must remember that certain individuals may be incapable of activities open to most men. There are those who cannot love deeply—at least not at a given moment in time.

Individual limitations and powers are important in ethics. Men want to know what is good for them as individuals as well as for them as members of the race or a given group. We must admit, however, that the individual is often a mystery even to himself. *What am I?* How do I answer this when at one moment I hate and at another love? Today I am joyful, and tomorrow I am in the deepest gloom. At times my body seems to weigh me down; at other moments it lifts me up. Certainly I am both rational and animal, but it is the shifting balance between the two aspects that puzzles men, and me in particular. Moreover, even if I admit that animal and rational each refer to a set of possibilities, I want to know what these possibilities are in the concrete.

As I grow, I realize that my possibilities change because either the world, myself, or other beings have changed. Sometimes we discover that something was impossible only because we thought it was. There are bright children who do not learn mathematics because they are convinced they cannot. There are adults who never learn to love because they believe no one can love them. Most men seem to have inadequate ideas of their own abilities. We cannot, then, identify ourselves even with a predetermined and completely fixed list of concrete possibilities. I am an open being in process and not subject to complete description.

The conclusions we have based on rather ordinary observation are reinforced when we look at the data of the sciences, which reveal constantly new possibilities for both individuals and the race. The sciences, by freeing us from the idea that many things must be so because they have always been so in our culture, present us with such vast possibilities that we almost hesitate to face them.

The sciences, including philosophy, reinforce our conclusion in yet another way. Conclusions and systems and theories are constantly being overturned because their discoverers and makers tried to identify man with some incomplete scheme of things. The neat world of the Freudian id, ego, and superego had its uses, but we are constantly discovering that more is involved. Monists, dualists, materialists, sensists, voluntarists, nominalists, idealists, and existentialists quarrel among themselves because each wants to make some partial vision of man and the world *the* vision, *the* philosophy of man. They err by making closed statements such as. "Man is *only* matter." The nature of man demands that we always make open statements such as, "Man is at least matter." We must, then, constantly be on guard against making a scrap of truth into a total description of man.

All this does not mean that we can say nothing of man. It means that we must proceed with caution, recognizing the unfolding and even the hidden potentials that enter into man. It means that we must not block our vision of what is or can be by too many hasty statements. It means that we must resist the temptation to simplify man at the cost of truth.

THE PARADOXES OF MAN

Even incomplete catalogues of the possibilities of the species or the individual indicate that man is a paradoxical being. He is composed of aspects which are, in some way, opposed. We are tempted to say that man is an impossible being except for the fact that he does exist. Man is a creature and a creator. He is determined and free. He is individual and social. He is material and spiritual. These oppositions are reflected in his knowing, for he has both sense and intellect. They appear in his tendencies, which are vegetable, animal, and spiritual. Man is located in time and space but seems to transcend it. He is a part of nature yet above it.

In the face of these paradoxes, as in the face of human complexity, the temptation is to simplify and reduce man to manageable proportions. This is self-defeating, since someone will soon discover that we have omitted an essential note and will evolve a new simplification which will in turn generate another reaction. Once again, we must accept man as he is and admit the limitations of our knowledge. What we build on may be beyond our own comprehension, but at least it will be more real than a simplified picture which eliminates some inconvenient side of man.

These paradoxes are of the essence of man, for the tension between the concepts represents the tension in man as he seeks to become himself and to find a unity that is at best only inchoative. The struggles between spirit and matter, between sense and intellect, between individual and society, may be inconvenient and even painful, but they are real and powerful generators of energy. They constantly remind us that man is a creature to be made, a set of possibilities to be realized, and not a nicely sculptured figurine on a mantelpiece. This will remind us that our ethical categories must be big enough to take in what man can be as well as what he may be at a given time. To put it another way, change and growth—or at least the possibility of them—are essential aspects of the human condition. For this reason the vision of an ideal is important, since it has a great influence on the strivings of men to realize their potentials. We are, after all, concerned with what man can be and ought to be, and not merely with what he is at a given instant.

THEOLOGICAL CONCEPT OF MAN

The ideals of men and their concepts of human potential are influenced by theology as well as by philosophy and the positive sciences. The influence must be recognized. Because the writer is a Christian with a theology, as well as a philosopher with his own personal insights, he must acknowledge some of the unavoidable influences of theology on philosophy. If nothing else, theology makes the thinker aware of possibilities which reason alone has not unearthed or perhaps cannot. The Christian believes that man is called to a destiny that transcends purely human possibilities but not the power of God. This knowledge makes him more hesitant about making closed and exclusive philosophic statements. It reinforces his philosophic openmindedness at the same time as it expands his sensitivity to possibilities.

The Christian, too, has a moral theology based on the destiny mentioned above. Revelation tells him that man is called to be perfect as God is perfect. It gives him Jesus Christ as a living model of the way this perfection is to be incarnated in the world of space and time. This ideal is, of course, beyond mere human imagining, but it does provide a concrete outline of the perfection which is possible for the man aided by divine grace. This ideal has a powerful attraction even for those who do not believe in the divinity of Christ. For the believer, it is a part of his being, so that quite unconsciously he sees reality in terms of Christ and what a Christian ought to be.

While we have tried to distinguish what comes from theology and what from philosophy, the attempt has not been completely successful. Though this is a defect from one point of view, it is a virtue from another, for it will mean that the reader will have been exposed to concepts of greater richness, even though they have not been established with full philosophical rigor.

While the influence of a theological image of perfection may be somewhat inconvenient, it is not any more of a hindrance than the culturally transmitted images which plague all thinkers. Unconsciously, men tend to theorize in terms of an image which is seldom made explicit, but lurks behind and beneath their thought. A thinker such as Aristotle made his image fairly clear when he described the high-minded man, but he also exposed some of its weaknesses to those who have another image as their base of operation. As Sidgwick notes, Aristotle's ideal is not like that of the Christian, for in the Aristotelian concept the high-minded man shuns all subordinate positions, is generally candid—though he affects irony with the common herd—but is not given to wonder or praise.[3] In our own society we would object to Aristotle's ideal as being undemocratic and snobbish, but our own purely philosophic image of the ideal type of man may not be any better founded.

The difficulty of formulating and validating an ideal must be faced honestly. Even if we had certitude about all the elements which should go into the ideal, we would still have trouble assigning priorities to various elements. Indeed the priorities would probably have to change with changing circumstances and needs. Kindness, for example, might have to be de-emphasized in time of war and played up in time of famine. The ideal for one group might be unsuitable for another. The artistically sensitive individual might not be able to survive the jungle, but would be a most useful type in a society which, having achieved abundance, still worshipped mere survival values.

If we were asked to list the qualities or values to be included, it would be necessary to compose a very long list. It would certainly include courage, wisdom, moderation, generosity, kindness, justice, and many other commonly accepted values. These qualities or values, however, are abstractions. We recognize the fact that they are fully meaningful only when incorporated in concrete activity. In the concrete, the values may conflict if we view each value as absolute. As a result, the relationship of values becomes very important. How shall we balance justice and kindness in a given situation? What does moderation mean in a situation of great danger?

The necessity of reconciling values or goods in both the abstract and the concrete means that the ideal involves some system of priorities, some system of making choices on a consistent yet flexible basis. Often we make ideals of the types we need to solve pressing problems. This is understandable, but it can be dangerous. The strong man can often prevent anarchy, but he may destroy freedom, intimacy, and love in the process. Again, the ideal may be described and promulgated by those who want certain things for themselves no matter what the cost to others. Thus the image of the docile worker, unable to run his own life, made it easy for early industrialists to exploit man, so long as workers corresponded to the image the owners proposed.

Although we do not believe we can arrive at a definitive philosophic ideal, we will, in the course of the book, discuss some of the elements which go into the ideal. In addition we will attempt to work out some crude method of balancing the elements in the face of a changing world. First, however, we must say something more of the paradoxes of man.

The problem of the ideal cannot be separated from the paradoxes and the tensions which we find in the adult human being. These paradoxes and tensions point to both the limits and the capabilities of the individual. They are at once a sign of the human condition and the cause of man's striving both to form and to realize something that he is not.

CREATURE AND CREATOR

Man is a creature, a made being who comes into existence at a given point of time and then leaves the world of time at the moment of death. He depends on something greater than himself for existence and even leans upon the created world about him for warmth and food and shelter. Saint Augustine spoke of man as being closer to nothing than to something. This, however, is not a purely theological insight, for the existentialist is painfully aware of the nothingness in man even though he may not admit the dependence of man on God. Though men flee the admission of this nothingness and dependence, it is there to haunt them whenever they are quiet for a moment or crash into the hard wall of reality which frustrates their desire.

The frailty and contingency of the world and of man should prevent us from placing the full meaning of life in the world we touch and see and move in. Those who do not believe in God or man's dependence on him may make do with a secular, this-worldly ideal. The present book assumes as established the existence of God, man's dependence on God, and a meaning beyond the limits of time and space.

Man is a dependent creature, but also a creator endowed with freedom. This is the paradox of paradoxes. Within broad limits, man is not chained completely but can impose himself and his will on reality. He need not forever shiver in the cold. He can and does build great cities to ward off the elements. He need not accept the brute fact of nature as an unchangeable datum. He has learned to unleash the secrets of nature and even to change its observed course. Man can impose new meaning on the world around him by rearranging the parts so that they stand in a new relation to his own being. So great is even this limited power of freedom and creativity that man is forever tempted to see himself not as *a* great creator but as *the* free creator.

No matter how great the temptation to exaggerate, man must ultimately admit that though he has freedom to create, this freedom is limited by the world in which he exists, by his own being, and by God, who holds him in existence. This limited freedom, however, must never be overlooked, for it enables man to become many things he is not. It is the instrument of human becoming. Man's freedom may be finite, but man cannot become fully himself—that is, realize his possibilities—without it.

While freedom is one of the values in the ideal, it is not easy to say how much freedom an individual has at a given moment. Culture, temperament, habit, physical condition, all influence a man's freedom. Sometimes they limit it; sometimes they increase it. Each individual's freedom is unique, so his responsibility is also unique. Furthermore, because freedom is subject to growth and decline, the responsibility of the individual may vary from moment to moment.

Cold, heat, the cutting edge of a knife, may change man's physical being or even destroy it. They do not, however, change man to the same degree as what he freely wills. What man wills becomes part of his inner being. Indeed it is in this sphere that man shares in the creation of his own being. The erection of a great museum is only the assembling of physical parts in accord with a directive idea. A freely willed act is the changing of the inner and spiritual side of man. What a man freely loves or uses becomes part of him. It is for this reason that freedom is so decisive in human life and in ethics.

Because the freely chosen influences the inner being of the individual, ethics is concerned with what man wills as well as with what happens to him as a result of outside forces. Hence, we will constantly be asking what man ought to will if he is to realize the good for himself.

Since this freedom operates in the world and in a man who lives in a complex world, man must be seen as a microcosm in a macrocosm. Both these worlds have fixities and both have open possibilities which can be realized by man. The line between the two, however, is not always clear. As a result, freedom is tentative, groping, and unsure of itself. It is exposed to risk and even the possibility of self-destruction.

MATTER AND SPIRIT

The paradox of man is most often experienced in the tension between matter and spirit. Matter both supports and limits the activity of the spirit, while the spirit both dominates and yields to matter. In some strange way, matter and spirit form a unity despite the tension between them. Matter is not a mere instrument of the spirit. The person, the I, is not identical with the matter of the body; yet the person, the I, cannot say that the body is not himself. The body is united to, but is not identical with, the spirit.

The body both divides and unifies. The tension is a sign that the union, the total person, is not fully achieved but a task to be accomplished. When we watch the growth of individuals, we see the gradual integration of spirit with the body which achieves a lofty, but still incomplete, realization in the lives of a few rare individuals. It is almost as if both spirit and body were raw materials, partially integrated with the person himself, but to be redone and made to interpenetrate each other over the course of time.

The growth in union is not, of course, automatic. We see cases in which the spirit can destroy the body, burn it out and desiccate it until the remaining person is an inhuman caricature. We see others, too, whose body takes over and drags down the spirit until it is hard to distinguish the person from an animal. Only training, reinforced by conscious free choice, seems to produce any sort of harmonious unity.

Ultimately, we do not really know how the body and the spirit are joined or cooperate. Thousands of pages have been written on the topic, and none of the theories is very satisfactory. The fact of partial union and growth in union, however, seems to be fairly obvious.

Although man's spirit and freedom are decisive, the body cannot be disregarded as if it were a mere appendage. Since the body also puts us into relation with the world around us, the external world must be considered lest we end up with an ethics of good will which allows a man to destroy himself and the world because his intention is good. Man's final meaning may be found outside the world of time, but the union of spirit and matter means that it is not, so far as we can see, found completely independent of time and space.

The fact that the union is seemingly not complete, but a thing to be achieved by free acts in time, means that we cannot consider the dynamics of either matter or spirit in isolation from one another. We must accept the tension and look to the interrelation of the aspects if we are to make decisions based on reality and not on our simplified picture of it.

DEATH AND IMMORTALITY

Death is a fact, but its nature is a mystery. We know that a particular body is no longer animated, but we do not know whether or not the spirit which gave life to that particular body is separated from all matter. Man is subject to agony and doubt as to whether the spirit lives on when it is stripped of this familiar body. Death ends life in time, but does it also end man's being? This is a crucial question.

If death ends being as well as life in time, then human life has no absolute meaning either inside or outside time. Man, in this hypothesis, is involved in an interesting tale composed of momentary sorrows and joys, but with no absolute finality. Man yearns for immortality because he yearns for meaning. Yet we must ask whether this is just wishful thinking, a reasonable hypothesis, or a certitude.

The Christian theologian, relying on divine revelation, has a fairly clear answer to the question. Man's spirit is immortal and

will ultimately be reunited to his body. Jewish theology hesitates
before this bold affirmation. Philosophers are divided for a variety
of reasons. Even those who take a stand in favor of personal immortality admit that they do not really know how the spirit exists
after the death of the body. Their assertion of immortality still
leaves us in anguish.

As a Christian, I believe in the personal immortality of the
spirit. As a philosopher, I know of no argument which will per-
suade an uncommitted thinker to give this idea his unqualified
assent. At the same time, the arguments advanced do make it
reasonable to act on the assumption that there is a personal immortality. The remainder of this book rests in one way or another
on this assumption.

There are men who do not believe in personal immortality and
yet live lives that are noble by nearly any ethical standard. In
view of the fact that, apparently, such individuals are not motivated
by either hope of ultimate reward or fear of punishment, their lives
are often singularly unselfish. It would appear that in some wonder-
ful way they have grasped the dignity of man and intuited the
nature of the good, even though they have not seen clearly one of
the aspects which rounds out the picture of man. Their lives have
been reasonable, even though their reasoning may have been incomplete.

TIME AND ETERNITY

The assumption of personal immortality means that man is capable
of existing in two worlds, and that the here and now does not have
its full meaning when divorced from the beyond. Once we admit
the fact of personal immortality, it is no longer easy to view life
in this world as an ultimate. The assumption of immortality further
emphasizes man's transcendence not only of time but of the historical process which takes place in and through time.

The fact that man lives in two worlds is a source of further
tension. Shortsightedness is at war with the long vision. The long
vision may cause us to neglect even the necessary in the here and

now. Like most of the tensions in man, it cannot be resolved in a general way, once and for all. The relationships change constantly. At one moment it may be necessary to charge into the hurly-burly of this world; at another, wisdom calls for a retreat. The perfect balance thus shifts from man to man, age to age, and even moment to moment. To say anything else is either to take man out of the world or to deny that his body and life in time have any significance. Or perhaps one might like to deny the existence of spirit and adopt some modern form of the old philosophy of pluck the pleasure of the day.

UNIQUE INDIVIDUALS AND THE COMMON HUMAN NATURE

The individual human being is unique. He is a person, an incommunicable, rational whole, who transcends the limits of nature in many respects. His own nature and his position in the world of nature do limit him, however. The uniqueness of his own being does not allow him complete escape from the nature which he has in common with other men. Unless we grasp both of these facts—the uniqueness of the person and the limits of the nature—we can fall into real error. If man was only a nature, then we could, in theory, develop an ethics of a very rigorous sort. Indeed, it might be so rigorous that freedom would be only a word. On the other hand, if man were not limited by a nature which he shares with others, every ethics would have to be completely individual. There would be no common norms. Actually, because man is a person and shares a nature which is common to all men, the truth is somewhat in between. There are common limits, but they do not cover everything. There are individual choices in an area of freedom, but they must occur in a framework of limitations.

It may not always be possible to decide where the line between the person and the nature is to be drawn in the concrete, but it is there. When we strip man of all his cultural accretions and search for the core common to all men, we may discover that it is very small indeed. No matter what its size, however, it is there and it is important.

I AND WE

Although an individual may have only a few things in common with all men, he is still involved in a variety of relations with both individuals and groups. Involvement with others is not merely a statistically normal condition, it is necessary for both survival and growth. The true isolate, who has never been associated with other men, is rare, because survival is almost impossible for him. The few "wild" children who have survived without human contacts appear to remain seriously stunted. An adult who withdraws from all associations with others is liable to go insane.

Modern thinkers insist that for a man, to exist is to coexist. The world he lives in belongs to others. He can refuse to recognize this, but the fact remains. He can hate other men, but he will almost certainly seek intimacy with at least a few. The experience of our own incompleteness and loneliness drives us to meet other men and to form a "we." This "we" is one of those realities which we can experience with real intensity, even though we may not be able to verify its existence with empirical tools. Those who are part of a real "we" know that it completes their beings. Those who have not had the experience will consider the "we" a myth.

No matter what we may say in the abstract, in the concrete our relationships with others are a part of our being. We cannot be fully ourselves without being related to others. In addition, we soon find that we must enter into relations with groups where the bond may not be the intimacy of the "we" but a common task to be performed for the benefit of all. Man, in short, is both individual and social. His growth and survival depend on both interpersonal and social relations.

In practice, there is often tension between the individual and society. Because no individual is ever fully mature, no one is ever sure of his exact relationship to others, or to the group as a whole.

The needs of both individuals and groups are constantly shifting. The relationships must change too.

The social nature of man is of extreme importance in ethics. Our earliest ethical values and principles come from our family and the society of which it is a part. Even as we grow towards some independence of judgment, we discover that we must pay a penalty if we disagree too strongly with society. We are often in the position of trying to discover norms which will enable us to live with other men and yet maintain our own personality and integrity.

The human person is a complex totality in process. It is no wonder, then, that thinkers find it difficult to answer the question, "What is man as a species or as an individual?" Man's freedom, openness to eternity, and changing relationships to the material world show us why our concept of man and the ideal are capable of growth.

Although the very richness of the human person is an embarrassment to those who like their world neat, it should not cause us to despair in our present inquiry. Even though the picture is not perfectly clear, we have some outlines and some points of departure.

MAN'S KNOWLEDGE

Man's knowledge is as mysterious as man himself. Analysis, reflection, research, and methodological controls can clarify the nature of certain aspects of knowledge, but the mystery remains. Thus far, there is no theory that explains how sense and intellect cooperate, yet they do. There are experiences, such as that of the beautiful, which are very real but escape all our ordinary categories of knowledge. Even in our society where so much stress is placed on scientific method, controlled observation, and measureable results, many of the things we know are not capable of systematic verification. In fact, the attempt to control or analyze much of our human knowledge leaves us dissatisfied because we often know wholes which cannot be broken down into parts without destroying what we really know.

When we attempt to communicate our knowledge to others,

words often fail us. This may be particularly true of someone who is trying to explain why he loves someone else. He lists all sorts of reasons but knows that these do not really add up to his real reason. The reality he knows cannot be reduced to bits of acceptable verbiage.

Not everyone knows in the same way. Some are capable of grasping the whole, the raw, the unstructured; others appear to be limited to knowledge that is generic, abstract, and capable of classification. In addition, there are the obvious individual differences in general intelligence and memory.

Our perceptions and our knowledge take place in a cultural context and are conditioned by the way in which we have been taught to organize our knowledge. In our culture we tend to organize our perceptions in the patterns of plane geometry; in other lands, sense reality is structured in terms of solids. To a certain extent we see and hear only what we expect to see and hear. We may not consciously advert to the color of a man's skin, unless we have been taught that skin color is significant. If I expect others to be friendly, I may not notice minor signs of hostility. If I expect a certain class of people to be boorish, I am liable to interpret many acts as insults. The expectation itself is a result of both personality and the cultural rules. While we are not completely trapped by the culture, there is no denying its presence and its influence. This should surprise no one, for culture is almost a second nature. It is so much a part of us that it is only with difficulty that we escape even some of its influence.

The culture has much to say about what sort of knowledge we prize and what sort of verification we will accept. In our own culture, for example, we give high value to knowledge which meets the norms of the "scientific" method. The method, in its turn, is valued because it leads to "practical" results which our culture values. At times, indeed, there is a tendency to make "scientific" knowledge the norm for all knowledge. A narrow scientism is not too helpful in ethics, for ethics involves the incommunicable person as well as the measurable world. At the same time, the results of scientific investigations in psychology, sociology, and anthropology can help us to enlarge our vision and to check some of the factual presuppositions of our ethical judgments.

ETHICAL JUDGMENTS

Ethical judgments involve several forms of knowledge. Some judgments are taken to be self-evident. Nearly all ethical systems start with such self-evident truths as pleasure is good; pain is evil; man is good; death is evil. Other ethical judgments involve the relationship of a factual situation to a norm or definition which may be considered self-evident or established by either induction or deduction. The judgment: This is murder, says that the concrete situation fulfills the definition of murder. The judgment that murder is wrong implies that the killing of a man destroys a basic good or goes against a general command to respect others. Many of our ethical judgments contain many qualifiers such as "in this particular case," or "in general." For example, we say that in general contracts are to be observed because we realize that some contracts may conflict with the public good or the rights of others.

All these judgments contain affirmations of value or goodness. In later chapters we will have to examine the justifications for them. At this point, we will merely indicate some of the problems involved.

While we admit that ethical knowledge, like all knowledge, has to start from some self-evident proposition, the self-evident judgment ought to be examined. For example, we may ask if a supposedly self-evident statement like "justice is good" is not really derived from some more basic position. In addition, we may want to ask whether a judgment is self-evident only in the context of a given culture or is clear to all men who look for the truth. Thus some men assume as self-evident the fact that pleasure is *the* good. Other men, while admitting that pleasure is *a* good, assert that there are other goods which are not reducible to pleasure. In short, the extent and universality of self-evident judgments need to be examined.

When an ethical judgment involves a relationship of a concrete factual situation to a norm, we should examine the factual situation to see if it is actually as asserted. If a man asserts that taking a loaded gun from a child constitutes stealing, it is well to see if the act really fulfills the definition of stealing. If stealing involves taking another's property when he is reasonably unwilling, we will have to ask whether the child with a loaded gun could *reasonably* object to its being taken away. Since definitions are often only shorthand expressions of the real ethical principle, we would do well to see that the definition itself has been properly worked out. Someone, for example, might define murder simply as the killing of a man. We should ask whether the definition does not need to be qualified to read "the *deliberate* killing of an *innocent* man."

Those judgments which involve qualifiers about the extent of the judgment demand particular care. We might discover, for example, that women in polygamous societies are treated as cattle, and so judge that polygamy is evil since it degrades a human being. It might be, however, that the degradation does not come from the polygamy, but from the basic philosophy behind the institution. If this were the case, we could not condemn polygamy for this reason. At the same time, if we could not isolate the precise cause of the evil, our knowledge of the association of polygamy and female degradation would create a well-founded suspicion that polygamy should be avoided. As a matter of fact, since polygamy can be both an *effect and a cause* of a twisted view of women, we would have a real reason for saying that it was evil, even though it were not the sole cause of the harm.

It seems to us, however, that in cases like this the judgment should say that polygamy is generally wrong. Furthermore, we should realize that additional research might lead us to the conclusion that polygamy is always wrong or to a modified conclusion that it is wrong only in certain circumstances. Good ethicians have always realized that our knowledge can progress in this way. However, there is often a popular tendency to make universals out of what are only generalizations. As a result, care is necessary.

ETHICAL JUDGMENT AND THE
WHOLE MAN

Knowledge exists in a concrete human person. It exists in a subject and relates a subject to other subjects and to the world around him. Ethical judgments and ethical knowledge involve the subject in a particular way, for they look ultimately to action and often to a change in either the subject or the world. Ethical judgments, then, are liable to involve the whole man—his feelings and emotions as well as his senses and his intellect.

There are subjective components in ethical judgments. In our everyday language, *subjective* evokes ideas of the arbitrary, the capricious, the unfounded, the idiosyncratic, and that which is cut off from the world common to all men. Without doubt there are things which are subjective in this sense. However, the adjective can also refer to that which exists in the incommunicable subject or person. The subjective in this sense does not necessarily imply the arbitrary or the unfounded. The subject transcends the world of nature but is also joined to it. Freedom, one of the great manifestations of subjectivity in this sense, is not crushed by the determinations of the objective external world which can be observed by all, but neither is it necessarily independent of or at odds with the world. As John Wild has pointed out in *Existence and the World of Freedom:*

Consciousness has a subjective center, but it is found to be always stretched out toward objects of some kind. These objects, and the way in which they are ordered, may differ from individual to individual and from culture to culture, but no self has ever been found in an objective state. As a matter of fact our experience is neither exclusively subjective nor exclusively objective but a relational structure to which neither term alone does justice.[4]

The ethical quality of an act is certainly not subjective in the sense of arbitrary. Neither is it merely a question of attitude or choice of the subject. Nor is it merely a "something" which exists in the world of non-subjects. As we shall see, it involves both the subjective and the objective poles of reality and the proper union between the two. In some cases, what exists independent of the knowledge and choice of the subject will set limits to the subject; in others, it will leave the subject free to create new meaning and reality. For the purpose of describing what is, we shall use objective to refer to what exists independent of the knowledge and choice of the subject, and subjective to refer to what depends on the knowledge and choice of the subject. Occasionally we may use the word subjective to designate the arbitrary, but this should be clear from the context.

It should be noted that the choices and opinions of the subject, whether arbitrary or not, are real and have real effects. If people think you are untrustworthy, they will treat you with suspicion and hinder some of your activities. The falsity of their opinion does not make its effects any less painful. If a society decides that membership in a given religious body is important, non-members will suffer, no matter how foolish the decision. These effects must be studied and taken into consideration. In any event, we must not let our terminology and categories get in the way of what exists, for categories are tools and not the end and purpose of ethics or any other science.

Ethical judgments involve the whole man, not only as he is but as he can be and ought to be. This is to say that in some way or other they often look to the future, to the realization of an ideal. To say that something is good is to imply that it is suitable for realization. To say that something is bad implies that it should be avoided. In short, the future and the things to be done or avoided in the future enter into the ethical judgment. For this reason our views of the limits and possibilities of man and of the ideal are as important as our descriptions of what a man is at a given moment. For this reason too, ethics can never be merely a neutral sort of science. It involves the knowledge not of the spectator, but of the player who is seeking to discover what the rules of the game ought to be.

RELATIONS WITH OTHER SYSTEMS

Although the relationship between our positions and those of other thinkers will be pointed out in the following chapters, a few points should be obvious even at this stage. Our positions with regard to man, reality, and human knowledge rule out many partial answers which disregard some vital aspect of reality, or force thought into too narrow a mold.

We reject any system which builds ethics on a single aspect of reality to the exclusion of all others. The materialism of the communist, the rationalism of Spinoza, and the sensism of the linguistic analyst all limit the inquiry by disregarding obvious factors. We do not deny that these systems have some truth; we only refuse to accept a partial truth as the whole truth.

We must also reject systems which limit the good to the realities and processes of this world of time. These, too, neglect vital aspects of man and produce answers which satisfy neither the heart nor the head, though they may have a specious simplicity. Hedonism, utilitarianism, and all forms of evolutionism are thus excluded by the broad vision of man.

The unique nature of man as both individual and social also precludes any system which either swallows the individual up in a collectivity or isolates him from the human whole. Both Hegel's idealism and Hobbes' egoism are thus untenable answers to questions about *the* good for man. Much the same can be said of collectivist interpretations of Aristotle or the atheistic isolation described by Sartre.

While there are many systems which have much in common with what we will attempt to evolve, we differ from some in that we do not believe it possible to evolve a blueprinted theory which covers every detail of life. We are not, then, trying to evolve a code morality of immutable and changeless precepts. On the other hand, there are enough fixed points to supply us with a framework of truths and principles that can be applied fruitfully to the shifting world. Our epistemology and metaphysics cause us to reject both pure situation ethics and the simpler code moralities.

Neither our epistemology nor our philosophy of man will permit us to propose a simple code morality which will give a blueprint of norms to cover every possible situation in life. We can hope, however, to develop some general principles and methods which will help the individual in determining the moral meaning of particular situations. Only after we have discussed some general, and at times fairly vague, principles and minimums can we hope to say much about a wisdom ethic.

Although we wish to develop a systematic approach, the recognized limitation of our knowledge forces us to put aside the dream of a neat, complete, and unchanging set of categories which will include everything with absolute precision. Because we work not only with a few immutables but also with the vast array of the changeable, uncertainty and risk are part and parcel of what follows.

We must, however, act responsibly. This means not only that we make a choice and accept the blame or praise but also that we respond to what is and attempt to give a coherent account of our choices. In short, we accept the human condition and attempt to do our best with the tools available.

THE WORK TO BE DONE

The philosophy of man outlined in these pages contains implicit judgments about what is good for man. We assume, for example, that it is good to act reasonably. Such an assumption needs to be examined and tested to see if it is consistent with more fundamental ideas of the good. In the chapters which follow, then, we must start to develop an orderly idea of the good and attempt to relate it to various aspects of human nature, the individual person, and the surrounding world. This work can be dull and exacting, but it must be done if the vague, the intuitive, the precritical judgments of men are to be made explicit enough for use in making reasoned judgments about good and evil in the concrete.

NOTES

1. Edward Joseph Shoben, Jr., "Towards a Concept of the Normal Personality," *The American Psychologist,* 12 (1957), April No. 4, pp. 188–189.
2. Clyde Kluckhohn, "Values and Value-Orientations in the Theory of Action" in Talcott Parsons and Edward A. Shils (eds.), *Toward a General Theory of Action* (New York: Harper & Row, Harper Torchbook Edition, 1962), p. 418.
3. Henry Sidgwick, *Outlines of the History of Ethics,* 6th ed. (Boston: Beacon Press, 1931), p. 63.
4. John Wild, *Existence and the World of Freedom,* © 1963. Reprinted by permission of Prentice-Hall, Inc., Englewood Cliffs, N.J.

POINTS FOR DISCUSSION

1. Attempt to outline your own theory of man and to sketch your image of the ideal man. Distinguish the attributes of all men, men in general, and men in your culture.
2. Compare your theory and image with that of some other person with a different background.
3. What are some of the author's unstated assumptions which lie behind his vision of man?
4. How has the experience of growth affected your own vision of man? Has it narrowed or broadened your thinking?
5. What theory of the good is implicit in the author's description of man?
6. What theory of the good is implicit in your theory of man?
7. What are the implications of the possibilities and dynamic side of human reality for our theory of knowledge?
8. Work out your implicit ideal and discuss your reasons for including various qualities.
9. What elements in your ideal are the result of your religion, your nationality, your personal inclination?

READINGS

On Man

Herschel BAKER, *The Image of Man* (New York: Harper & Brothers, Harper Torchbook Edition, 1961).

W. Paul KILEY, S.J., *Human Possibilities* (New York: Philosophical Library, 1963).

Dorothy LEE, *Freedom and Culture* (Englewood Cliffs, N.J.: Prentice-Hall, 1959).

William A. LUIJPEN, *Existential Phenomenology* (Pittsburgh: Duquesne University Press, 1963).

Jean MOUROUX, *The Meaning of Man* (Garden City, N.Y.: Doubleday, Image Books Edition, 1961).

On Culture and Ethics

Abraham EDEL, *Ethical Judgment: The Use of Science in Ethics* (New York: The Free Press of Glencoe, 1964).

May EDEL and Abraham EDEL, *Anthropology and Ethics* (Springfield, Ill.: Charles C. Thomas, 1959).

3/ THE GOOD

INTRODUCTION

The complexity of man and of his position in the world should indicate that any attempt to define the good must cope with a confusing array of answers to the question, "What is *the* good?" In the history of western thought, the title has been given to pleasure, to power, to self-realization, to what is approved by society, as well as to that which calls for expressions of approval by the individual. The variety of answers has tempted some men to say that there is no answer to the question. Despite this, men talk and judge and act as if there is a good, and that, objective in some way.

The existence of value judgments in all societies and in all men is a fact which cannot be denied. Though the judgment itself is often described as subjective, there is a certain constancy in preferences which indicates that the user of the word *good* is referring his judgments to some norm. Furthermore, it is clear that men strive to realize order in their work which corresponds to some idea of the good. Even though men may disagree about the precise content to be assigned to the term good, in many cases there are broad agreements about the goodness of objective realities. Almost universally, men value life, health, respect, and group living. So too, intelligence, knowledge, and power are everywhere respected. While there are cultural differences which affect the hierarchy of valuation, there is great agreement about many goods.

THE PROBLEM

In the present chapter we wish to find whether there is some objective basis which can be used to unify our use of the idea of the good in a general sense. Then we will attempt to work out a method which can be used in applying this idea to concrete problems.

THE WORD GOOD

The linguistic analysts have devoted a great deal of attention to the use of the word *good* and related terms. Although most of the analysts are non-cognitivists who deny that the ethical statement says anything about real qualities, they do make certain important points. Words like good involve evaluation, emotion, recommendations, and commands. To say that something is good is not purely and simply a statement of fact. A statement about what is good or bad frequently tries to communicate several things, including the attitude of the speaker. This should not cause us to overlook the obvious fact that people generally have reasons for the value statements they make. Thus, if asked why a certain car is good, I will point to its durability, speed, design, safety or economy of operation, all of which involve some objective factors. Men do believe that there is some basis for the evaluation, the emotion, the recommendation, and the prescription that go with or are implied by the use of the word good.

We may ask, in fact we should ask, why they say that durability, speed, design, and the like make a good car. Moreover, we will ultimately want to find out if there is a common meaning behind all uses of the word good, and the reasons assigned for using the word.

THE FUNCTIONAL MEANING
OF THE GOOD

When we are dealing with artifacts such as hammers, machines, and tables, we call them good when they are capable of doing what they were made to do or what we want them to do. This is to say that we judge them functionally as means or instruments to a goal selected either by the maker or the user.

While we do say that a thing or an act is good because it serves an end or a goal, we must face the fact that sometimes we will say that the goal itself is evil. A bomb is a good—that is, an efficient— means of killing an innocent man; but few would agree that the end in this case is a good. We must then discover what we mean by a good end or goal.

When we speak of things which are not human artifacts, we sometimes speak of them as if they had a goodness quite independent of their usefulness to man. While we may evaluate a horse in terms of its ability to serve man, we often say that it is good because it meets certain criteria of what a good horse is, quite independent of its utility. In these cases, we refer certain qualities, such as the condition of the coat or teeth, to a criterion. We are saying that the horse in question is what a horse ought to be.

Such usage leaves us with questions about the criterion. Does the criterion imply a function? Can the criterion be justified, or is it merely an expression of an arbitrary choice? Is the criterion only a reflection of a group consensus or does it have deeper roots in reality itself?

INSIGHTS FROM ARISTOTLE

In attempting to answer the question, What is good? Aristotle looked to the dynamic element in the world of our experience. The things we know directly—that is, in the world about us—do not merely exist, they tend towards a further state of existence. This tendency is actualized by operations and acts which center on various objects, most of which will keep the being in existence and which will expand the existence. The fertilized egg in a human mother becomes a human child if all goes well. Acorns become oaks and even chemicals manifest observable regularities. Men live in societies and set up rules for social life. These are facts of experience. They are not, however, brute facts. They imply relationships to what *is not* but can be; relationships which we detect with our intellect and not merely with our senses.

In any class of beings we know, these tendencies have a certain determination and direction, although we cannot always isolate it. The natural sciences are concerned with discovering these tendencies or directions and enshrining them in mathematical formulas. Even the social sciences are interested in discovering such regularities. Indeed, much of human thought is concerned with the discovery of the constant direction of movement in reality, both animate and inanimate.

The tendencies of reality manifest not only what is but what can be. They cause the mind to look ahead, and the person to strain towards the future. As time passes, we form ideas of what will satisfy these tendencies. We see a relationship between what is and what can be or will be.

Aristotle observed tendencies in both men and other beings of experience. He called the object or act which would satisfy a tendency a *good*. In this way, he attempted to relate the meaning of the concept to something that existed or could exist. Note, however, that it is the relationship of an object to a being with a tendency that stands at the center of his description. We are, in short, dealing with a dynamism and not merely with a static state of affairs.

It should be obvious that different things satisfy tendencies in different ways. My tendency to stay in existence is partially satisfied by my tendency towards food. The tendency towards food is served by everything that contributes to the production and distribution and preparation of food. Farming, transport, and cooking are all means to satisfying a tendency, but they satisfy it indirectly. In general, we will say that something which satisfies a tendency indirectly is good as a means. Those things which satisfy a tendency directly we will call good as an end.

Some things are ends with regard to one tendency and means with regard to another. Thus, food may be an end relative to my tendency to seek nourishment, but only a means relative to my tendency to stay in existence. This is to say that some tendencies appear to have much of their value as means to another tendency. If this is so, we will ultimately have to ask if there is some master tendency to which all other things are related as means to end.

The Aristotelian approach has certain definite advantages. It includes a variety of objects as good, while limiting the goods as ends. Because the good as means can change, the definition also allows for variation on this level. Finally, it is relational, and yet anchors the good in some objective structure.

Although the Aristotelian approach can be applied to all beings, we are primarily interested in man and his good. In the rest of this chapter we will concentrate on the tendencies of man.

The goods as ends are fairly limited, for as far as we can see, man tends naturally and spontaneously only to a limited number of things. He tends to existence, to knowledge, to the reproduction of his kind, and to life in a group. At first glance, nearly everything else would appear to fall in the realm of means. The realm of means is broad and offers much variation. Thus there are a variety of means to knowledge and social life, so that it is quite possible for different people to consider quite divergent things as means to a common end. Democracy, aristocracy, and monarchy are alternate means of governing a society. Each has advantages and disadvantages, so that there can be reasonable differences in opinion about which is best in a given situation. Moreover, since our knowledge of means increases in time, the theory helps us to see how even a given society can change its valuation of given means as its knowledge increases. At one time the United States believed in *laissez-faire* economics. Experience showed the society that not all sectors operated well under conditions of freedom. Today it regulates large sectors of the economy.

Variations in groups and individuals are not merely the result of arbitrary choices. Maslow notes that there appears to be a hierarchy of needs, so arranged that the higher or more specifically human needs do not emerge clearly until lower needs, which man shares with animals, have been satisfied.[1] Once physiological needs have been satisfied, a set of safety needs appear. When both physiological and safety needs are fairly well satisfied, man feels the need for belonging, for love and esteem. Finally, there arises a need for self-actualization.

An individual or a group which has not been able to satisfy the more basic needs may never exhibit the higher ones. Life can be organized around mere survival, and this will affect the ideal and the ethical norms of the group or individual. In short, the degree of development can often explain variations.

HIERARCHY OR RELATIVE POSITION OF ENDS

Reality, however, is far more complex than this. In a given being of our experience, we observe that there are tendencies and that the satisfaction of one tendency may be only a means to the satisfaction of another. Furthermore, we must recognize that there are conflicts between tendencies. In many men, for example, an overactualization of the tendency to pleasure can block the tendency to knowledge. As a result, it is necessary to face the problem of the hierarchy of tendencies and of goods. We must also face the fact that what satisfies a tendency in one being may thwart a tendency in another. Aspirin may cure one man's headache but cause another man to suffer an upset stomach. You may flourish on a diet of raw onions, while another man cannot keep such food down. While this may be an annoying fact, it introduces us to one of the basic problems in ethics, the ordering of goods among themselves, no matter how you define the good.

In many cases, we attempt to assign hierarchy by accepting the judgment of wise men or the prevailing judgment of the society of which we are a part. Such a procedure is relatively simple, but it does not get us to the bottom of the matter. Sooner or later, we have to ask why one tendency should be given priority over another.

Because the tendency to intellectual knowledge is specifically human, we almost spontaneously give it a *priority of dignity*. In our own culture, where knowledge is the key to so many other things, knowledge rightfully has a very high place. However, we know that food and drink are so necessary to continued life that often we give them a *priority in time*. In the concrete, then, tendencies that man has in common with other beings may take priority over specifically human goods. Similarly, though we almost spontaneously give the life of the individual priority over the life of the group, there are many cases where we put the group first, since so many persons depend on the group for survival.

CHRISTIAN INFLUENCE

The naturalist—that is, the ethical thinker who wants to keep the good inside the world of time and nature—has to struggle endlessly with the problem of priorities. In some way, we sense that even Aristotle's goods as ends are relative, at least to each other if not to something beyond time and space. The Christian thinkers, starting with theology, look beyond time and space for a point of reconciliation. It should be noted that though the Christians started with a revealed theology, they also tried to develop a natural or philosophic theology to support their position.

For the Christian, God is the absolute good. Man tends to God and can be satisfied only by being united with God. Consequently, priorities in the world are to be assigned in accordance with the relation of an act or state to the possession of God. God is the absolute good. He contains within himself all other goods, for he has infinite existence.

If we look at man, we soon discover that in most cases he is a restless being, unsatisfied by the goods of this world. The finite things around us are unstable, fleeting, and subject to decay. We are all aware of the fact that our life in time will end in death. We may dream of a day when sickness will be conquered, but we all know we will suffer some illness. While we may accept life and its limits, we know that the absolute good is not in the here and now.

Our restlessness is rooted in those powers which are specifically human. Our mind is never really satisfied; it reaches out for more and more knowledge. We are aware that we could be something more than we are. The scholastic philosophers said that the mind and the will of man had an infinite capacity, since they were not intrinsically limited by matter. Only an infinite being could, then, satisfy the being of man. Only God could be the end and the absolute good for man. To put it another way, man's freedom and intellect open him up to the infinite and indicate that he is ordered to the infinite.[2]

Not every man perceives this ordination to the beyond, yet we suspect that every man feels it in some way. Even men who will not admit the existence of God often try to create infinites in this world. In our own time men have held up the state, or mankind in general, or even scientific knowledge as absolutes to which a man should give himself completely. Even these things tend to pass away; men ultimately see through sham absolutes and man-made "infinities."

The openness of man and his ordination to God do tell us something important about man himself. Man is a unique being with a peculiar dignity. He alone in the created world appears to be ordered to a union with the infinite and to a life beyond time. He is not, however, a means to the perfection of God. God, being infinite, can receive nothing from man. Man is ordered to God as to his own perfection. Man is, in some way, an end in himself, since he is not a means to anything else. Man, however, is not *the* end in itself, for man as we know him is still in the process of becoming. He can exist fully only when he is united to God.

The human person's unique relationship to God affects his relationship to the subhuman world. The person is the center of the world. Rocks and dogs and cabbages exist for the person. They are means to be used by man as he moves towards his own perfection and towards God. Although the subhuman world may be vast, complex, and beautiful and the person may be very small in quantitative terms, the person is still the unique creature who both crowns and transcends the visible world.

If we accept man as a quasi-end in himself, we find ourselves dealing with a whole series of beings who have basically equal value. The relationship between men is not simply a means-end relationship, but one between equals, a relationship between ends. Furthermore, since men depend on social life for the provision of many means, such as food and housing, ethics must face the need for reconciling the claims of individuals and societies. In other words, an ethic founded on the dignity of a person who is necessarily a social being cannot be purely egoistic.

It is interesting to note that many men who do not admit the existence of God or man's relation to God have intuitively grasped the dignity of the individual. This fact is important, since it provides a place for dialogue between those who may not agree on all elements of philosophical anthropology. There are points where the dialogue may break down or become a squabble about the emphasis to be given to this life or the life hereafter, but there is room for large agreement about what are goods in the concrete world.

Simple agreement about the dignity of man does not solve the problem of hierarchy. It really provides only a minimum framework and a direction. It does not immediately provide us with a concrete image of the perfection of man, nor does it tell us exactly what activities and institutions move man towards his perfection and so towards God.

INTUITION OR PROOF

Behind all this analysis lies an intuition that existence, all other things being equal, is good; and that what tends to existence or increases existence may be labeled as the good. It is an intuition which is not always understood in its full implications, though men almost spontaneously have it in some vague way. The errors of men are not based on an ignorance of the good of existence, but on an identification of existence with some partial aspect, such as power or pleasure. The theory we are presenting holds that the good is essentially metaphysical, the fullness of being as found in God and as shared or shareable by man. All other things, though they have their goodness insofar as they exist, are only means relative to man, since none of the beings of our experience below man is capable of the fullness of being or existence. Power, pleasure, virtue, wisdom, knowledge, and all the other things which we consider as goods, are goods inside this framework, though principally as means to the expansion of man in his movement towards full existence.

From a certain point of view, we may argue that if God exists, he is certainly good, and that, therefore, all beings are good insofar as they participate in him. This is true, but it seems that the argument ultimately rests on the fact that we have had some basic intuition of the meaning of the fullness of being, so that our argument is more of an explicitation of an intuition than a demonstration in a proper sense.

At this point the reader must take a stand. Before he does so, however, he might ask himself if most of the things men value and consider as good are not in some way related either to the satisfaction of basic tendencies or to a desire to expand one's own existence. Those things which do not fit in the first categories of satisfaction and desire for an expanded existence are likely to be expressions of the existence itself. In other words, the reader should clarify his own judgments of goods and evils and see whether they are not, in some way, unified around the idea of existence.

In analyzing one's own stand, remember that abstract ideas such as justice, prudence, respect, fairness, which are typical of the ethical vocabulary, really refer to relationships which recognize either the means-end relationship or the relationship between men. For this reason, we believe the analysis will be more fruitful if the reader concentrates on concrete relationships.

THE MEANS

If we accept the fact that man is, in some way, ordered to God, we must then ask what means are available for the attainment of this goal. Even if we prescind from this ordination to God, while continuing to accept the perfection of man himself as an end, we are faced with the same question, What means are suitable?

The moral theologian, who has divine revelation at his disposal, can give answers based on explicit or implicit divine commands. In the Judeo-Christian tradition we have not only the ten commandments but the great law of love, which commands us to love God and to love our neighbor as ourselves. Although the moral theologian must wrestle with the concrete meaning, the limits, and the extension of these commands, he does start off with the advantage of some specifics guaranteed by the divine wisdom. The philosopher or ethician is not quite so fortunate. He must examine himself and the world he knows in order to decide what means are suitable.

The only means available in the world of experience are man's endowments and acts, the world around him, and the myriad forms of social organization by which men help one another. These are the only possible means that we see, but other means are possible. Anyone who admits the existence of God must also admit the possibility that he can supply us with special aids. Indeed, the great religious traditions of the West assure us that the special divine aids, generally called "graces," are the decisive means. Though ethics, as a part of philosophy, can neither prove nor disprove the existence of such "graces," it certainly takes into account the possibility that "graces" can exist. The very fact of this possibility limits any answer that philosophy may give to the question, What are the means to the end? As a result, the philosopher can never decide what are the sufficient means to the ends of man; and the individual human being can never know by unaided reason exactly where he stands in his journey towards the end. This ignorance of his exact position in time is one of the factors which leaves a man without a religious faith in a state of mental anguish.

It is also the factor which renders ethics an essentially unsatisfactory science, no matter how great its utility.

Though we cannot see what means are *sufficient,* it is possible to give a sort of tentative answer to the question, What means are necessary? Thus, because continued existence in time is, *as far as we can see,* a necessary condition, if not a means to everything else, we can argue that those things which are necessary for existence are necessary means. This conclusion, however, is not so neat as it might appear at first glance. It is possible, from a philosophic point of view, that God only treats men's acts as conditions necessary for attaining the end, and not as means which make a positive contribution to that achievement. This is certainly not very probable, since we assume that God has some reason in giving man his powers and his processes. However, since we cannot read the mind of God, we do not know the answer by unaided reason. Despite this, the only reasonable *assumption* is that in some way, either as a condition or as a means, some of man's acts are necessary for the attainment of man's ends. Because it is an assumption, it is also the weak point in ethics; the point about which we do not have certitude, but only a reasonable working hypothesis.

Even if we wish to prescind from man's relationship to God, there are serious problems to be faced. If we say that the good, the end of man in time, is the full development of his being, we must still decide what constitutes that full development. In other words, we return to the problem of the ideal mentioned in the last chapter. Even when an ideal has been embraced, it is still necessary to decide which activities and institutions best serve this goal. The goods to which man tends naturally are certainly a part of the ideal, but the ideal must contain much more than this. The creation of a world in which all men have a chance to be full men is a part of the ideal, but the shape and dimensions of this world are not immediately evident. In short, the work of ethics is not completed when a few basic lines have been drawn.

Let us summarize some of the basic points we have made thus far. God is the good, the infinite existence. He is also the end, for he alone can satisfy the deepest tendencies of man. The individual person is, in some way, an end in himself, because of his relation to God. Ultimately, however, the person fulfills himself and realizes his full being and goodness only in union with God. It is reasonable to assume that man's perfection in time is, in some way, either a cause or a necessary condition for the attainment of that union. While the exact nature of man's perfection in time is not easy to sketch, his relationships to other men and his basic tendencies to existence, knowledge, and social life point to some things that are good as means.

OBSTACLES TO KNOWLEDGE OF THE GOOD

The foregoing pages have attempted to outline a metaphysical basis for the use of the word good. The basis we have outlined is not immediately self-evident to every human being. A man brought up in a society where mere survival is a constant preoccupation may never have time to reflect on the depths of his own being. He may end up restricting the good to those things necessary for mere survival. There are individuals who have been convinced that they are useless or that all men are beasts. Such persons will have serious difficulty in recognizing the goodness of the individual and of existence itself.

The intuition of the good appears to involve more than mere knowledge. It demands commitment. Without commitment, the good will remain an object of contemplation, an abstraction which lacks the power to attract the whole being of man. Those who fear commitment will have difficulty intuiting the nature of the good. The young are especially subject to these limitations. First, because they are at loose ends in the world and afraid of committing themselves when they do not see all the consequences, even though they may sense them in some vague way. Secondly, because the young are still struggling to find their own identity and the focus of their own being, they may be incapable, at a given moment, of seeing the depth and the breadth of humanity which is a necessary pre-requisite for the intuition of the good.

The work of Maslow provides partial confirmation of the role of maturity in the knowledge of the good. He remarks that in high achievers and self-developers—that is, in mature personalities —little distinction seems to be made between judgment of the facts and judgment of the good.[3] When the personality is fully inte-grated, or at least integrated to a high degree, the person does not feel threatened by reality or by his own commitment. At the other end of the scale, of course, we have the psychopath, who, though he may be able to recognize the difference between good and evil in the abstract, has no emotional resonance or commitments, so that the idea of the good is purely abstract and inoperative in his personality. In between, we have all sorts of personality disorders which can block out the notion of good in particular areas, be-cause they have blocked out the appreciation of parts of the personality or of reality itself. Perhaps it is for reasons like these that the great philosophers believed that philosophy and ethics were beyond the comprehension of all but the mature.

The social and personal factors mentioned above impede not only the knowledge of the good but the judgment as to the relative goodness of acts and objects in particular circumstances. Thus it may be that a whole society can be blinded to a type of goodness and even to the essential goodness of a human person considered as the center of value in this world. To a certain extent this blindness and ignorance may be inculpable, because there is, in the practical order, no way of removing it. This should not surprise us, for there is good, if not conclusive, evidence that the great moral breakthroughs in the history of civilization have occurred when some moral giant had an intuition which he was able to reduce to laws and directions that led an entire people to a higher level of morality and civilization. Since such breakthroughs occur in other fields of knowledge, it should not surprise us if it is also true in the far more complicated and humanly involved area of ethics.

SOME CONCLUSIONS AND IMPLICATIONS

In some way the full development of man is dependent on the satisfaction of the basic tendencies to existence, society, and knowledge. As lower tendencies or needs are fulfilled, tendencies to love, esteem, and a broader self-actualization become more marked. Only God, however, can bring about full self-actualization. We can, then, consider as good not only those things which satisfy basic tendencies but those which prepare the way for and satisfy the higher tendencies. Since the higher tendencies do not emerge fully without the satisfaction of the lower tendencies, we must pay attention to the order of development as well as to the hierarchy of goods.

Although there are certain things necessary for the full development of every man, it should be clear that individual capacities will vary, so that there may be room for great freedom once the proper fundamentals have been taken care of. Indeed, there can be great variation in the concrete means used to satisfy even basic tendencies. We cannot, then, make a complete list of specific concrete goods without reference to studies of specific groups and situations. At the same time, there are basic general goods which every man seeks to realize as he develops. Existence, knowledge, and social life are valued by all groups. No society values suffering in itself. Every society sees killing, indiscriminate lying, and theft as harmful to the group. These are, then, some ethical universals.

RELATIONSHIP TO OTHER THEORIES

The theory evolved in the previous pages does not deny that the goods proposed by other thinkers are genuine. It merely denies that any limited good can be *the good* for man. This is a necessary consequence of the acceptance of a broad view of the complexity of man. As a result, our criticism of other theories comes down to saying that they rest on a narrow and incomplete theory of man so that their concept of the good suffers from the same defect. Our own theory, though still poor in detail, provides at least some underlying objective meaning to the vast variety of meanings assigned to the word good. In addition, it also provides some unity and so a basis for comparing goods which at first sight might appear incommensurable. Thus the goodness of concrete actions, states, and institutions is to be judged by its relation to the full development of the person who is, in some way, ordered to union with God, the infinite being.

While the metaphysical theory presented in this chapter is strongly teleological, it should not be confused with utilitarianism. In the first place, the good is not only beyond mere pleasure but beyond time. In the second place, the good is not found in some collectivity, such as the greatest pleasure for the greatest number, but in the final development of the individual human person, who is more than a mere cipher in a calculus of pleasure. Finally, as we will see more fully in the following chapter, the moral good will involve not only the effects of an act but the way in which it is willed and made a part of man.

Like all teleological theories, ours has a relativistic tinge. This should not blind one to the fact that one absolute—God—and one quasi-absolute—the individual person—stand at the center of the system. Each of these is, in its own way, an end, an intrinsic value, and not merely a means whose value is relative to its ability to produce desired results.

As presented, this theory might seem to minimize the existence of intrinsically good or evil acts even while admitting to some absolutes. This is certainly not our intention. A deliberate act which goes directly against the end of man is certainly intrinsically evil. Blasphemy is an example of such an act. What we do wish to stress is the difficulty of defining acts which are intrinsically wrong. There are external acts which are almost universally unsuitable for the attainment of man's end, but which God might permit or command in special circumstances where he, with his wisdom, sees them as means. So too, there are acts which seem at first to be universally harmful, but which further study indicates can be helpful in some circumstances, when factors thought to be constant—or even factors unnoticed at first—are changed. In short we do not wish to deny the existence of the intrinsically good or evil *act,* but to maintain an attitude of humble caution.[4]

Our emphasis on the complexity of man and of the circumstances in which he exists might lead some to conclude that we have adopted a sort of situation ethics in which each decision is unique, so that no generalization is possible. Quite the contrary is true. Man needs generalizations if his moral life is to be more than a set of problems resolved by guesswork or appeal to a vague inspiration. What must be stressed is that generalizations are human creations and often subject to revision or refinement as our knowledge of man and the world increases.

Like Kant, we give great emphasis to the value of the person. However, the differences should be noted. The person, as we see him, is an end, but an end to be realized and not a center of unlimited freedom untouched by the demands of the external world. Thus the external acts of man as well as his motives are important, since man must use the external world if he is to reach his goal.

The natural law theories set forth in many scholastic textbooks are in most respects similar to the present theory. There are, nevertheless, differences which should be noted, even at this stage of our presentation. In the first place, most of these textbooks seem to assume that human acts *are* certainly means to man's final perfection outside time. While this may be true in theology, we prefer to adopt a more moderate and modest view. The philosopher can reasonably assume that human acts and institutions are means to, or necessary conditions for, the attainment of God. He should not, in our opinion, claim to have more than a reasonable assumption. Further, though we admit that God has built the basic tendencies into man, we recognize the difficulty of distinguishing the inherent from the culturally impressed. In view of this, and the fact that man's freedom is a part of God's plan, we shall be more hesitant than most in interpreting the meaning of tendencies.

There are strong personalist elements in the theory we have

presented. The person as a whole, and not nature alone, is the center. At the same time, we recognize the fact that the person operates within some limits posed by nature. In short, we do not agree with those who see man as free to create his own essence any more than we agree with those who think that the essence provides a nearly complete blueprint.

THE WORK TO BE DONE

A basic stand on the nature of the good does not tell us how to decide on the priority of specific goods in the concrete world. It does not tell us how we should make choices in a given situation. We need at least a set of formal analytic tools which can be used for deciding on priorities and separating the relevant from the irrelevant in a concrete case.

NOTES

1. Abraham H. Maslow, *Motivation and Personality* (New York: Harper & Row, 1954), Chapters 5 and 8.
2. The identification of *the* good with *the* infinite being solves several problems in the history of ethics. In the first place, you resolve the tension between happiness and the good. Happiness as a complete fulfillment of all man's capacities and tendencies can be arrived at only by possession of the infinite good. Thus the state of union between the two is a union between the ultimate subjective good of man, happiness, and the ultimate objective end, God.
3. Abraham H. Maslow, *Toward a Psychology of Being* (Princeton, N.J.: D. Van Nostrand, 1962), p. 79.
4. The concept of the good developed above also removes a large part of the tension between good as value and good as an end, which has characterized much of ethical writing in the West. The good as value stressed good as a concept in a line of formal causality and denoted an intrinsic quality. This idea was found in Plato, the Stoics, and to a certain extent in Kant. The good as end stressed the good in the order of final causality, so that the goodness of many things was extrinsic since they were valued only as a means to the end. Aristotle, the Epicureans, and the Utilitarians embraced such a theory of the good. In

the present theory, the end is intrinsically good in itself, even though we may arrive at the knowledge of its goodness by means of teleological orientation. Further, some things which are merely means and as such have a goodness by relation to the end may also be intrinsically good, at least insofar as there is something in their very nature which makes them a means, quite aside from the free choice which orders them to the end. As we shall see in the course of future chapters, not only a human person as such is an intrinsic good but also such acts as knowledge and altruistic love, which perfect man because of their very constituent nature.

POINTS FOR DISCUSSION

1. Study the theory of the good in one or more systems and see if it corresponds with the way in which people speak of the good.
2. Work out the hierarchy of goods which you have been using. How do *you* justify your hierarchy?
3. Does our increasing knowledge of the extent of the cosmos reduce the significance of the human person?
4. How do those who reject or ignore a relationship to God justify their position on the dignity of man?
5. Discuss the effects of increasing maturity on your own ethical judgments. How has your concept of your own identity influenced these judgments?
6. How does commitment influence our perception of what is good?

READINGS

Linguistic Analysis

Alfred Jules AYER, *Language, Truth and Logic* (New York: Dover Publications, 1946).

R. M. HARE, *The Language of Morals* (New York: Oxford University Press, 1964).

P. H. Nowell SMITH, *Ethics* (Baltimore: Penguin Books, 1954).

Charles L. STEVENSON, *Ethics and Language* (New Haven: Yale University Press, 1944).

Stephen TOULMIN, *Reason in Ethics* (Cambridge, England: The University Press, paperback edition, 1960).

Situation Ethics

Joseph FLETCHER, *Situation Ethics: The New Morality* (Philadelphia: The Westminster Press, 1966).

Paul LEHMANN, *Ethics in a Christian Context* (New York: Harper & Row, 1963).

Natural Law

Thomas E. DAVITT, S.J., "Law as Means to End—Thomas Aquinas," *Vanderbilt Law Review,* 14 (December, 1960), pp. 65–99.

A. P. DE ENTREVES, *Natural Law: An Introduction to Legal Philosophy* (London: Hutchinson's University Library, 1961).

Josef FUCHS, S.J., *Natural Law: A Theological Investigation* (New York: Sheed & Ward, 1965).

Yves R. SIMON, *The Tradition of Natural Law: A Philosopher's Reflections* (New York: Fordham University Press, 1965).

4/ CHOICE
AND DISCRIMINATION

INTRODUCTION

Agreement about the general meaning of the good does not solve the problem of choice. We have no instincts which will guide us automatically to choose those acts and objects which will maximize our existence and bring us to ultimate fulfillment. We need experience in order to make good choices. We also need some means of measuring our experience and relating it to both our perfection in time and our ultimate fulfillment beyond time. Without experience and without criteria or measuring sticks, we will not be able to make choices which relate our activities to the increase of goodness.

Every thinker must face the problem of choice and discrimination. A philosopher who says that the good is pleasure must recognize the fact that there are different types of pleasure. Since we cannot have every and all pleasures at a given moment, he must rank and classify pleasures before he can make reasoned choices. If love is made the ethical ideal, we must evaluate the suitability of various expressions of love. How do we make decisions when my love for one person conflicts with my love for another?

In the present chapter we will concentrate on developing criteria which can measure the relation of an act to our perfection in the world of time. Such a limitation is necessary, since unaided reason does not know which individuals have reached ultimate perfection, any more than it knows who has been definitively cut off from union with God. Philosophically, we have no way of comparing the ultimate successes with the ultimate failures. At best, we can only make the reasonable assumption that our growth and fulfillment in time make some contribution to ultimate perfection beyond time.

In line with our assumption that there is a relation between man's growth in time and his ultimate perfection beyond time, we will argue that what promotes human existence and growth is *in some way good*. On the other hand, what hinders man's existence or arrests his growth is *in some way* evil. The phrase *in some way* is extremely important, for there are many things which simultaneously help and hinder. A tranquilizing drug may calm my nerves, but it can also make a person lazy and unconcerned. Amputating a gangrenous leg may save a life, but it leaves a man crippled. Moreover, there are many occasions when we must choose between goods. Is it better to take a vacation at the seashore or in the mountains? Should I rescue a child or its mother from a burning building when there is time to save only one? How, in short, do we assign priorities?

A useful criterion must help us not only in assessing priorities but in assigning responsibility. Am I guilty of an unethical act whenever I permit some evil to occur? Am I responsible for all the consequences of my actions? When must I accept the blame for my mistakes and when may I reasonably refuse to admit any guilt?

DIFFICULTIES

A truly useful theory will attempt to answer all the above questions with an economy of principle. If the answer involved too many principles, we would then need a subtheory to determine the priority of principles themselves. The ideal of simplicity is not easy to attain for a variety of reasons.

The number of factors which help or hinder man are almost infinite in number. Each day we discover that something we once considered neutral has a real value or disvalue. At one time, for example, smoking was merely considered a dirty habit. Now we know that it is dangerous and at times deadly. How do we assign priorities to a vast number of disparate things like cabbages, love, honor, automobiles, whiskey, courage, and vitamin pills?

Any relatively adequate theory must take into account both the inner and the outer world of man. The fact that these two worlds are fused and interpenetrate complicates the situation considerably. If we separate the worlds for the purpose of analysis, we may find that we have falsified the problem itself. Too sharp a division might lead us into an ethic of external consequences or into an opposing ethic which considers only intentions and good will. A hundred years ago many people viewed the enforced separation of whites and Negroes as something purely physical. Today we know that segregation attacks the basic dignity of man and can harm the spirit if not the body. Good will, or lack of an evil intention, cannot change these effects radically. Effects are important. On the other hand, if we do not intend the good, we may change the world without really changing ourselves. Man cannot grow without the support of the world about him, but the largest sphere of growth appears to be within him in the world of love and freedom and knowledge.

Possibly the greatest difficulty arises from the fact that we do not have a complete picture of what the ideal should be. The ideal is both vague and shifting, for several very basic reasons. The ideal grows as experience and analysis uncover new potentialities, needs, and goods. A person may start out with mere survival as his ideal, but he should learn that he needs love in order to be a man. The experience of love should enlarge his vision of what he can do and make him aware of the need for patience, courage, and prudence. A deepening experience of group life should reveal the fact that the ideal should include loyalty, fidelity, truthfulness, and self-control. The ideal, of course, is not merely a collection of qualities, but a constellation of goods to be obtained and harmoniously integrated.

It is more than the sum of its parts. It is an image, a dynamic picture of what a man can be. The relative importance of qualities and their interrelation cannot be presented in an abstract formula, for not all things are possible for all men, nor would it be possible for one man to realize all his potentials in a single instant. As a result, the ideal is influenced by the concrete state of affairs at a given moment.

Even the Christian theologian, who has the concrete ideal of Christ, will emphasize one characteristic rather than another in accord with the capabilities of individuals and the needs of the times. Today, for example, the theologians give great emphasis to the need of imitating Christ by serving men who live in poverty. At the same time, they appear to give less stress to contemplation and the life of personally imposed penances. So too, some may want to stress the meekness of Christ, while others insist on his strength. While this is mainly a question of emphasis, the emphasis does have an influence on action.[1]

All these difficulties, whether from the complexity of factors, our increasing knowledge of human potentials, or the shifting configuration of even a vague ideal, impose certain limitations on the present chapter. We shall not attempt to give a sample, but shall content ourselves with presenting some ways of determining what is suitable for inclusion in the model. In addition, we shall attempt to integrate a system of simple priorities with a basic theory of responsibility. The result will be a formal scheme of analysis without too much specific content, but it will enable us to unify our handling of the specific in later chapters.

THE PROBLEM OF RESPONSIBILITY

In our culture we distinguish between the goodness or evil of a man's actions and the goodness or evil of the man himself. We may be quite clear that the killing of innocent men is evil, but we hesitate to say that a man is evil because he has killed another in an automobile accident. We want to know whether the accident was caused by lack of foresight, or by carelessness, or whether any malice was involved, before we condemn this individual. If the driver has not been careless or malicious, we do not attribute moral or ethical guilt to him even though we see the death of an innocent party as a very human evil. We distinguish between the evil done and the ethical quality of the person because we distinguish responsibility for our actions from the mere effects. We also distinguish between evil effects which are inevitable and evil effects which we will or permit under certain circumstances. In one way or other, we imply that the ethicality or morality of an action cannot be judged without reference both to effects and to those interior dispositions which make a man responsible for a given act or omission.

There are good reasons for these distinctions. Nearly everything we do involves at least the chance of harm to ourselves or others. If we were responsible for every evil that flowed from our activities, we would exist in an almost continual state of ethical guilt. Every time I cross certain busy streets I risk death. Am I unethical because I take such risks? Most medicines I take have harmful effects along with the good ones. Am I unethical because of this? Am I unethical and responsible every time I risk evil or foresee evil as somehow involved with my activities?

We make distinctions and ask questions about our responsibility, not only to avoid excessive guilt but also because we recognize the importance of interior acts. What I freely will becomes a part of me in a special way. What I freely embrace is taken in by my freedom. My freedom leads not merely to contact but to a sort of union with what I freely choose. The distinctions are a recognition of the difference between a truly free act and an act which came from a man without real human involvement.

In general, we may say that a man is *at least* responsible for what he freely wills as either a means or an end. This is to say that a man is responsible for what he makes a part of himself by freely embracing it. When a man has willed something in this way, we do not merely praise or blame what he has done, we praise or blame the man himself. These willed acts are treated as being in the ethical or moral realm, since they involve man's freedom and creativity. The willed act is no longer in the realm of the accidental; it has been incorporated into man in a special way.

The words "at least" were underlined in the paragraph above, lest people think that man was responsible for only what he willed as a means or an end. Is the drug manufacturer who foresees that some people will be killed by his inadequately tested drugs excused from all responsibility on the grounds that he does not will the deaths as either a means or an end? Is the reckless driver innocent of the death of those he hits merely because he did not intend their deaths? Most of us will answer these questions with a definite *No.* In general, we limit our responsibility for effects to those that we foresee or should foresee as either certain or probable. While we may not will everything we foresee, we are involved in the effects, for foreknowledge creates some possibility of controlling our acts and their foreseen effects.

Are we responsible for all the effects we foresee as either certain or probable? Is the teacher who flunks a student with an average of thirty responsible for a nervous breakdown which he foresees as probable? Is a surgeon responsible for the death of patients when he knows that this operation will succeed in only one out of four cases? These questions cannot be answered easily if we remember that the teacher who does not flunk a student with an average of thirty may (quite apart from the question of abstract justice) destroy his reputation for fairness and make his teaching far less effective. Similarly, if the surgeon does not perform the operation in question, death may be a certainty within a few short months. In short, we must take into account the foreseen effects of what we omit as well as of what we do.

In practice, most of us answer the above questions by balancing effects. We say that the teacher and the surgeon are not responsible for the harmful effects they risk or permit if the goods that they will as means or ends equal or outweigh the harmful effects. This procedure needs to be refined, but it is basically sound. We recognize the fact that foreknowledge does not give us complete control of everything. The forest ranger in his tower may see someone about to drive over a cliff, but he has no way of stopping him. A teacher knows some students will misunderstand him no matter how hard he tries to be clear. Both the ranger and the teacher have foreknowledge but lack the power to prevent the evil in question. If we tried to avoid all involvement with foreseen evil, we would be doomed to inactivity in many crucial situations. A surgeon who refused to perform any operation that involved some risk of death would not save many lives. A policeman who refused to patrol a riot area would be of little use to people threatened by violence. Furthermore, even inactivity would not enable us to escape the charge of being unethical, since my inactivity often has many harmful consequences. Both the surgeon and the police-man in our examples would cause more harm than good by their refusal to take risks. The same would be true of a teacher who resigned merely because it was inevitable that a few students should misunderstand him. In short, there are evils we cannot avoid without becoming responsible for even greater evils.

SOME NECESSARY REFINEMENTS

The need for balancing unintended harmful effects against the intended good effects is not to be taken as saying that the end justifies the means. The harmful effects of which we are speaking are not intended as either means or end. They are side effects which contribute nothing to the good and indeed are in some way obstacles to the overall good. The death of a patient or the mis-understanding of a pupil contributes nothing to the end of either the surgeon or teacher. Harmful side effects of a drug which cures arthritis contribute nothing to my health. I may catch pneumonia by diving into an icy stream in order to rescue a child, but the pneumonia does not help to rescue the child. Certain headache remedies may upset a person's stomach, but the upset does not cure the headache. When in doubt, ask if you could obtain what you intend even if some miracle stopped the evil effects. If the answer is yes, the evil is probably not a means to your goal.

In the cases we have cited, the end does not justify the evil effects themselves. At best, the end to be obtained only justifies our permitting or risking the evils in question. As we shall see later on, there are cases where the end cannot justify even this. Later in the chapter we will also consider the problem of justifying minor or physical evils even when they are willed. At this stage, we can make only the following limited statements. We are not responsible for all the consequences of our acts. In some cases, the end or good to be obtained can justify risking or permitting unintended side effects which are not means to the end.

OTHER FACTORS

If there are alternative means available for attaining the good with fewer harmful side effects, we cannot escape responsibility if we refuse to use the alternative. If an aspirin will stop pain with no risk of addiction, we are not justified in using morphine, at least not when aspirin is available and is adequate for the job at hand. If the teacher can prevent misunderstanding by preparing his classes more carefully, he must do so. If the surgeon can reduce the risk of death by using an equally effective but less dangerous procedure, he should do so.

We are responsible for unintended effects which we can avoid by reasonable efforts. When there are alternatives, we have some control of the effects, so that a failure to control implies an indifference to the good which is, in effect, a rejection of the good. It is for this reason that we hold people responsible for the results of ignorance or error which could have been removed or avoided if reasonable efforts had been made. We shall return to this particular problem in Chapter 7.

In practice, we must consider not only alternative means to the end but the certainty and probability of all the effects of each alternative. This means that the size of the risk is to be considered in balancing intended goods and unintended evils. We risk death whenever we cross a busy street. No one, however, will accuse us of an unethical action so long as we have some reason for crossing and take ordinary precautions. In this case, the risk of death is not great, while there are real goods to be obtained. People would judge us differently if, in order to impress people, we risked our lives by drinking a quart of whiskey in a half hour. In this case, the risk of death is high and the good small, if not imaginary.

My responsibility for the unintended effects of my actions varies with my causal contribution to the effect. The teacher who knows that some students will misunderstand him even though he is clear, also knows that the students are often inattentive, ill-prepared, or just plain lazy. The real blame for the misunderstanding can rest with the student and not with the teacher. When we fire a worker who is failing to work, we may injure his family. However, it is the worker who is the major cause of the harm. In such cases, where the major cause of the evil is outside us, our responsibility is diminished and we need less of a reason to run risks.

In general, responsibility decreases as causal influence diminishes. If we were responsible for effects over which we had little or no control, we would often be forced to omit good actions because of the stupidity or malice of others. If inefficient workers are not fired, good workers will be harmed. If teachers must stop teaching because inattentive students will misunderstand, good students would be penalized. Other factors may oblige us to omit actions which have little influence on intended side effects, but all other things being equal, our responsibility decreases when much of the causality flows from other agents.

A PRELIMINARY SUMMARY

In determining whether or not a person is responsible for the unintended but foreseen effects of his actions, we attempt to balance the goods intended with the evil consequences. We are asking if a person has a proportionate reason for risking or permitting evil. The proportionality of a reason depends, in part, on the availability of alternate means, the size of the risk involved, and the extent of the agent's causal influence. As yet, however, we have not considered the two most important criteria of proportionality: the hierarchy of goods and the urgency of need.

THE HIERARCHY OF GOODS

The problem of hierarchy, or of priorities, appears not only in cases that involve the risking or permitting of evils but also in cases where a person appears to be willing an evil precisely as a means. A parent spanks a child in order to teach him that a stove burns. An employer docks the wages of a worker in the hope that the worker will start showing up for work on time. A surgeon cuts off a leg to prevent death from blood poisoning. In each case, some sort of harm is willed as a means to a good, and yet ordinarily we do not say that the agent is guilty of an evil or that he is unethical or immoral. Why? Is there something different about these evils? Are there cases where the end does justify willing an evil?

While we do not accuse the employer, the surgeon, or the parent of an unethical act, even though they have willed an apparent evil as a means, we take quite a different point of view in cases like the following. A man kills another man and eats his body in order to keep himself from starving to death. A woman in moderate circumstances steals dresses from a store so that she will be stylishly dressed for her daughter's graduation. A child lies to his mother in order to avoid punishment. In all these cases we tend to say that the good intended does not justify the evil used as a means. What is it about these evils which prevents us from invoking proportionality?

There are no completely satisfactory answers to these questions, but two attempts at rough classification can provide some tools for analyzing the hierarchy of goods and evils. The first method distinguishes between a physical evil and an "ethical" (moral) evil. The physical evil may be willed as a means when there is a proportionate reason. The "ethical" evil may never be willed for any reason whatsoever. While the distinction has some use, it does not tell us much about the difference between the two evils, nor does it explain why we may will the one evil for a proportionate reason, but not the other. Is a slap in the face a physical or an "ethical" evil? It would seem to depend on whether the slap was intended to insult or snap a person out of hysterics. While intention, or the end willed, is certainly important, it does not tell us anything about the means considered in itself. Stealing seems to involve only the loss of a physical good, yet we condemn deliberate stealing as an ethical evil. There must, then, be something more at stake than the merely physical.

The evils which we permit a person to will when he has a proportionate reason all seem to have this in common. They do not, of themselves, go against the end of man, his essential dignity, or his rights. When there is a proportionate reason for the act, this type of evil actually promotes the end, the dignity, and the rights of man. On the other hand, the evils which may not be willed for any reason go against either the end of man, his dignity, or his rights. The man who murdered and ate his companion in order to escape starvation treated a fellow man as a thing, deprived him of his rights, and possibly cut him off from his full development. The woman who steals a dress in order to look stylish at her daughter's graduation has not only violated the storekeeper's right to his property but has raised prices for others and attacked that good social order which is necessary if men are to lead their lives properly. The child who lies to escape punishment has deprived the parent of information he needs in order to do his duty and has injured the social confidence necessary for the conduct of an orderly household. Directly or indirectly, each of the acts we would more or less spontaneously condemn either violates a right or destroys some good that is necessary for the perfection of one or more individuals. Such evils are at odds with the perfection of man in time. The end cannot justify such evils because they are against the end.

In order to simplify the problem of expression, we will distinguish between major and minor evils. A major evil is one which is against the end because it involves either a violation of rights and essential human dignity or the loss of a good necessary for the maintenance of human dignity. A minor evil involves the destruction or loss of a merely physical good or some purely useful good which is not necessary for human dignity and which is not the object of a right. It should be noted, however, that even a minor evil cannot be willed, risked, or permitted without a proportionate reason. The reason is simply that such activity is unreasonable, a refusal to work for the end by all possible means. Such a refusal is implicitly a rejection of intellect, which is a necessary means, and so equivalently a major evil.

The distinction between minor and major evils is not completely satisfactory for a number of reasons. Even after we have clarified the meaning of rights in Chapter 6, we will still have to admit that such terms as human dignity and human growth are vague and designate different concepts in different cultures. Similarly, the concept *necessary* does not specify a fixed set of objects in each and every culture, although some things are considered universally necessary. While these difficulties cannot be disregarded, they should not discourage us. At this stage we are only developing a formal scheme, a sort of blank check that needs to be filled in.

THE NECESSARY AND THE USEFUL

No matter how vague the terms necessary and useful may be, there is a minimal content. All men need food and liquid in order to stay alive, and life is generally necessary for the attainment of human perfection. Food and drink, in their turn, cannot be easily obtained without some knowledge. In certain areas, food and drink cannot be obtained without social cooperation, so that social life is also a necessity. Similarly, since most of our knowledge comes from others, society is necessary on a second count. We can, then, show that a large number of things are necessary for mere survival. We even have an empirical test of such necessity. If we remove these goods, men die.

Social life serves not only survival but growth as well. It provides security, so that man can function with a minimum of fear. It can help to create that freedom necessary for man to make his own choices. To attain such ends, society needs standards of order, the assignment of roles, and some agreement about values. Indeed, the web of things necessary for society spreads out far and wide, even if the group is viewed only as a tool necessary for survival. Systems of exchange or sharing, methods of communication and decision making, are all necessary in some form or other.

Over and above those things which all men need for survival we have the needs of classes of men and of individuals. Children need not only food but intimacy in order to grow and cooperate with others. Children need to learn to control their emotions in order to be accepted by others. Particular individuals need to experience beauty, to express themselves, and to solve the mysteries of the world about them.

Both groups—classes and individuals—have biological, psychic, and social needs which can be determined with greater or less precision. There are, however, a large number of goods which, while not necessary, are highly useful. Some of these useful goods may even be necessary for a particular ideal which the individual has set up for himself. When we are dealing with the merely useful or with things that are necessary for an individual only because of a previous choice, we have passed into the area of the ideal and of individual freedom. No longer are we dealing with the minimum necessary for survival, psychic stability, or social cooperation for necessary goods. We are in an area where it is not a question of basic dignity but of full growth. We shall return to this in the next chapter when we ask if a man is obliged to do the better thing and to work for an ideal.

While the distinction between the necessary and the useful poses some problems, it does permit us to work out a rough hierarchy of goods. The classification is crude, since each term designates a space on a continuum. At times the spaces appear to overlap. The highly useful is often barely distinguishable from the slightly necessary good. How will we classify a college education in contemporary American society? What position shall we assign to aspirin, newspapers, soap, a church building? The attempt to answer these questions will indicate why the necessary-useful scale is a shifting one. The scale helps, but it does not solve all problems.

The necessary-useful scale can provide particular help in determining whether or not there is a proportionate reason for risking or permitting a major evil or for willing, risking or permitting a minor evil. I may not cut off my leg to provide a conversation piece at cocktail parties. I may cut it off to save my life. The woman mentioned earlier may not steal a dress in order to appear stylish, but most would permit her to take food if she and her family were starving to death. A parent may spank a child in order to teach him a lesson, but he may not beat him in such a way as to cause bodily injury, since no overall good would be attained in this way.

We depend on other men for our survival and growth. Other men have a dignity equal to ours. For these two reasons the consideration of the necessary and the useful must look to both the needs of others and the needs of societies. The calculations which enter into the judgment of proportionality must not be purely egoistic, lest the social nature of man be denied in practice, if not in theory. This will become clearer in the chapters on rights, love, and society. At the very start, however, the social dimension must be stressed, since selfishness can tempt us to substitute an egocentric pragmatism for an ethic that recognizes the value of all men.

URGENCY OF NEEDS

Human needs vary not only in object but in urgency. Both food and liquid are necessary for survival, but they differ in urgency. I can go without food for a fairly long time, but a few days without liquid will lead to death. At times, then, liquid may be more necessary than food. Even on a higher level, the place of urgency must be considered. In a general sense, we can say that knowledge is necessary for the full growth of the individual. However, not every type of knowledge is necessary. A man can grow without knowing much about space exploration, but he can hardly grow without knowing something about his own being and the expectations of those with whom he must live. The latter type of knowledge is more urgent and must be gained early in life.

Urgency, even if culturally conditioned, can be a real factor in judging proportionality. The urgency of the poverty program should make us ask if we are ethical when we spend large sums on less urgent tasks such as space exploration and road beautification.

In practice, the urgency of one necessary good can justify our choosing it over a necessary good which can be obtained at a later date. Urgency increases necessity and so changes the concrete balance. A student needs to sleep and to study. Sleep may be more urgent when lack of it harms the student's health and makes study impossible. During examination periods, of course, students consider study more urgent than sleep.

Urgency, the hierarchy of goods, the probability of evil, causal influence, and the availability of alternates must all be considered in weighing proportionality. All these factors influence our responsibility for the foreseen but unintended effects of our actions.

THE ETHICAL AND THE UNETHICAL

All the foregoing pages have been a preparation for the discussion of the difference between good and evil in general and the ethical and unethical, or, as some may prefer to put it, the moral and the immoral.

The goods and evils we consider in the ethical order have two characteristics. First, they are good or evil for man. Secondly, they are goods and evils which man incorporates into himself by his knowing and willing. The ethical order is primarily concerned with the activities and institutions for which man is responsible. The ethical includes both the subjective and the objective, and the personal and impersonal side of reality. Our definitions of the ethical and unethical must reflect this union of the two aspects. The following formulas will summarize what has gone before.

1. *It is unethical to will either the rejection of the end or a major evil whether as a means or an end.*

2. *It is unethical to will even a good if this involves risking or permitting a major evil without a proportionate reason.*

3. *It is unethical to will, permit, or risk even a minor evil without a proportionate reason.*

These three formulas restrict the use of the terms unethical and ethical evil to free and deliberate acts or omissions which go against the end of man. When a man acts in this fashion, we condemn not merely the consequences of his actions, but the man himself. In these cases, a man has made the evil a part of himself by freely willing it or by permitting or risking it without a proportionate reason. If such activity is habitual, we may even refer to him as an unethical man.

The ethics compressed into three formulas is not purely and simply an ethics of consequences. It is also an ethics of intentions and motives. While the consequences of our acts are extremely important, they are not decisive. The decisive element is found in our foreknowledge and willing. Our intention may be decisive, but it cannot change the objective order. There are goods and evils which must be considered if man is to grow.

Although the term unethical will be used in a restricted sense, we do not mean to imply any indifference to the other evils that afflict man. The evils that are permitted or risked for a proportionate reason are evils even though the overall effects may be weighted on the side of the good. If we are forced to let one of two men die because time will only permit us to save one, we should feel sorrow and anguish even though there is no foundation for guilt. The ethical man will be constantly striving to remove the evils in the world. He will be looking for alternate methods of obtaining the good without harmful side effects. At the same time, he need not feel that he is unethical just because success has not been instantaneous.

The definitions ought to make us temperate in our judgments of others, even when we must condemn their acts. Ordinarily, we do not know what the other person knew and willed. We do not know how he calculated the proportionality involved in so many cases. We should be slow, then, to call a man unethical even when the evidence shows that he was wrong. While fairness to others may demand that we judge persons but rarely, loyalty to the good may demand that we condemn their actions publicly and prevent them from doing evil. A man may think it correct to beat his child until it is unconscious, but may I tolerate his act if I can stop it? The state may think capital punishment is justified, but I will work for its abolition, since I believe it is wrong in our society. In short, toleration of individuals is not the equivalent of the toleration of evil.

There are times when even temporary toleration of evil may be justified. In some cases we are powerless to remove the evil immediately. In other cases rapid removal of the evil may generate even greater evils. If the state in which we reside has no child-abuse law, there is probably little we can legally do at a given moment to stop a man from beating his child into unconsciousness. We can, however, work for the passage of a law which will stop him. There are inequities in our economic system which should be removed, but cannot be removed overnight without causing untold hardship to many innocent people. We may have to put up with such situations for a time until changes can be made. We are not excused from trying to change the system, but only excused from the responsibility for producing instant results.

THE ETHICAL GOOD

The ethical good is not merely the absence of ethical evil as we have defined it. Sometimes men do good through inadvertence. A purely routine greeting to someone may cheer him up or make him feel that someone cares about him. The good is real and not to be downgraded, but it is not an ethical good since the act was not deliberate. The good was not intended and so did not become a part of the man who gave the greeting. An ethically good act must involve willing the good in some way.

Merely willing a good does not create an ethical act. If the known harmful effects of the good outweigh the good, we are involved in an unethical act. What, however, are we to say of those cases where the agent wills a good and erroneously, but inculpably, believes that the good effects outweigh the evil effects? We will not accuse him of an unethical act so long as his error or ignorance is inculpable, but can we say that he has performed an ethical act? Here is an individual who honestly believes that he must offer a human sacrifice to God. Has he performed an ethical act when he kills his child in the name of religion?

Undoubtedly, the man who is subjectively in good faith, though he is in serious error, incorporates good into himself. At the same time, the act in question produces more harm than good in the objective order. The act, in its totality, is so flawed that we hesitate to call it ethical. Because the individual is not responsible for the result of inculpable error or ignorance, we cannot call the act unethical. Perhaps we should call it a subjectively ethical act and reserve the term ethical without qualification for acts which are both subjectively and objectively good.

Leaving aside the question of terminology, the situation we have described points up the tragedy of human life. Our limited knowledge often leaves us in a position where our good will does not rest on the real. Our ignorance or error can create victims. Our intentions may not be fully realized because our knowledge of means is inadequate. It is for this reason, as we shall see in a later chapter, that moral knowledge is a necessary good for man.

The fully or unqualifiedly ethical act involves both the intention of the good and the production of effects such that the intended goods at least balance out the unintended evils which are risked or permitted. While this may be too restrictive a definition, it does point up the fact that it is this type of act which we must strive for, even though we do not always realize our goal. We cannot be content with the subjectively ethical without running the danger of indifference to the good. We shall return to this point several times in later chapters.

The ethical man is concerned not only with avoiding evil but with realizing the human potential for growth. He does not look for excuses, though he may have to use them. He is looking for opportunities to maximize the good. He wants to create good for others and make the good a part of himself by means of his own deliberate choices. He may use code morality or definitions of the unethical conduct as minimum guides, but he is seeking to go beyond the minimum. He is an idealist in that he searches for the more perfect, but he is a realist in that he honestly faces the limits of reality, of his own knowledge, and of the men about him.

As the ethical man reaches greater and greater maturity, he may have less need for the formal analytic scheme we have developed in this chapter. He can develop a feel for the good and spontaneously make excellent judgments about complicated situations. In the beginning of the ethical life, however, most men need some formal scheme to aid them in deciphering the meaning of their activity. To some extent, however, formal schemes are like scaffolding that is necessary when a building is going up but can be torn down when the job has been finished.

In theory, the ethical man should be able to do without scaffolding. In practice, he may need it throughout life. As we grow older, we meet new situations of ever greater complexity. A mere glance will not tell us all the effects of a political, economic, or social system. The interrelation of causes is so great that even the refined analytic tools of sociology, economics, and political science hardly suffice for an understanding of what is going on. As a result, the ethical man may actually have to develop new analytic tools in order to cope with these ethical problems which arise from the nature and functioning of institutions rather than from the simple face to face contacts with individuals. In ethics, as in other areas of life, there is always something more to be done.[2]

In the following chapters we will consider some of the goods which the ethical man must bring into existence as well as the useful goods which may form part of the ideal. The next chapter will delve a little more deeply into the problem of priorities and the place of freedom in forming the ideal.

NEGATIVE ANALYSIS OF ACTS

The beginner in ethics is often confused by the array of factors to be considered in making judgments about the ethical quality of an act. While the following systematic form of analysis is no substitute for experience, it may introduce the beginner to an orderly method of breaking down a problem and arriving at a decision.

Stage 1.   *A.* What is willed as a means and as an end?

        B. What objective evil or good results from, or is found in, the means and the end?

NOTE: Omissions and their effects must be considered.

Decision 1. *A.* If the end is deliberately rejected or if a major evil is willed either as a means or an end, the analysis stops here. You are dealing with a clearly unethical act.

NOTE: A major evil goes against a man's rights or destroys a good necessary for either an individual or society.

        B. If the above is not true, go on to stage two.

Stage 2.   *A.* What are the side effects which are *foreseen* as either certain or probable but are *not willed* as either means or ends?

        B. What is the good or evil of each foreseen but unintended side effect?

        C. What is the certitude or probability of both the intended and unintended effects?

        D. What is the urgency of the goods involved?

       E. How great is the causal influence of the intended act and its intended effects?

Decision 2.   *A.* If there is no proportionate reason for willing a minor evil, or no proportionate reason for risking or permitting a major evil, the analysis stops at this point. You are dealing with an unethical act.

       B. If there is a proportionate reason *in the abstract,* go on to stage three.

Stage 3.   *A.* Is there an equally good method of attaining the good intended with less evil or less risk of evil as side effects?

Decision 3.   *A.* If the answer to the above question is Yes, you should use the alternative, since *in the concrete* you have no proportionate reason for risking or permitting the evils which you can avoid without losing the good.

       B. If the answer to the above question is No, you may act, since you have a proportionate reason for permitting or risking the unintended evils in the concrete as well as in the abstract.

This analytic method requires the person who uses it to make an honest effort to study the contents to be inserted. In particular, he must study the effects of the intended action. Such study involves more than the use of common sense. Whenever possible, the ethical man will consult with experienced people and seek to find out what scientists may have written on the subject. He will also be aware of the need for updating his knowledge in those areas where new research has a bearing on the suitability of various activities for human perfection. Above all, he will remember that ethics is not concerned merely with avoiding evil but with a search for the good.

RELATIONS TO OTHER SYSTEMS

Most of the differences between our treatment and that of other thinkers is to be found in the discussion of man and the fundamental nature of the good. Something, however, should be said about the relationship between our terminology and that used in many of the traditional treatments of the subject.

Writers in the scholastic tradition distinguish between the *befitting* (*honestum*), the *useful,* and the *pleasurable* good.[3] We have eliminated the term pleasurable good because experience indicates that some pleasure is necessary for human life, while all pleasure is at least useful if treated as a means. In short, we have absorbed the pleasureable goods into our other categories. The befitting good is described as a good which is sought because it contributes to the perfection of man's being as a whole. For all practical purposes, this is identical with our ethical good in an unqualified sense.

Most writers distinguish between intrinsic and extrinsic goods. The extrinsic good includes the useful or instrumental good; things which may be used as means, even though we do not value them for themselves. Money, for example, is an extrinsic good for everyone but a miser, who loves it for its own sake. The intrinsic good is valued for itself, that is, as an end. Knowledge can be considered as an intrinsic good insofar as it is the end of the intellect. However, in our view, such particular ends as knowledge are, in the last analysis, means to the attainment of human perfection and union with God. In order to avoid confusion, then, we prefer to reserve the term intrinsic good for God and the human person as a whole. Only persons, whether divine or human, can be called intrinsically good in an unqualified sense.

Catholic moral theologians have long considered the moral determinants of a human act to be the moral object, the motive, or end, and the circumstances surrounding the act. We have not followed this useful opinion for several reasons. It is difficult to decide how the theologians decide what pertains to the moral object of an

act. They do not have handy criteria for the inclusion or exclusion
of circumstances in the definition of the moral object. Our own
method of analysis tries to provide these criteria and to relate them
to factors that are accessible to men of good will. Indeed it is our
impression that many contemporary moral theologians are already
operating on a basis similar to the one we have developed.[4]

The naturalistic ethicians hold that the good is somewhere within
the world of experience and not outside it. While we do not agree
with this statement, we must admit that in practice our methods
have strong naturalistic implications. Because we do not see the
direct relationship between particular acts of man and his final
union with God, it has been necessary to work out a system for
analyzing the goods in the world of persons and nature. We are
aware, however, that this approach is incomplete and depends for
its meaning on the assumption that the world of time has some
relationship to the world beyond time.

Quite obviously, we differ from those who say that an act is good
or bad only because God commands or forbids it. While God can
issue commands, the ethician, as opposed to the moral theologian,
has no way of discovering what those commands may be except by
examining reality and its impact on man. The religious man should
not be content with mere ethical analysis. He should listen to both
the word of God and the wisdom of his own religious group. At
the same time, the religious man does well to seek the reasons for
divine commands so that his faith may be supported by his reason.

THE TASK AHEAD

The full meaning of everything covered in the present chapter
depends on an understanding of the limits on our freedom, our
knowledge, and our rights. The next three chapters will treat of
these concepts. As yet, we have not clarified the difference between
the goods which we must choose and the goods which we may
choose or reject. The following chapter will treat of obligation and
the place of freedom in the ethical life.

NOTES

1. *Cf.* Jacques Leclerq, *Christ and the Modern Conscience* (New York: Sheed & Ward, 1962), p. 173, for some illuminating observations on moral theology.
2. For examples of the type of analysis and information that may be necessary, *cf.* Thomas M. Garrett, *An Introduction to Some Ethical Problems of Modern American Advertising* (Rome: Gregorian University Press, 1961), and Johannes Messner, *Social Ethics* (St. Louis: B. Herder Book Co., 1949).
3. *Cf.* Austin Fagothey, *Right and Reason* (St. Louis: Mosby, 1953), p. 34.
4. *Cf.* John G. Milhaven, "Towards an Epistemology of Ethics," *Theological Studies,* 27 (1966), pp. 228–241, and John G. Milhaven and David J. Casey, "Introduction to the Theological Background of the New Morality." *Theological Studies,* 28 (1967), pp. 213–244.

POINTS FOR DISCUSSION

1. How do other ethicians try to solve the problems of discrimination, choice, and responsibility?
2. Is there any completely satisfactory way of solving these problems?
3. Do even moral theologians, who start from a divine revelation, have to face these problems? Why?
4. What methods of discrimination are used by moral theologians in the various churches?
5. Examine and discuss the informal methods of discrimination used by men with no formal training in ethics or moral theology.
6. Why is it impossible for the end to justify the means when the means are of a certain type of evil?
7. Why can the end sometimes justify risking or permitting even major evils?
8. How, in the concrete, do you decide whether a good is necessary or merely useful?
9. How would you classify different types of pleasure? Why?
10. Do the ordinary moral and ethical precepts in our society rest on a view of the good similar to that developed in chapters three and four?

READINGS*

Peter A. BERTOCCI and Richard M. MILLARD, *Personality and the Good* (New York: David McKay, 1963), pp. 411–428; 486–507.

Joseph DE FINANCE, *Essai sur l'agir humain* (Rome: Gregorian, 1962), pp. 348–381.

Thomas J. HIGGINS, *Man as Man* (Milwaukee: Bruce, 1948), pp. 29–77.

Abraham H. MASLOW, "Psychological Data and Value Theory" in Abraham H. MASLOW (ed.), *New Knowledge in Human Values* (New York: Harper & Row, 1959), pp. 119–136.

William H. WERKMEISTER, *Theories of Ethics* (Lincoln, Neb.: Johnsen, 1961), pp. 91–284.

Sidney ZINK, *The Concepts of Ethics* (London: Macmillan, 1962), pp. 207–225; 256–291.

* All these readings involve other approaches.

5/ OBLIGATION AND FREEDOM

INTRODUCTION

Our ethical vocabulary is not exhausted by such words as good, evil, and responsibility. We also use ethical terms such as *ought, must, obligation, duty,* and *moral necessity.* While these terms designate a relationship to the good, they are not synonymous with the good. Common sense tells us that not all goods are obligatory, because not all goods are possible at a given moment. It would be good to be a doctor, a lawyer, a teacher, a stone mason, a homemaker, a ditch digger and the President of the United States. We are not obliged to be all these things at once because we are not capable of doing this. Indeed, most men would be incapable of being all these things successively. On the other hand, we generally feel obliged to protect our health, to earn a living, and to cooperate with other men. There would appear to be a difference between goods we consider obligatory and those which are merely good.

THE PROBLEM

Our experience of obligation is different from our experience of the good. Obligation involves some sort of constraint, limitation, necessity, even though we are free to act against these barriers. Obligation involves experiencing our freedom and its limitations simultaneously. It can even be a painful experience, since often we are constrained to give up some goods in the name of duty. A mother feels obliged to stay home and nurse her sick child even though this involves giving up income, recreation, and service to a sick neighbor. No one will force her to nurse the child, but she feels the inner necessity to do so. She probably embraces this duty with joy and enthusiasm, but this does not change the fact that she feels the necessity.

This experience of constraint or necessity, coexisting with freedom, is generally distinguished from irrational compulsions. We recognize that a neurotic may be constrained to walk home and check the lock on his door two or three times. Perhaps we feel compelled to step on cracks in the sidewalk, to buy a new hat, or to break milk bottles, but generally we do not say we are obligated to do these things. Implicitly, we assume that there is some difference between a feeling of moral restraint and such compulsion. We assume that there is a reasonable basis for the feeling of ethical obligation, while we either assume or know that there is no reasonable basis for our neurotic compulsions.

In the first part of the present chapter, we must not only find a basis for the distinction between the obligatory good and the merely good, but we must also unearth the basis for our separating the experience of moral or ethical necessity from neurotic compulsions.

HYPOTHETICAL OBLIGATION AND
OBJECTIVE NECESSITY

If a man wanted to go to Europe a hundred years ago, he had to go by boat. Today, if a man wants to be a physicist in a university, he must go to college and graduate school. If a man wants to be a world champion weightlifter, he must undergo rigorous training. Once a man sees the necessity of the means for the end he has chosen, he will feel obliged to use that means. The boat, the school, and the training are all objectively necessary for the ends in question. The individual, however, will not feel obliged to use these means until he has decided to attain the end. The obligation is hypothetical. If you will the end, you are under a necessity to will the necessary means. The necessity of the means arises from the objective order, not from the choice of the individual.

Many of our obligations are hypothetical. You are bound to obey the rules of the Elks if you choose to be a member. You are obliged to sell your car to an individual if you have agreed to do so. You must speak English if you are going to teach in most American schools. The list might be extended endlessly. In each case, however, the necessity arises both from my free choice and from the objective situation. The objective situation is not, however, the same in every case. The necessity of using a boat a hundred years ago arose from the state of technology at that period. The need for rigorous training has its roots in the nature of the human body. The necessity of obeying group rules arises from the nature of group activity. The need to speak English is rooted in the fact that this language is the principal vehicle of communication in a given culture.

While the necessities are real, they are not absolute and unchangeable in all cases. Today a man can go to Europe by either plane or boat. In Spain a teacher does not need English. In most cases, a man can get out of these hypothetical obligations by changing his mind about the end he desires. An individual can decide not to go to Europe, not to become a champion weightlifter, not to join the Elks.

Often we are involved in chains of hypothetical obligations. A man has to go to Europe because this is necessary for his business. His business is necessary for the support of his family. A man may agree to sell his car because he needs money in order to pay for an operation which is necessary to preserve his life. We may ask, however, if the man is obliged to support his family only because he has chosen to do so. Is a man obliged to preserve his life only because he decides that this is good? To put it another way, are there necessary ends which, when recognized as such, create obligations within the individual quite independent of his choices?

ABSOLUTE OBLIGATION AND OBJECTIVE NECESSITY

In the last chapter we pointed out that experience has shown us that certain things are necessary for the survival and growth of man. Food, drink, social life, and knowledge are necessities for continued existence, and continued existence is, as far as we know, necessary for human perfection and the attainment of union with God. We must ask, however, if union with God is necessary. Better yet, we must ask if God is so necessary that once man sees this he will feel obliged to work towards God even though he does not choose God as his end. If there is no necessary end, there is no absolute obligation. In such a hypothesis, man is obliged only when something is necessary to an end he has freely chosen.

In Chapter 3 we noted that God, the infinite being, was the only being capable of satisfying all man's tendencies. Man necessarily tends to this supreme good whether he knows it or not. Human restlessness and discontent are rooted in the being of man. Man has no choice about being a project, a person to be realized. This results from his nature and his position in the world. For these reasons we say that God is the necessary end, quite independent of the choices of men.

Every individual does not clearly recognize the fact that his being is necessarily directed to the infinite, to God. This means that there are men who do not feel under the necessity of striving for the infinite we call God. Every man, however, does feel the pull of the infinite, even though he cannot name the object of this pull. Every man feels under the necessity of striving for something outside himself. Indeed, in the course of history, men have set up many pseudo-absolutes in order to give some meaning to this drive. Some men set up power and pleasure as the objectives which will satisfy this drive, even though experience always proves the futility of these as ultimates. Others set up the race or the state as the supreme and necessary good. Man, in short, creates absolutes, but there is only one absolute and necessary being which can satisfy his being: God.

Actually, the most common substitute for God is the human person. This is not surprising, for the human person is an end in himself. He is not a means to anything, even though he is incomplete and dependent on God. Moreover, the perfection of man in time is reasonably assumed to be the means to the perfection of man beyond time. For these reasons, a humanist can construct a lofty ethics. Unfortunately, because men can see that man is not capable of fulfilling all the longings of man, humanism often leaves men unsatisfied or resigned to achieving less than the realization of the full human potential.

When a man sees that only God can satisfy his infinite longing for completion, he will feel necessitated to strive for God. He will experience an absolute obligation, even though he has not chosen God as his end. Man, however, does not necessarily direct all his activities to the attainment of God. The necessity he feels does not destroy his freedom. He can turn away and say that it is better to be an incomplete creature than to depend on God. Man can blot out the realization that God is necessary. He can escape the feeling of obligation by refusing to think of it. Indeed, we see men who do not even want to consider the real possibility of God because they know they might then see his necessity and have to admit their own limitations.

Even the man who does not run from the necessity of God does not always act in accord with his knowledge. He can and does put other things first, aware all the while that this is not reasonable. An absolute obligation does not coerce man's will. We are free even when we feel constrained. Though we may see where the supreme good is to be found, we are still able to choose lesser goods. Knowledge and experienced constraint do not ensure full reasonable activity, for we are men in the process of fulfilling ourselves.

DEFINITIONS

In our view, *an obligation is a moral necessity arising from the knowledge of an objective necessity.* We say "moral" to indicate that the necessity is compatible with freedom. We are not talking of a physical or psychic determinism. The obligation, as defined, exists formally in the person who experiences the necessity. However, because the foundation is objective, we can speak of a person having an obligation to do something even though he may not know of it.

The obligatory good is the necessary good. Necessity distinguishes obligation from the merely good. The necessity of a known objective foundation distinguishes an obligation from a neurotic compulsion. If the necessity is only imagined, or if it is only felt and no objective necessity can be assigned, we are not dealing with an obligation.

An *ethical* obligation exists when the objective necessity is related to the necessary end. I am ethically obligated to eat because eating generally is necessary for life, which is generally necessary for human perfection, which—so far as we know—is necessary for the attainment of the final end. Even a hypothetical obligation can be an ethical obligation if the end willed is necessary for the final end or if the fulfillment of the obligation is necessary for the preservation of some necessary good. For example, even though the obligation of fulfilling a contract arises only as a result of my free choice, I am ethically bound, since the fulfillment of contracts is necessary for social life.

In the preceding paragraph we inserted the word "generally" in several places. The reason is simple. There can be exceptions. Moreover, when there are apparent conflicts of obligations, the hierarchy of goods and of necessity might demand that eating be subordinated to some other necessary good. Similarly, I may be excused from observing the terms of a contract because changed circumstances have made it against the public good, so that the fulfillment of this particular contract would no longer be useful for social life. In practice, then, we will see that many of our positive obligations will be hedged around with conditions.

GENERAL OBLIGATIONS

The first and most general obligation is the *avoidance of all ethical evil*. We must not will something which is against the end, since this would be to avoid the basic obligation of striving freely for the end. The obligation of following the three formulas developed in the previous chapters is absolute. It does not admit of conditions or exceptions.

Our general negative obligation is the avoidance of ethical evil. What are our positive obligations? How shall we determine them? Our general positive obligation is to strive for the end beyond time and the fulfillment of the human person in time. We must, however, ask which specific acts are necessary for this double end. As we have noted earlier, merely avoiding ethical evil will not suffice to perfect a man. It should also be clear that purely general statements of positive obligations will not be particularly useful in making decisions.

Later chapters will consider specific positive obligations. They will not, however, attempt to present an exhaustive catalogue. Different things are necessary at different times and places. An Eskimo may be obliged to learn fishing, while the same skill may be rather useless to a desert dweller. It is necessary that some men in our society study medicine, but such an obligation does not fall on each individual. Each culture and society must work out its own systems, and these give rise to varying necessities and obligations. At the same time, we can see general obligations to provide for nourishment, the training of children, and the collection of knowledge necessary for survival. The form of these obligations must be studied in a given context.

Often, our *prima facie* obligations seem to conflict. In such cases we have to go behind particular norms and expressions to discover the actual priorities of obligations. We shall have to ask which good is more necessary and more urgent. We shall also have to discover who has the primary responsibility for bringing the goods into existence. Chapters 7 and 9 will consider some of the methods for resolving doubts and assigning priorities in these difficult cases.

THE GREATER GOOD

While a man is certainly obliged to bring into existence those specific goods which are necessary, we may ask if he is obliged to maximize the good, to strive for an ideal, even though many of the specific goods are only useful when considered in the abstract. Must a man strive to develop his talents to the greatest possible degree? Does ethics oblige a man to go beyond the minimum set up by the necessary and to strive for the concrete optimum possible at a given time and place?

In order to avoid confusion and the charge of "perfectionism," we wish to make several observations before attempting to answer the question about the obligation to maximize the good. In the first place, man cannot be obliged to do what is concretely impossible for him. We are not asking about an obligation to do what is abstractly more perfect, but about what is more perfect and possible in the concrete situation of an individual. In the abstract, the works of the mind and spirit are more perfect than the works of the body, but in the concrete, digging a drainage ditch may be the better thing to do. Secondly, we are not concerned merely with what is the better thing at a given moment, but with the greater perfection of an individual over the course of his life. Right now, it may be better for me to read than to exercise, but the long-run good may make it better for me to run around the block and tone up my muscles. Finally, because we are looking at the concrete greater good over a long period of time, we are interested in a balance of goods, a constellation of goods which expresses a maximum.

Let us consider a concrete case. John Stack is the twenty-one-year-old son of very wealthy parents. He enjoys excellent health and has unusual intellectual talents. He is a gentleman who would never deliberately hurt anyone's feelings and can be very generous when called on for help. John has finished college and is living a life of leisure, since there is no need for him to go to work. His education would qualify him to go on to medical school or to go into a drug company as an executive trainee. He could also enter his father's medical supply business or go to law school. John decides that he will not take any of these opportunities since he does not have to.

John Stack is a pleasant enough young man who appears to observe the minimum ethical requirements. We cannot say that he is obliged to be either a doctor or an executive or a lawyer. Yet we must feel that there is something wrong about his decision to live a life of leisure. We sense a waste of talent, an indifference to the needs of others, a lack of real concern with ultimate values and goals. There is a refusal to use his gifts to the fullest which betrays a certain amount of selfishness.

The refusal to utilize our talents and opportunities is really a refusal to grow. It is equivalent to saying that some narrowly conceived good is more important than the achievement of our perfection in time. In the concrete, John is saying No to the sick he might help either as a doctor or as an executive. He is permitting an evil to continue for no proportionate reason. Thus, he falls into a type of ethical evil by refusing to maximize the concrete possibilities that are open to him.

For these reasons, we believe that there is an obligation to maximize the good, though the form and shape of this maximization is left to the free choice of individuals. Although we may not be able to assign an exact necessity to any one of the possibilities, we cannot reject them all without falling into evil. This does not mean that we should be constantly worrying about whether or not we are doing the perfect thing at each moment. Such worry is profitless, since it consumes energy while producing nothing of value. The obligation to maximize does imply that we should be alert and ready to take the opportunities which do present themselves. We should not worry, but we should avoid an easy complacency which is equivalent to an indifference to the good of man.

From a purely pragmatic point of view, the man who only does the minimum will find it hard or impossible to maintain even that low level. For this reason, if for no other, he must decide what will move him more effectively to his full perfection. Indeed, though ethics must be concerned with the minimum do's and don'ts, the truly creative moral life takes place in the vast area of freedom which exists between the limits. It must challenge the individual's ideals and not merely help him draw up a list of safety regulations.

USE OF FREEDOM AND CREATIVITY
IN THE ETHICAL LIFE

To view the ethical life as no more than adherence to a narrow code is to reduce man to a stereotype or a skeleton without the flesh of creative individuality. There are limits within which man must move, but these do not so much confine as point to the area where man is challenged to realize the unique, the noble, and ultimately the perfection of the truly human. Indeed, because this area between limits is the field of human freedom, it is the world of the truly personal and human. Here man transcends mere nature and moves towards the divine, towards the actual fullness of being which is man's destiny. To strive for less is to sink back to the constricting world of matter, of half-joys and human mediocrity.

The saints and great humanitarians were often men and women with ordinary talents. They were not, however, afraid to use their gifts or to commit themselves to an ideal. They did not run away from risks when something great was to be accomplished. Gandhi in India, Schweitzer in Africa, are admired not because they avoided evil but because they freely chose to be themselves and to go beyond the ordinary ethical demands of their societies.

OBLIGATION AND FREEDOM

While obligation does not destroy freedom, it limits its exercise in the ethical order. This makes the notion of obligation repugnant to those who conceive of freedom as the highest if not the unique good. As a result, discussions of freedom and obligation often generate more smoke than light. While some of this confusion is probably irreducible, careful distinctions between the various types of freedom can clarify the problem by showing the proper value of various freedoms.

Earlier chapters have already shown that freedom is a necessary precondition for ethics, as well as one of its constitutive elements. It is only in the free act that man grows or diminishes precisely as a person, even though all his activities affect his well-being. At the same time, some limitation of freedoms is necessary if man is to maximize his good. Where one draws the line depends on the nature of a particular type of freedom and the concrete situation in which the individual is located.

In the *Idea of Freedom*[1] Mortimer Adler summarizes the main meanings as follows:

1. *Circumstantial freedom of self-realization:* a freedom which is possessed by any individual who, under favorable circumstances, is able to act as he wishes for his own good as he sees it.
2. *Acquired freedom of self-perfection:* a freedom which is possessed only by those men who, through acquired virtue or vision, are able to will or live as they ought in conformity to the moral law or an ideal befitting human nature.
3. *Natural freedom of self-determination:* a freedom which is possessed by all men in virtue of a power inherent in human nature whereby a man is able to change his own character creatively by deciding for himself what he shall do or shall become.
4. *Political liberty:* a freedom which is possessed only by citizens who, through the right of suffrage and the right of judicial appeal against the abuses of government, are able to participate in making the positive law under which they live and to alter political institutions of their society.
5. *Collective freedom:* a freedom which will be possessed by humanity or the human race in the future, when through the social use of the knowledge of both natural and social necessities men achieve the ideal mode of association which is the goal of mankind's development and are able to direct their communal life in accord with such necessities.

Circumstantial freedom is certainly a means to growth of the human person. A certain minimum of it is even a necessary means, for unless the individual can exercise not merely his will but his whole being, he will be subject to strain, to doubts about his own worth, and to the narrowness of the world which is imposed upon him. At the same time, circumstantial freedom cannot be un- limited, for other men live in the world outside, and their rights must be respected if this sort of freedom is to be a real good and not merely the subject of a slogan.

The ethics of circumstantial freedom cannot be written without reference to concrete situations. In general, for example, freedom of expression is to be encouraged, but in time of war we often discover that other goods are threatened by loose talk. Similarly, though one man has a right to speak, another has a right to be protected from the effects of lies and fraud. There is a balance to be attained if all men are to profit from freedom of this sort. We shall treat some of these problems in Chapters 6, 7, and 12.

The acquired freedom of self-perfection is, within our frame- work, the goal of all other freedoms. In some sense it is the goal of man in time, at least indirectly. This is to say that it is a state of internal perfection or fullness, but incomplete insofar as man is made for the infinite. Yet, since it is at least a partial realization of the specifically human, it can be considered the end of man in time to a greater or lesser degree.

Such freedom is a result of the activity by which man builds himself in the inner sphere. It is the core of the truly personal which, though influenced by all else in the macrocosm, is the unique and truly personal possession of the individual. Simultane- ously, it is also the fuller openness of man to all the potential means in himself and in the world around him.

We must strive to take possession of ourselves and to create ourselves by realizing the potentials which are open to us. If we refuse to do this, we shall act like things and objects, tossed about by the winds of opinion and molded by forces which may be alien to our own being and hostile to our full perfection. We must use our natural freedom of self-determination if we are to possess the acquired freedom of self-perfection.

The acquired freedom of self-perfection is not necessarily at odds with rules or conformity to social norms, or with the observance of ethical obligations. This freedom is only at odds with blind conformity and coerced obedience. The man who conforms freely and on a reasoned basis does not lose his freedom, he fulfills it. The person who rebels blindly may be more of a slave than the individual who freely embraces a law. Unreasoned rebellion may be a sign that a person has not learned to possess himself. He reacts rather than acts; rejects rather than chooses; seeks to escape rather than to find fulfillment.

Blind, unreasoned conformity may be the lesser of two evils, but it can hardly be called ethical or human. Such conformity may not only stop growth, it can lead a man to embrace evils just because he is used to embracing whatever he is commanded to embrace. Blind conformity, indeed, is a refusal to be a man and to bear responsibility for one's free choices.

The natural freedom of self-determination, which is generally called free will, is the power which makes the acquired freedom of self-perfection possible, and makes circumstantial freedom a meaningful moral category. It is one of the necessary means or capacities which constitute man's basic dignity. As a mere power, it does not exhaust man's nobility, nor does it assure the actualization of the self. It can be used destructively to diminish both self-perfection and circumstantial freedom.

Although all men with a developed intellect possess the power to make some free choices, the power needs to be developed. The scope of my self-determination grows as I see more alternate means to the end. My ability to make choices increases as I escape the power of illusion, of uncontrolled emotions, and of a diminished self-image. This is to say that the power of choice grows as we grow toward maturity.

We must increase our power to choose freely if we are to maximize the good. In practice, this means that we must conquer those fears, anxieties, and other feelings which can block our vision of alternatives and either freeze us in inactivity or stampede us into unthinking action. In addition, we must choose and make commitments so that we increase our confidence in our ability to make reasoned choices. If we do not believe in our power to rule our lives, the power is useless.

Our free choices close off some possibilities and open up others. We want to choose so as to maximize the opportunities for growth. The man who chooses to get drunk may kill his pain temporarily, but he also limits his potential for action. Has he increased or decreased his freedom? The same question may be asked of the student who drops out of school because he hates to study, or of the man who chooses to live as a hobo.

Political liberty is almost a form of circumstantial freedom. However, it stresses man's active exercise of freedom in a particular way. Man can be man without it, but it would appear that political liberty is necessary for the full development of the human person, since such liberty is necessary if the world around is to be a full expression of the manifold perfections of man. Indeed, unless we believe in some form of enlightened despotism, political liberty would appear to be an obligatory ideal. Thus, while admitting that other political arrangements might be temporarily necessary, there is an obligation to work for the state of society in which the individual can flower completely.

Today we must ask questions about the need for political freedom or active participation in the governance of even nonpolitical groups. Is political freedom an ideal in corporations, universities, and the church? Does the relationship of political freedom to growth mean that every institution should seek to maximize the participation of members in the decision-making process? We are inclined to think that growth demands participation, but as yet we lack the institutional forms necessary for the orderly integration of participation with other functions of nonpolitical groups.

Collective freedom is not meaningful within the framework we have developed, for it presupposes that the race or the collectivity is more important than the individual. In both theory and practice, it involves the subjection of individual man living in the present to an abstract collectivity that may or may not come to be. Thus, at present, it really involves denial of the first four freedoms as permanently meaningful moral categories.

IMPLICATIONS AND SUMMARY

It should not be thought that there is an abstract and static ideal balance which will maximize man's freedom of self-perfection. At one time, the maximization may require great restrictions on circumstantial freedom. At another time, restrictions may be hostile to the full development of man. For example, in a society tottering on the edge of anarchy or famine, a strong government and heavy-handed limitation of some freedoms may be necessary. In more stable and affluent societies, the same limitations would be unjust, because they smother the fires of creativity by subordinating the growth of both the individual and society, not to survival, but to vested interests and the blind worship of the status quo.

If the dynamic and changing values of freedom in the concrete are forgotten, moves to increase or decrease circumstantial freedom may result in the destruction of the individual or in his enslavement to either personal or social anarchy. In any event, circumstantial and political freedom are meaningless unless the individual has the wisdom and the strength to utilize them. It is naive to think that the mere removal of obstacles creates the power to acquire true inner freedom. The undisciplined individual, victimized by the anarchy of his own passions, cannot be free, no matter how many restrictions are removed from the society around him.

Man's freedom, like man's perfection in general, is something to be acquired. It is not an innate gift which flowers automatically in a benign environment. To lose sight of this is to build ethics on an illusion.

Since the acquired freedom of self-preservation is the more fundamental value or good, it must be cultivated and protected by both society and the individual. Above all, one must remember that this freedom is never fully acquired in time nor made a permanent possession. Man must struggle to keep what he has gained and to increase it. Those who believe in the virtue of some primitive spontaneity are not realistic, since the spontaneous is often counterfeit, a result of passion, stupidity, or immaturity. The truly mature individual enjoys a sureness of judgment and a wholesomeness of vision which is a reflection of his integration and assured self-identity, but, his spontaneity is valid because it springs from a structured and controlled personality, *not merely because it is spontaneous.*

The remarks in the preceding paragraph give some hint as to the value of habit and routine. Both reduce the human quality of many acts, but they can, if properly ordered, increase true freedom by saving energy and by carrying people over the rough spots in life. A well-thought-out routine, for example, frees the individual from concern with incidentals and gives him a momentum which can be applied to tasks of greater importance. Good habits support freedom by reducing conflict and tension which eat up energy that could be better put to creative uses. To put it another way, self-discipline is one of the necessary means to the creation of a true sphere of human freedom. Here again, the fight is not between freedom and limits, but between limits which increase true freedom and those which inhibit it.

The ideal involves the free integration of both the necessary and the useful into the individual. It gives a place of honor to the freedom of self-realization, for it is in this freedom that all other goods are raised to the truly human level. In later chapters we shall discuss the place of intellect, love, and life in the realization of man's inner freedom.

RELATION TO NATURAL LAW THEORIES

The theory of natural obligation developed above is similar to many natural law theories. It rests on the assumption that there is a given direction in human life which results from the essence of man as created by God. In this it agrees with nearly all natural law theories, though it differs insofar as our position on the essence of man and his relationship to the world is distinct. The theory of natural obligation should not be confused with Hobbes' natural law, which assumes that man is essentially selfish; nor with Locke's natural law, which is really a disguised divine positive law. Although our theory is realistic, it has little affinity with the rationalistic concept of Grotius, who would deduce all precepts from a few basic notions. We stress the fact that the concrete content of a natural obligation cannot be derived except by both analysis and experience of the real.

A careful reading of standard textbooks in ethics will reveal some important differences. First, we do not look at the natural law as a detailed codex which reveals a fixed, detailed plan in the mind of God. This blueprint idea has led to much confusion and ridicule, since it gives the impression that we can get answers to all questions by deciphering nature as given.[2] The task, as we have indicated, is not so simple. More important, blueprint versions of natural law theory do not stress the fact that man's creative response is also a part of God's plan. For this reason our own approach is more schematic and flexible. Although this may surprise people, such a position is quite close to that of such thinkers as Saint Thomas.

At the root of all our positions is the idea that the world is partly a changing expression of God's unchanging will and partly a creation of man and his culture. As a result, we feel that the ethician should be wary of deductions made from the abstract essence of man and should stress the concrete relationship between the person as a whole and the various aspects of reality, whether created by God or man.

RELATIONS TO OTHER SYSTEMS

Probably the most famous voluntaristic theory of obligation has been proposed by Kant. It is a pure formal theory which finds the source of obligation in the human will itself, independent of both the divine will and the structure of external reality. As Maritain has noted in his *Moral Philosophy*,[3] Kant makes his moral agent an agent who is absolutely self-sufficient and who acts rightly without needing to perfect or fulfill his being. The command of the law which is obligation arises not from any finality, but from the fact that it is conformed to the criterion of universality and non-contradiction. The object of an act does not specify either its goodness or its obligatory character. This is done by the form of universality and noncontradiction. If consequences are considered, it is only to determine whether the command is compatible with universality. Thus the nature of the will (practical reason) is ultimately what gives rise to obligation and the command.

While Kant's exposition is brilliant in terms of his epistemology, which separates the inner and the outer world, it rests on an exaggerated vision of man's autonomy. Man is dependent on the world as well as on God. His freedom is not absolute, but conditioned and often feeble. In view of a realistic metaphysics, which appreciates man's limitations and his position in the world as well as his relation to God, Kant's theory must be judged incomplete. He is correct in seeing that loyalty to one's intellectual nature and freedom is of vital importance. He is incomplete when he divorces the nature of the spirit from its position in reality taken as a whole. What is needed is a more comprehensive theory which accepts the fact of man's multidimensional position in the world and before God.

However, a word should be said about those theories of law and obligation which identify it with force, physical or social. Many thinkers hold that obligation arises only from a sovereign will which has power to enforce its rulings. This is the equivalent of reducing all morality to force. In such a theory, Hitler was wrong and the Allies right only because the latter group won the Second World War and was able to enforce its will. There is, in short, no norm to use in criticizing force except force itself. While these ideas are scandalous, they are logical deductions in a system which does not admit the spiritual side of man. After all, more-or-less is the norm in the world of pure matter, and this more-or-less is most conveniently expressed in terms of mass or force.

Force, as we shall see in our chapters on rights and societies, has a legitimate place in human life. It cannot, however, be the root of

obligation or of right in any theory that admits the true nature of
the human person and the hierarchy of goods that flows from this.
Here, as elsewhere, the real conflict is not in ethics but in the
underlying theory of man and of his knowledge.

BY WAY OF SUMMARY

Obligation, like moral good and moral evil, involves both the
interior and exterior of man. As a result, the content of particular
obligations can be determined only after a study of both areas and
their mutual interplay. It is in view of this that the concept of man
as person in the world and the theory of epistemological limits are
decisive in working out obligations. Ethics, then, is inseparable
from the rest of philosophy and from the data of other sciences,
both natural and social.

NOTES

1. Mortimer J. Adler, *The Idea of Freedom* (New York: Doubleday, 1961),
   Vol. II, pp. 5 ff. Copyright © 1958 by the Institute for Philosophical
   Research. Reprinted by permission of Doubleday & Company, Inc.
2. *Cf.* Thomas E. Davitt, "Law as Means to End—Thomas Aquinas,"
   Vanderbilt Law Review, 14 (1960), Dec. No. 1, p. 91, for a critique of
   the "blueprint" theory.
3. Jacques Maritain, *Moral Philosophy* (New York: Scribner's, 1964),
   p. 101.

POINTS FOR DISCUSSION

1. List some of the obligations which people attempt to impose on you
   and test them to see if they are based on an objective necessity.
2. List some of the hypothetical obligations you have assumed and
   decide whether your choice was justified.
3. Do we assume special obligations when we choose to become a
   doctor, a teacher, a husband? What is the source of these special
   obligations?
4. List and discuss necessities which arise not from the fixed nature of

things but from the existing social structures, e.g. the need for a college education.

5. In what way can you maximize the good?
6. In what way can you perfect your own freedom of choice and self-realization?
7. Where in our society can circumstantial freedom be improved?
8. Discuss the problem of political freedom within the various organizations of which you are a member.

READINGS

Peter A. BERTOCCI and Richard M. MILLARD, *Personality and the Good* (New York: David McKay, 1963).

Thomas E. DAVITT, "Law as Means to End—Thomas Aquinas," *Vanderbilt Law Review*, 14 (1960), Dec. No. 1, pp. 65–99.

Emil MERSCH, *L'obligation morale* (Paris: Alcan, 1927).

Alexander SESONSKE, *Value and Obligation* (New York: Oxford University Press, 1964).

6/ RIGHTS AND THE ETHICS OF POWER

INTRODUCTION

Men speak not only of right and wrong, good and evil, ought and ought not, but of their rights to do or have certain things. They assert their right to life, liberty, and happiness, as well as the right to a job, to freedom of expression, and to security against the unreasonable. These assertions involve an ethical claim. They do not merely assert possession of the thing to which they have a claim. They do not merely assert that they have the physical or political power actually to secure the object in question. In some cases, to be sure, the claim is purely political in origin, the result of a legal concession; but most often men in our days base their claim on their own dignity or on their own activity. In short, they assert the existence of natural rights.

While men may not use the term *natural right,* nor have a developed and coherent theory of rights, there can be little doubt that as men realize their own dignity they assert their claims to the respect that human dignity demands. To be sure, their vision of both their dignity and its demands may be limited and conditioned by the social context in which they live. Often, too, men will not assert claims to things which they cannot obtain because the laws or customs are against them, In the West they may appeal to the law, the constitution, or their own power as justifying their claims. In time of crisis, however, or when society is the creature of an exploitive class, the oppressed see that it is not power, society, law, custom, or constitution which gives them rights, but their own worth as individuals. All these social facts and enactments may be means necessary to protect human dignity, but they are not the cause of the dignity nor the root of rights.

Although the formal theories of natural right have had their ups and downs in the history of the West, they recur because crises are forever showing us that there must be something behind and above society itself. When things are going smoothly for us, and society supports our dignity, we do not feel the need to drive back to ultimates. Let the problem of totalitarianism or widespread injustice in the racial sphere come to the fore, and we must seek the ultimate roots of rights in something more fundamental than the existing social order.

The existence of natural rights (ethical claims which exist independent of the social enactments such as laws or customs) is obvious to anyone who admits that man is a unique being with a dignity that demands respect. The structure, shape, and interrelations of rights are, however, problematic. This is to say that the notion of right, like the notions of good, of obligation, and of freedom, creates real problems when one attempts to refine it in such a way that it can be a guide to decision making in the concrete world of men. Most of this chapter, then, is concerned, not with the general question of whether or not natural rights exist, but with the interrelations of rights and their significance for the problems of power.

THE EXISTENCE OF NATURAL RIGHTS

Once a stand has been taken on the nature of man and the existence of obligations which flow from what man is, the existence of natural rights should be obvious. If man is an end or value in himself, he must respect his own dignity. Since his basic dignity is the same as that of other men, he cannot respect himself unless he respects others. The dignity of man, then, creates claims or obligations independent of any positive enactments or of the ability to enforce one's will. A child may be powerless, but he still has a claim to respect that I cannot disregard without disregarding myself. For this reason, a right is called a moral or an ethical claim, since it does not depend on power.

Human dignity exists independently of society and independently of a man's condition, and it creates obligations. A man may quibble about the exact nature of the demand—that is, about its precise content—but he must recognize some claim as soon as he admits that the other is not a thing but a person like himself.

This is not pure theory or the result of a deductive process. Whenever we wish to dodge obligations to other men, treat them as things or make exceptions to our general ethical principles, we find it necessary to dehumanize the other person in our own mind. In time of war, for example, we work ourselves up to a point where the enemy is a faceless beast guilty of every atrocity. The reason is simple: unless we see him as subhuman, it is difficult to justify the killing and destruction we will inflict. In times past, many Southerners could justify their oppression of the Negro only by denying the existence of his soul and conceiving of him as an animal or a half-man. In my own opinion, we succeed in justifying capital punishment only because we manage to view the condemned as someone who has at least temporarily lost his humanity.

Tribal morality which treats insiders by one set of rules and outsiders by another is often based on the assumption that only members of the tribe are truly human. The insulting language used to describe outsiders is an emotional, if not intellectual, expression of this distinction. There is, of course, far more than this involved, but the essential point should be clear. When we admit the humanity and dignity of the other, we admit his rights and our obligations towards him. When we want to avoid obligations and the admission of rights, we try to re-create the other to the image and likeness of something that is less than human nature as we understand it.

While we have pointed up the force of rights by saying that we cannot violate the dignity of another without violating our own worth, this should not lead one to think that the ultimate root of rights is found purely in self-interest. It is the value of the other which commands respect and would command respect even if, by some impossible supposition, I would suffer no harm. Indeed, the highly ethical man may seldom if ever avert to the impact of his acts on himself, since he responds to the value of the other as a man and only implicitly to his own value. At the same time, the aspect of self-interest must not be disregarded, for the universal claims of human dignity make it necessary to work out a social system which makes it possible for all men to fulfill themselves.

The fact that man demands respect by his very nature does not, however, give us the content or the object of rights. Nor does it enable us to mediate between conflicting claims which men make. It is for this reason that distinctions are necessary. There is a hierarchy and constellation of rights, just as there is a hierarchy and a constellation of goods and of obligations, for these are expressions of the structure of man and his dignity, as well as of his position in the world. Reasoning and study are necessary if workable definitions are to be developed. To a large extent this is the work of special ethics, but even general ethics should supply some of the analytic tools.

TYPES OF NATURAL RIGHTS

While a natural right is a claim to respect for one's dignity, this notion is so formal and so lacking in content that it needs considerable refinement before it can be used as a tool for making decisions. After all, when men urge their rights they do not merely say that you must respect men, but that you must respect them in a certain way. Men assert that their life, or their liberty in a given area, demands respect. They may claim that this respect demands that they be given a certain job or be aided in a certain way. The ethician must face the fact that unless he can give criteria for the content of rights, his insistence on the dignity of man may only lead to endless squabbles.

An inspection of the things which men claim reveals that *some of the objections and acts are necessary for the existence and growth* of the individual. The right to life is the best example of this sort of claim. Often, however, the claim involves *merely useful goods*. Thus, the right to freedom of speech does not involve something necessary for the existence of the individual. In fact, when we analyze this right, the claim really asserts that a man should not be unreasonably interfered with in expressing himself. After all, everyone recognizes that no one has the right to shout "Fire!" in a crowded theater when there is no fire. Similarly, most will agree that a man has no right to destroy the reputation of his enemy by spreading lies about him. The right to freedom of speech, then, is conditional. This is in line with our remarks that merely useful goods must be subordinated to necessary goods, while necessary goods are subordinated to the ultimate dignity of the individual. For the purposes of this book, we will distinguish between a *quasi-absolute right,* which involves a claim to a necessary good, and a *relative right,* which involves a claim not to be unreasonably impeded, even in one's search for useful goods.

As is so often the case, a simple distinction only indicates the two extremes and says little about the territory between. Things can be more or less necessary and more or less useful, with the result that abstract definitions must be fleshed out by study of the concrete situation. After all, it is only in the concrete that we see the real interactions between individuals. To put it another way, we can understand the full ethical significance of a right only when we see the actual impacts of its *exercise.* This is true even of what we have called quasi-absolute rights. Thus, the right to life does not automatically involve a right to use any and all means which might be necessary to preserve life. In the concrete there may be no right to a given means, because its use would involve the violation of someone else's right.

In the concrete world, it is also necessary to advert to the fact that some rights are inherent in the dignity of man, at least in their general shape, while others come into existence only when the individual has performed certain acts or acquired certain characteristics. Thus, I have a right not to be unreasonably impeded in my attempt to acquire property, but I do not have a right to a particular piece of property unless I establish *title* by purchase, or development, or gift. To put it another way, some contingent act is necessary to relate an individual to a particular piece of property. Similarly, a man has a right to a particular job only when he has fulfilled certain qualifications relevant to the performance of the job.

The title has several important functions which help to clarify the complexity of the system of rights and obligations. Titles are necessary where human dignity itself does not relate the individual to a particular concrete individualized good, although it may relate him to a class of abstract goods. Unless there is some way of relating him to the particular good, his right remains ineffective and his claim may even give rise to disputes unless there is some agreement as to what constitutes title. Title, then, has a symbolic function. It puts others on notice about the existence of a very concrete claim to a particular good. Like all symbols, it is effective only if it is based on some sort of agreement. For this reason we generally need custom or positive law or contract to establish agreement. At this point there may be a certain amount of arbitrary decision making. However, so long as the agreement attempts to respect the basic dignity which is the root of the right, it cannot be considered unjust. This should not blind us to the fact that the symbols can be manipulated in the interests of exploitation. Thus, a powerful group may agree that a title exists only when a person has certain qualities which are irrelevant to the basic right. Color and religion, for example, have been made qualifications for holding political office even though they have nothing to do with political competence.

A right is not only a claim to something, it is a claim against someone else. More often than not, it obliges others not to injure the good or to interfere with my reasonable pursuit of the good. This negative claim on others does not guarantee that the holder of the right will actually get what is necessary for the support of his human dignity. Thus, a hard-working man may exist in a society in which no one impedes him from getting a job, but in which no individual has an obligation to give him a job. In one sense his right has been respected. In another sense, his right is meaningless, since he cannot, by any means, establish a title to a particular job and against a particular employer.

If the right to a job, to medical care, and to similar necessities is to be meaningful, the right must affect some person or group of persons. We believe these claims can be urged against society as a whole. As we shall see in a later chapter, society must create conditions in which each individual can satisfy his needs—that is, exercise his quasi-absolute rights in a positively meaningful way. This is an important point, for if society is obliged only to provide for noninterference, and not to create positive conditions, many rights become relatively meaningless. Unless the existence of such positive social obligations is recognized, many moral claims become purely theoretical, since they cannot be urged against anyone, with the result that no one is really bound to show any real respect for the individual who cannot realize himself without the aid of others.

THE LIMITS OF RIGHTS

The distinctions given in the introduction to this chapter indicate some of the points which must be considered in determining the relationships between various rights. A more careful study of limits and the distinction between quasi-absolute and relative rights will help, however, to indicate a more precise way of describing the exact content of a given right.

Since rights derive from the dignity of man and are directed to his perfection, they are *limited by the final end of man*. A man never has a right to commit an ethical evil, since this is against his dignity and his end. He can neither treat another man as a means nor own him, since this would be equivalent to treating the other as a means. Rights and their exercise are thus *limited by the rights of other men*.

The mutual limitation of rights poses real problems. I may not permit or risk harm to another without a proportionate reason in the area of quasi-absolute rights or necessary goods. I cannot will to limit the other's search for even relative goods except for a proportionate reason. Proportionality or reasonableness can be determined by the rules given in earlier chapters, but the notion remains vague and allows the existence of many grey areas. For this reason, society must provide means for settling conflicts of rights. This is necessary for good public order and because, though an impartial body is not infallible, it will come closer to justice than an interested party who may tend to exaggerate his own claims. We shall return to this question in our discussion of the difficulties of application.

It should be noted that though the system of law and customs used by various societies is often based on objective considerations, this is not necessarily the case. There is little objective reason why women and children should come first except that they are less capable of protecting themselves. What is necessary, however, is some accepted order which will prevent panic or the use of sheer power. In short, there are areas where the social order is a greater good than claims to relative goods or privileges.

These difficulties should not blind us to the fact that the quasi-absolute right takes precedence over the relative. The starving man can have a claim to a watermelon which a rich farmer does not need for his subsistence. Moreover, as we shall see in a later chapter, love can overpass the purely juridical approach which deals only with minimal relationships.

PROBLEMS OF APPLICATION

The problem of conflicts of rights serves as an introduction to the problem of application. To apply the principles one must be able to decide *who is a person; what aspects involve quasi-absolute rights;* and what constitutes a *reasonable interference* with the exercise of a right, whether absolute or relative. The problem in each case has two aspects. First, it is necessary to develop criteria for application. Secondly, it is necessary to be on guard against the prejudices which blind us to significant factors.

The problem of "who is a person" is crucial in questions involving life and death and will be treated in Chapter 10. Here and now we only note that we have high certitude only when we see a being exhibiting signs of intelligence. In many cases we have only indirect indices of personality which give us more or less certitude, or possibly only probability, that we are dealing with a person. Often, then, we will have to base our choices on practical certitude rather than on a rigorously demonstrated conclusion. In line with what we have written in Chapter 2, we consider as persons those who manifest signs of human intelligence and the offspring of those who show signs of human intelligence.

Having an absolute certitude about our own personality, we may be tempted to give ourselves the preference on the ground of a higher degree of certitude. This is a fallacious procedure, since I am always more sure of my own humanity; and if the difference in certitude were decisive, all conflicts would be settled in my own favor. Furthermore, when I know the other to be human, I must treat him as human, even though my affective assent may not be strong.

What aspects of the other involve quasi-absolute rights—i.e., claims to things necessary for his movement toward perfection—cannot be decided without reference to the concrete order. However, the pragmatic test is to ask whether men in general can be men without the good in question. This test is easy enough when the thing in question affects continued existence or the continued functioning of the intellect. It becomes difficult to use, however, when we consider other goods which are more or less necessary, or more or less useful. How shall we classify a job in a society that provides for all members whether they work or not? How shall we classify expensive and prolonged medical care when medical facilities are limited? Is a college education a necessary good in contemporary American society?

We will have difficulty classifying some of these goods and a man's right to them for several reasons. A job is not as necessary in a society that provides alternate means of family support as in one that says, Work or perish. The existence of alternatives can modify necessity. Prolonged and expensive medical care may be necessary for the survival of an individual, but the limitation of facilities may make it proper to allocate the resources to others who can recover with less cost. The exercise of a right to even a necessary good may be limited by the rights of others and the need for maximizing the good to be obtained from the facilities. A college education is not a necessary good for each and every individual, but society certainly needs a large number of college graduates. Since the necessity is social rather than purely individual, society may have something to say about who gets a college education.

Most of our rights are relative, that is, a right not to be unreasonably interfered with in our pursuit of useful goods. Many problems, then, center on determining the reasonableness of an individual or group who interfere with the pursuit of such goods. The rules of proportionality developed in Chapter 4 are rules of reasonableness. They apply to this area as to others. They cannot, of course, justify willing the suppression of a quasi-absolute right or necessary good, but they can justify risking or permitting such harm, or even willing the limitation of a relative right. The test is whether or not the good willed equals or outweighs the harm flowing from the limitation. Unfortunately, as we have noted over and over again, it is difficult to make an impartial judgment, so that societies have set up complicated systems or laws to insure uniformity and some impartiality. This is a recognition that a man may not be a good judge in his own case.

Are we reasonable when we keep women out of executive positions on the ground that business is a man's world? Is a society reasonable when it takes away part of a man's income in taxes? Is a union reasonable when it forces workers to limit their output? These are the type of questions which must be answered before we can decide if a relative right has been violated.

Because we often leave the judgment of reasonableness to the legislature, the courts, or the governing bodies of various private groups, we must also ask questions about the precedures of judges, law makers, and executives. Does the method of dismissing a boy from school minimize arbitrary judgment? Do legislative hearings give all interested parties an equal chance to present their case? Does a poor man have as much chance for justice as a rich man when both appear in court? Questions like these must be asked and answered constantly if we are to protect even relative rights.

All our institutions cannot guarantee perfect respect for rights. If men confine themselves to seeking only the minimum relation of respect implied in the theory of rights, ethics will not yield the proper results. For this reason, the obligations of love and the generosity of love which by-pass the analytic and gnat-straining approach are a necessary supplement. This is not to play down the importance of rights but to point out that they do not offer a full framework for the good life and complete human development.

CULTURAL FACTORS

Our efforts to decide *who is a person* and what constitutes *reasonable interference* are complicated not only by our own selfishness and emotional states but by the culture of which we are a part. Our perception and value judgments are culturally conditioned. This is to say that we tend to see reality through a set of tinted spectacles placed on us by society. We can remove the spectacles at times, but it is difficult, since the refusal to see things the way others see them may brand us as abnormal, insane, or disloyal.

In some schools the administration and faculty assume that they hold all authority and have a right to make any regulations which they consider necessary, useful, or convenient. A faculty member who argues that convenience is not a reasonable cause for limiting the freedom of students to wear beards may find himself an outcast. He has taken off the spectacles of the group and challenged their view of reality and of ethical principles.

If a group believes that property rights are absolute, it will assume that a landlord may reject a tenant for any reason whatsoever. The person who challenges this belief on the grounds that the right of others to fair treatment limits property rights will find himself under social pressure. Indeed the penalties imposed may cause him to adopt the view of the group and to ignore the rights he sees being violated.

In those cultures where women are viewed as chattels or as weak beings in need of great protection, the tendency will be to increase the area of "reasonable" interference. The culturally induced assumptions of fact can thus affect our judgment of the limits of rights. Similarly, if a people believe that any speech against the rulers is extremely dangerous, they will tend to limit freedom of speech without questioning their assumptions.

In our own culture, we speak of inalienable rights to life and liberty. In practice, however, we limit these rights and their exercise. The categorical statements of the First Amendment appear to forbid any federal interference with the freedom of the press. Moreover, the amendment has received many different court interpretations.[1] These views reflect the changing values of both the judges and the society they represent. The words in the Constitution may remain the same, but their meaning changes with the changing times. It is important to remember that even the formulas of the ethicians are short-hand versions of a larger truth and that their meaning is strongly influenced by the cultural context in which they are read.

Although in many cases the received cultural views lag behind the insights of moral leaders, there may be cases where the culture holds up very lofty ideals. This may well be the case of the American ideal of equality.

A RIGHT TO EQUALITY

All men are equal in their basic human dignity, but not all men are equal in talent, power, intelligence, social station, and opportunity. Are men entitled to be equal in all things? Is absolute equality an ideal which men have a right to and society an obligation to support?

Some inequalities are, at first glance, natural. Physical constitution, health, imagination, and memory appear to be unequal as a result of birth. Because of this, we are tempted to say that all men do not have a right to equality in these areas, since such a right would be meaningless. On second thought, however, we realize that much of the inequality in these areas is not natural but a result of environment, social milieu, and the free choice of other men. Despite inherent limitations, the puny child might have been strong and healthy if provided with adequate nutrition and medical care. The seemingly unimaginative adult might have been a creative artist if exposed to the right education and family background. This is not to say that all inequality can be banished but that the spread can be reduced if opportunities are made more readily available.

In the American society, equality, or at least the availability of opportunity, is a political and a social ideal. It is not merely a question of providing equal protection of the law to all, but of allowing all to develop their talents and human potential to the fullest. We do not think of the right in terms of noninterference with the pursuit of useful goods, but of a right to positive help in developing talents and eliminating the inequality which does not spring from nature but from defects in the society, the family, or the economic order.

Realistically, positive equality of opportunity can never be completely realized. Some sources of inequality, such as the family, cannot be abolished without extreme harm to both individuals and the community. Moreover, since man becomes conscious of new needs almost as fast as old needs are satisfied, the resources of the community almost always lag behind the needs of men. Indeed most societies lack the means necessary to create complete positive equality of opportunity. These facts, however, do not make the ideal any less an ideal. The limited resources may make the exercise of a right to equal opportunity difficult, but the right remains. Perhaps we should say that the right is a claim which requires society to move towards the ideal rather than a strict claim to equality here and now.

Some inequality seems to be necessary for the functioning of society. Not all can rule directly, not all can be doctors or lawyers or clergymen. Social life demands that there be differentiation of function and some subordination. Kept within the limits we will discuss in a later chapter, neither differentiation nor subordination seems to be a violation of any right. Unfortunately, the necessary differences and inequalities can be connected with those inequalities which block men's growth. Let us illustrate.

In any large group, it is necessary to have the function of ruling assigned to a distinct group. This gives rise to an inequality that is necessary for both the society and the individual. This is not unjust in itself, but it can lead to a violation of rights if those who hold political power use it to grant favors to friends. In business it is generally necessary to give economic rewards in accord with merit as measured by productivity. This again is not unjust, but if it gradually leads to a situation where only productive merit is considered, some men will be doomed to misery through no fault of their own. Finally, though division of labor is necessary and just, it can lead to situations where one man is considered less a man because he cleans the streets, digs ditches, or acts as a servant.

In the real world, social and economic institutions can tempt us to value men in terms of their roles, status, or functions. While this is not necessarily evil, it can become an evil if we value men exclusively in such terms. The respect we owe a man just because he is a man should be the primary factor in determining rights. If we allow status, role, function, or income to replace basic human dignity as the source of rights, we will inevitably end up disregarding the rights of others and our own moral obligations.

RIGHTS AND POWER

The theory of natural rights does not appeal to some people because it is all too obvious that the right itself does not contribute to the perfection of the individual unless it is respected, protected, and made effective by providing the power necessary for its exercise. For some individuals, right is too much of an ethical or moral category; too far removed from the world of action and control and resistance. In the real world, a right has meaning only if it is backed up with some sort of power—psychological, political, or physical. Such individuals see the factors which translate the claim into external action as more important than the claim itself.

While such objections are based on a misunderstanding of the metaphysical and ethical nature of natural rights, they have considerable merit. Indeed any theory of rights which neglects or oversimplifies the relationship of right and might is not very useful. As we have already noted, the existence of society is necessary if rights are to become concretely meaningful. To put it another way, rights must be interpreted, protected, and enforced by social action if they are to be more than purely theoretical entities. This, however, is not the same as saying that the right is the might of the state, the individual, the law or custom.

If might is right, whether the might be legal or physical, there is no recourse against tyranny but might itself. In such a theory there is no criterion of justice or injustice except force of some sort. The winner is simultaneously the good man; the loser is necessarily either evil or neutral. For these reasons, if for no other, the theory of natural rights is reborn every time men think it dead. Often it takes a Hitler or a Hungarian revolution or an atom bomb to remind men that force is not a sufficient, or even an efficient, criterion of right. Horrible facts drive men back to asking ultimate questions about ultimate values and ethical categories.

THE ETHICS OF DEFENSE

Most writers in ethics have held the right to such things as life and property implies the right to use force in the defense of such goods. In line with general ethical principles, the ethicians limit the use of this defense by means of the principle of proportionality. In the concrete, they say that force may be used only when peaceful means have failed. Moreover, no more force may be used than is necessary for the defense of the good in question. Finally, the force ought to be proportional to the good defended. It would hardly be ethical to kill a man in order to prevent him from stealing a dollar from a millionaire.

The right to use force does not always imply an obligation to use it. For example, a man may judge that it is better to submit to force than to be responsible for inflicting harm on an unjust aggressor. At the same time, a case can be made for the obligatory use of force when the person attacked is essential to the functioning of a family or a society.

In general, ethical problems of self-defense, war, and revolution do not focus on the basic right to use force but on questions concerned with the concrete exercise of the right. When am I attacked? May I kill another man in self-defense if this the only way to save my life? The first question asks for concrete criteria of application. The second question asks if I may use all the force necessary for my defense.

"When am I attacked?" appears to be a simple question. In practice it is hard to answer. Certainly I am attacked when the aggressor is already shooting at me or is rushing towards me with a hunting knife. The immediacy of space and time make the attack clear. In modern times, however, self-defense may be meaningless if I have to wait until the first shot is fired or until the aggressor is inside my living room. The actual attack may begin ten thousand miles away and the blow may arrive even before I am aware of the enemy's decision. As a result, we now raise questions as to the legitimacy of anticipating attack or of meeting it on foreign soil.

The problem of attack is very secondary compared to the second question, "May I kill another in self-defense if there is no other way to save my life?" The replies fall into three main groups.

1. Yes, and you may even will his death.

2. Yes, if you do not will his death but are only permitting or risking it.

3. No. You may neither will nor risk nor permit the death of another.

The answers obviously depend on the value assigned to human life and on a person's general theory of responsibility. Since we will not treat of the value of life until a later chapter, we will not state our own answer at this point. Here it is sufficient to note that the problems of self-defense is not as simple as we often assume.

The justification of force in self-defense is based on the supposition that force can be a reasonable means in certain circumstances. The use of force, however, is at best a lesser evil, a last resort. Because it is an evil, we must certainly work for the abolition of force as an instrument in human life. At the same time, we must remember that a refusal to use force can lead to even greater evils. If I will not to defend myself or my neighbor, I may be handing the world over to those who believe might is right.

POWER AND THE PROMOTION OF RIGHTS

While ethicians will admit rather readily to the use of power in the defense of many quasi-absolute rights, there is considerable hesitation about the use of power in the effort to make real the right to equality and freedom from unreasonable interference in the pursuit of merely useful goods. The hesitation is understandable. The relative rights are not clearly defined at times. There can be several legitimate opinions at to what is reasonable or unreasonable interference. Furthermore, it is assumed that disputes in this area can be settled by peaceable means. The authorization of the use of power in the promotion of relative rights might thus lead to a sort of anarchy.

Events in our own time have made us aware of the fact that many rights can be meaningless unless power and sometimes force are brought into play. The effort to organize unions often created violence, and was successful only when the power of the state was brought into the picture. The civil rights movement has often caused violence because the courts and the legislature on the local level did not operate fairly. In the last analysis, advances in civil rights have depended on the intervention of the central government and the application of both political and economic power. The experiences of the union movement and the civil rights movement seem to indicate that there are many rights which will be relatively sterile if not backed up with power of one sort or another.

The need for power, though not necessarily for coercive power or violence, should not surprise us. The existing structures, processes, and ideologies of a society can stifle rights even without anyone intending them to do so. Moreover, once these structures, processes, and ideologies exist, a sort of inertia sets in, with the result that considerable power may be required to change them. Power, of course, tends to be met with power, so that the promotion of rights and the expansion of the area of legitimate freedom can sometimes produce explosive situations. At the same time, we must recognize the fact that there are unsettled and vague areas of rights which, since they are not covered by existing laws, are often defined by those who hold power. This power is then clothed with a sort of legitimacy based on possession or long tolerance. When it is attacked, it pleads legitimacy as well as invoking power.

A deeper examination of some examples used earlier may help to indicate the nature of this power in possession. A university administration has long been used to making regulations about student dress and appearance. It assumes that it has a right to do so, since all universities did this at one time and because the regulations have been accepted. Whether or not the university has the right to make such regulations, it has the power to enforce them. The administration can fine, suspend, or dismiss a student who will not conform. Students and faculty members may object that such regulations are an unreasonable interference with the right of the individual to seek such useful goods as comfort, cheaper clothing, or the expression of individuality. Two rights are asserted, and the adjudication of the dispute depends on the interpretation of what is reasonable. As a rule, the government will not enter into such a dispute when a university is technically private. Furthermore, the trustees and administrators, who normally judge disputes in the university, are involved in a conflict of interest. Is it ethical for the students and the faculty to use power and even the threat of force to protect their view of the rights in question?

In practice, disputes of this sort will generally be settled by power. Must students consent to the power of the school, or may they organize a countervailing power? A school can be embarrassed by the unfavorable publicity that results from picketing. Pressure from alumni can make the trustees think twice. Massive disregard of the regulation can make it dangerous to suspend or dismiss students. Indeed, if the faculty agrees with the students, the administrators can find themselves subject to extreme social pressure. Is it unethical to invoke any or all of these power plays against those who claim to have the right to make dress regulations?

Although these questions cannot be answered without a consideration of the nature of authority which is treated in a later chapter, several points should be noted, lest one assume that the possession of the power is equivalent to a right to use it without opposition. Very often power is necessary to make another see the justice of a claim. Power may be necessary for communication —which is, of course, a necessary prelude to the settlement of disputes. Secondly, the temptation to resort to power is often an indication that the existing structure does not make allowance for real communication or provide for effective systems of accountability. Thirdly, power is a commonplace tool in many of our day-by-day relationships, even if we do not recognize the fact. The important professor who threatens to go elsewhere if his salary is not raised is using power. The housewife who pickets a supermarket, the editorialists in the local paper, the preacher in the pulpit, all have and use power to change the way things are. In many cases, these people are not defending a quasi-absolute right, but only trying to enlarge their sphere of legitimate freedom.

Although might may not be right, it would appear that there are many cases where might settles disputes about right. Certainly the right as a moral claim needs to be backed up with power so long as not all men are sensitive to all claims of other men. This is not to say that conflicts should be settled by power, but rather that the possession of power by both sides may be a necessary condition for rational discourse and for the formation of truly free agreements.

POWER AND BELIEF

Power, or the ability to make someone else do what I want, is not a simple question of physical force. It can depend on personal magnetism, superstition, customary expectations, and belief. In the last analysis, much power depends on the other's belief that I can impose sanctions. By a sanction is meant the bestowal or deprivation of some good which the other considers valuable. Your ability to destroy me will not give you the power to bend my will to yours unless I believe that my life is more important that the good you want me to give up by doing your will. The ability of a university to dismiss a student will not give it power to enforce dress regulations unless students consider membership in the school more important than their freedom to dress as they please. In addition, even when the students rate membership in the school higher than the freedom of dress, the ability to dismiss will not have its effects unless the students believe that the administration will use it.

Because much power rests on beliefs about the ability and willingness of the possessor to reward or punish, changes in beliefs, values, and expectations can produce vast shifts in power. Shifts in power can cause the reexamination of the foundation of many supposed rights. When the former power holder can no longer unilaterally impose his will, those who were dependent on him want more than former power and custom as justification for alleged rights. Indeed, at this point, it is necessary to use rational discourse to convince the dependents that there is a real moral claim.

Many of the disputes about rights in contemporary society have their roots in two factors. In the first place, many minority groups or subservient groups have come to the realization of their dignity. Secondly, they have discovered that they have the power to enforce the rights which they feel flow from their dignity. Students, for example, have come to see that they are not university children but members of associations which often treat them as children. At the same time they have learned that agitation can increase their political freedom—that is, active participation in the university. Whether or not one approves of the methods used, it is necessary to examine the basis of student claims, lest the assumption that past practice is an ethical justification lead to misunderstanding and power plays.

IS POWER ETHICALLY NEUTRAL?

In practice, power is seldom ethically neutral. The meaning of power does not depend solely on the deliberate uses made of it. The reason is simply that power has effects, good or bad, by the very fact that it exists. After all, if I believe that you have power and will use it, my conduct is affected even if you never use it. You may not be aware of my beliefs and their effects on my conduct; you may not have used the power, let alone abused it; but my life is different; my freedom is limited and the exercise of my rights may be abridged. These effects can hardly be called ethically neutral.

If my belief in your power is completely unfounded, there is little you can do about it. However, if the belief is founded, we can raise questions about the ethics of the mere possession of the power although it is never used in fact. We must ask not only about legitimate and illegitimate uses of power but about the legitimacy of the possession of power.

The political scientist and the political philosopher have long been concerned with the legitimacy of power. Many of our laws and social institutions are designed not only to prevent and remedy actual abuses of power but also to block even the risk of abuse. The check and balance system in the American Constitution is an outstanding example of an effort to reduce the risks of even legitimate power. If we look behind the political disputes about government intervention, social programs, the power of corporations and of churches, we will see that the real issue is often concerned rather with the fact of power and its potential abuses than with the actual use or abuse itself.

In the political realm we have never achieved perfect social control of power. You can split it up, but it will tend to coalesce. You can set up countervailing powers which limit one another, but unorganized groups can be unprotected. In any event you cannot eliminate power, because it is necessary for the operation of society, the protection of rights, and the removal of obstacles to progress.

Even imperfect control is better than none. However, in the nonpolitical realm of the church, the corporation, and the university, the control may be very imperfect. In the same institutions the question of legitimacy is being raised with increasing frequency. This is to say that there are serious problems in the social ethics of nonpolitical organizations. While these problems cannot be treated in an introductory book, it should be clear that no theory of rights and power can be reasonably adequate without reference to the power of private groups over their members.

BY WAY OF CONCLUSION

As a man's vision of his own dignity expands and deepens, he sees his rights as more extensive than he had believed. The new vision often challenges old ways of doing things, vested rights, and existing power structures. The vision is the stuff from which revolutions are made. Whether the revolutions are moral ones or merely senseless wars will depend, in part, on the way ethical theory grapples with the problem of power and the definition of concrete rights.

The present chapter has not offered precise rules for settling conflicts of relative rights because it is not easy to settle some of the underlying issues, which will be treated in the chapter on Society. Even social theory cannot supply definitive answers to questions which involve fact as well as principle. When is the order of a society more important than the circumstantial freedom of the individual? Who shall judge the reasonableness of the limitations of freedom?

NOTE

1. *Cf.* Edward G. Hudson, *Freedom of Speech and Press in America* (Washington, D.C.: Public Affairs Press, 1963).

POINTS FOR DISCUSSION

1. How do varying views of man and reality give rise to varying concepts of rights?
2. Which civil rights of Americans are purely civil and which are also natural?
3. What natural rights are inadequately protected by existing civil law?
4. Granted that a man does not have a right to do something unethical, is it always reasonable to impede his freedom to do something unethical?
5. Who has the right to judge between the claims of conflicting rights? Is the right to judge absolute?
6. List and analyze some of the new rights being claimed by various groups; e.g., the right of students to participate in the government of the university; the right of Negroes to attend still unintegrated schools.
7. To what extent is it ethical to use or risk violence in seeking to make rights effective; e.g., the right to open housing; the right to freedom of speech in a university?
8. What situations in the world are hostile to the basic dignity of man and so a violation of his rights, even though you may not be able to give the right a name?
9. Work out a reasoned list of rights for various special groups, such as students, teachers, church members, managers in a business.
10. Discuss the ethical significance of one of the various forms of power.

READINGS

Glenn ABERNATHY, *The Right of Assembly and Association* (Columbia, S.C.: University of South Carolina Press, 1961).

Walter GELHORN, *Individual Freedom and Governmental Restraint* (Baton Rouge, La.: Louisiana State University Press, 1958).

Howard Mumford JONES (ed.), *Primer of Intellectual Freedom* (Cambridge, Mass.: Harvard University Press, 1949).

Bertrand DE JOUVENEL, *On Power* (New York: Viking Press, 1948).

Joseph PIEPER, *Justice* (New York: Pantheon Books, 1955).

7/ETHICS, INTELLECT, AND FREEDOM OF CONSCIENCE

INTRODUCTION

The foregoing chapters have been so analytic that they may create the illusion that ethical decisions are made in a purely mechanical way. We may also have given the false impression that individuals make their decisions in a vacuum and with a cold rationality. Since this is obviously not the case, it is necessary to face the problems connected with the formation of both general ethical attitudes and concrete ethical decisions. Many of the questions raised cannot be answered in any completely satisfactory manner, but an effort to answer them can deepen our awareness of human responsibility, of the need for constant study, and of the obstacles to ethical growth.

In particular, the present chapter will underline the problems arising from early moral training, a cultural lag in the community, and the incompleteness of our knowledge. The consideration of these problems will lay the foundation for a brief treatment of the agonies of ethical doubt and the dilemma posed by a man's obligation to follow his conscience.

CHILDHOOD TRAINING

Almost as soon as we are born, those around us start teaching us "right" from "wrong." Some of our actions are rewarded with a smile, with warmth and comfort. Others incur frowns, indifference, or even punishment. Parents, parent substitutes, relatives, friends, and the neighbors are involved in the process of teaching us the rules, mores, ethics, and etiquette of the family and the society in which we have to live.

At first the values, principles, and conclusions implicit in the actions of the adults about us are quite external. In time we internalize them, make them part of us, and accept the values concerning right or wrong. The body of principles, values, and ethical conclusions we accept has a great influence on our perception of the world and on the way in which we act. The influence of this early training and internalization of values is not, however, always helpful. Clara Thompson, in writing of the Freudian Superego, which is sometimes identified with conscience, notes:

Because of it the child fears not just the reality-disapproval of society, but attitudes of society which he has incorporated within himself. This "conscience" contains much that is irrational and harsher than the real demands of society. So in time anxiety is produced by the struggle within the person of the harsh Superego and the powerful forbidden instincts.[1]

The uncritically internalized demands can thus be an obstacle to growth and to moral judgment. Indeed, such a "conscience" may cause untold anguish without enabling the person to cope with the new and complicated areas of reality that he meets as an adult.

There are numerous individuals whose concepts of right or wrong were frozen at the stage reached early in childhood. They suffered from a selective conscience, since they had been sensitized to only a limited number of values or principles. They may have absolutely prudish ideas about sex but no concept of social responsibility. Others can be excessively sensitive about etiquette or courtesy but unresponsive to the real needs of other people. As a rule, these individuals have never tried to organize their moral thinking but have been content with a few simple rules which do not cover most of the real ethical problems in life.

Those whose ethical sensitivity is circumscribed often experience real agony when they are faced with complex situations in which they are torn between their simplified ethical principles and the demands of the situation. Their frame of reference is too narrow to enable them to handle many of the complicated problems which face businessmen, political leaders, teachers, doctors, and administrators. The result is often a compartmentalizing of their ethical life. For such individuals ethics often refers only to simple personal relations, especially in the home. The civil law is left to take care of everything else.

In surveying psychological literature, Brown notes that moral knowledge and conduct have a certain specificity.[2] This is to say that people tend to have particular moral norms but to lack general norms to cover cases they have never met before. For example, a man may see taking another man's silverware as a theft but have no exact idea of what constitutes theft. As a result, he may not see price fixing, expense account padding, or income tax evasion as forms of theft. Some men may have clear ideas about the nature of lying but fail to see the evil involved in the half-truth or the suppression of the truth.

These limitations of the undeveloped conscience must be recognized if we are to avoid problems by telling men to follow their own conscience. Conscience and moral knowledge do not grow automatically, any more than correct attitudes are created by a sort of spontaneous generation. Indeed, unless a man studies constantly, his conscience can be immature and his judgment untrustworthy when he meets new and complex situations.

Because growth is not automatic in the moral sphere, it is necessary to prepare for ethical knowledge and continually to enlarge our ethical categories. It is equally necessary to study the concrete world with which the ethical man must deal if his life is to be a coherent whole.

GROWTH AND ETHICS

Our growth in ethical knowledge and sensitivity depends not only on our early ethical training and our ability to transcend its limitations but on our general maturity. Unless we pass successfully through certain crises and form sound basic attitudes, we will not be able to cope with the complex situations we meet as adults. In his book *Childhood and Society*, Erikson analyzes the crises of growth which must be surmounted if a person is to mature.[3] Even a simple listing of these crises will indicate their importance for the ethical life.

> Basic trust versus basic mistrust
> Autonomy versus shame and doubt
> Initiative versus guilt
> Industry versus inferiority
> Intimacy versus isolation
> Generativity versus stagnation
> Ego integrity versus despair

The person who cannot surmount the first crisis will tend to perceive others as hostile, and hence to miss their dignity and value. Those who cannot come to a sense of their own autonomy will forever fear the acceptance of responsibility. The person who lacks industry, initiative, and a sense of his own integrity or identity will hardly be able to exercise his freedom fully. Indeed he may become a victim of every opinion which his acquaintances approve of. Certainly the person who is unable to resolve the tension between intimacy and isolation will hardly grow in that love which appears essential to both interpersonal relations and social life. The implications of each crisis have been developed by Erikson in a second book, *Insight and Responsibility*.[4] The point to be stressed is that growth crises influence attitudes, emotions, and value perceptions, which in turn influence both moral judgments and behavior.

While no such classification of the growth stages of adults is available, some similar process seems to occur in adult life. Maslow, for example, finds that self-actualizing people have characteristics which are not found in average people.[5] Some of these characteristics are important for ethics. The self-actualizers have an easy self-discipline, greater self-knowledge, and increased objectivity. This means that such individuals have psychological characteristics which make it easier for them to appreciate and follow the moral precepts of the great religions. It would also seem clear that the self-actualizer has a better chance of making sound moral judgments of his own.

The fact of growth in both childhood and in adult life points to the need for continuing moral education and growth in self-knowledge. This growth demands not only increased objectivity but increasing knowledge and control in the area of affectivity and emotion.

AFFECTIVITY

The values, principles, and ethical conclusions we learn in childhood are highly charged with emotion. For this reason, if for no other, they grip us strongly. Even when we have seen the folly of some of our childhood training, we may still find it extremely difficult to act against it. An individual who was taught as a child that Negroes were inferior, and punished for associating with Negro children, may as an adult find it difficult to treat a Negro fairly, even when his adult experience and intellectual convictions tell him that his parents were wrong. One who was trained in childhood to fear his body and his sexuality can in adult life remain uneasy in his marriage relations for years after he has realized that married sexual love is a beautiful and humanly enriching thing. Unfortunately it is easier to change ideas than emotions.

Although the problems connected with emotions and affectivity are fairly obvious, they are not easy to discuss. We lack adequate language and categories for our affective life. Furthermore, emotions are often so personal, and even irrational, that they defy exact description. In the concrete world, it is often difficult to say whether our conscious judgments cause our emotions or our emotions cause our conscious judgments. Despite these difficulties, a few remarks may help us to focus on some important aspects of affectivity in the ethical life.

In what follows we are not talking simply of pleasure and pain but of much deeper experiences. Pleasure and pain may be important signals sent out by the body, but as Allport notes in *Pattern and Growth in Personality,*[6] nature's signals seem to become less and less reliable as a man develops. These signals may give us valuable clues to the state of the organism, but they are not a sufficient guide for action. The emotions such as fear, anger, joy, and euphoria are much deeper manifestations of our reaction to things. They are concerned not merely with the state of the organism but with the state of the person as a whole. For this reason, they can have a much greater impact on our perception of the good.

THE CONTROL OF AFFECTIVITY

Some individuals have too little affective life. They view everything with either cold detachment or quiet withdrawal. Nothing carries value for them except the protective shell which keeps out the demands of the world. Sometimes, of course, the lack of expressed affectivity can hide a seething rage or deep hurt. Often it is only a protection against the hurts that result when one becomes involved with others. This occurs in institutionalized children and even in adults who had repressive childhoods.

Lack of affective life seriously limits both our value judgments and the force of our ethical decisions. While some individuals seem able to act ethically on the basis of principles which are not reinforced by feelings, they would appear to be the exceptions rather than the rule. Most of us need to have our value judgments supported by feeling. Indeed, to a certain extent we must be able to feel in order to experience the values we are to judge. Our delight in something helps us to see its goodness. Our pain and sorrow warn us that something is wrong. Neither our delight nor our sorrow is a sure guide, as we shall see later, but it is difficult to perceive values and disvalues without them.

In those cases where apparent lack of affectivity is merely a cover for seething rage or deep hurt, we may be faced with a really difficult problem. The person who conceals all his emotions from others may lose contact with himself. He may be confused as to when he should be affectionate, angry, afraid, or concerned, and so back away not only from many human contacts but also from the making of judgments about the rightness or wrongness of situations. Where affect is truly absent or deficient, the problem is to develop it. This, of course, is not an easy proposition, nor an overnight one. In many cases the development of normal emotions may require the services of a skilled counselor or a psychotherapist. The help of such professionals should not be despised, and indeed may be obligatory if the whole growth of the person is being blocked.

Some individuals are so dominated by feelings and emotions, and in general by the affective approach to life, that reason cannot keep control. Reason may be swept away as the person plunges ahead, relying exclusively on emotion to determine what is right or wrong. Unfortunately, feeling without reason can lead to as many harmful effects as reason without feeling. Emotional persons often have the world blow up in their faces. They mean to do the right thing but manage to overlook significant factors. They may be led by love and tenderness but miss the objective nature of the situation. In these cases, affectivity blocks rather than promotes sound ethical decisions.

More often than not, the overemotional person overreacts. The display of feeling and the consequent actions are not proportioned to the objective situation. We can see that an emotion is disproportionate when it focuses not on the total situation or its major components, but on a minor detail. Thus, the woman who rages against her husband's habit of leaving his clothes strewn around, even though he is a good husband in all other respects, is lacking in a sense of proportion. Similarly, the people who can involve themselves passionately in working for the betterment of animals but are blind to the needs of people have a poorly balanced affectivity. The emotion does not correspond with the objective value of the objects. Such emotions do not make for growth and integration, but for isolation or inner anguish.

Although we cannot make out an exact chart, we all recognize that some reactions are not in accord with reality. Fears, hopes, anxiety, and elation may be justified or unjustified, and we judge this by relating them to reality or to the public judgment of reality. This does not mean that they are not real. On the contrary, even the twisted emotion, feeling, or affectivity is very real. The problem is that they do not jibe with the rest of reality and do not help a man to relate himself to others, so that the feelings which should unite, isolate. To put it another way, a man has created an affective state which does not fit in with that reality which he must order to his growth.

BY WAY OF SUMMARY

Our ability to make good ethical judgments depends on our childhood training, our maturity, and our affective life. This implies a need for constant growth. It also implies that people who have distorted ideas developed in childhood or adolescence need to rethink their basic attitudes. The necessity of developing affectivity which can sensitize and support us never ceases. At the same time, the emotions must be judged and focused if they are to help us to cope with reality.

THE ADULT AND THE COMMUNITY

Not only the child and adolescent but also the adult who has reached real maturity must face the difficult task of relating their own values and ethical principles to those of the various groups and societies to which they belong. At one and the same time, the adult finds himself trusting and distrusting community and group standards. The distrust rests on several foundations. In the first place, history proves that community standards have often been inadequate. Secondly, the community is often a fiction in a pluralistic society characterized by rapid change. Thirdly, the community or the subcommunities are often incapable of justifying their positions in rational terms. Finally, the mature individual distrusts group pressure toward blind conformity.[7]

Not long ago, American society was almost universally blind to the problem of the Negro. Community standards did not admit the existence of a real ethical problem. People who felt uneasy were quieted with assurances that the Negro would find his way along the path of other groups who had pulled themselves up by their bootstraps. In other cases, the community absolved itself by attributing some inherent weakness to the Negro population. Mature individuals and even the young have now seen through these excuses, with the result that the latter suspect community standards in other areas. Only a very complacent individual would say that the young do not have a point.

The lack of community consensus in many areas is bewildering to both young and old. The churches do not agree among themselves, and the home is often at odds with the school. The liberal establishment embraces one set of values, the conservative another. Adults may agree about some standards, but the teenage culture tries to impose another set. Whom do you trust? Whose consensus is right? These are the unanswered questions which cause many men to solve great moral issues with slogans or vague appeals to democracy, the American way, or even the free enterprise system.

Unpleasant though it may be, all of us—young and old—are aware of the hypocrisy that motivates many of the slogans and small-group agreements. All too often we see a group morality setting up moralizing defenses. The Negro is to be denied equal access to housing in the name of private property. Workers are to be kept from organizing in the name of right-to-work laws. Medicare was to be beaten down in the name of a personal relationship with the doctor which many of us have never experienced. Pornography was to be justified in the name of art or of profits or even of freedom of speech. Cynicism was sure to follow when children discovered that parents and teachers did not live up to their own norms. Cynicism was bound to grow when people discovered that lofty moral language was a public relations tool for many groups.

Suspicion of established groups probably grows more rapidly when people discover that the groups cannot give a rational account of their positions. Young people, for example, want to know why they should be chaste before marriage; why cheating is wrong; why they should not set out to get all they can from others. Often, of course, the young want reasons to bolster their own ideals, though some undoubtedly are looking for a way out. Unfortunately their questions are not really answered, or they are answered with such ambiguity that even adults despair of arriving at a reasoned position.

Some of the reasons passed out as justifications of moral precepts actually confuse the young and the old. If certain things are unethical "because they are just not done by nice people," we equate morals with mores or even with etiquette. This does not make much sense to those who are already in revolt against many of the polite conventions. The conformist, however, must sense that ethics and morality cannot be of really deep significance if they change like women's dress styles.

The work of Piaget indicates that though children between four and eight years of age accept adult norms as absolute, children beyond eight tend to develop rules of conduct in their peer group.[8] These rules are subject to change by group agreement. The morality of these rules is supposed to be based on the respect felt for the group and its members. This may explain why such problems arise when a man cannot respect a group and why men find it hard to form objective judgments of morality.

In our search for ethical sensitivity and correct ethical judgment, we should be particularly wary of the "self-evident" values and truth which permeate a given culture or subgroup. In our American culture, for example, we tend to worship efficiency, to measure a man by his income or school marks, and to exalt popularity. While efficiency, income, and popularity are not disvalues or evils, it is not at all evident that they should occupy high places in the hierarchy of values. Consequently, if we blindly give them pride of place, we may find ourselves sacrificing compassion to efficiency, friendship to income, and personal integrity to popularity.

Although adults are not used to looking to the young for ethical guidance, we should recognize the fact that in our times the young may have escaped the appeal of values which used to be considered self-evident. Rightly or wrongly, many young people challenge our involvement in the Vietnam war because they feel that the value of life is being subordinated to a vague nationalistic patriotism. Similarly, young people may have a very valid point when they challenge dress regulations on the ground that a man should not be judged by the way he clothes himself.

Not only the "self-evident" community values but our own first truths need to be challenged occasionally. Is it really important to be first? Is it ethical to wish to dominate? Is my own sense of gratification a prime value? Are my ideas of success really sound? These are questions that should be asked over and over again, lest our values and ideals be subtly distorted over a period of time.

In American society the appeal to community standards may actually arouse hostility. The reason is simply that many people already feel smothered by the pressure to conform in a thousand little ways. Younger people in particular question the community's regulations about speech, dress, and manners. To be sure, they then conform to their own subgroup standards, but they can at least feel that they have had a hand in making these norms. As a matter of fact, since we live in a pluralistic society, people merely create new subgroups when they find that the standards of older subgroups are not acceptable to them. Conformity to subgroup standards can be extremely dangerous, but the failure to conform can result in deep loneliness. This loneliness too can be dangerous, for most men need the support of a group in order to form and maintain ideals. In the real world, neither blind revolt nor unthinking conformity can give an ethical solution to the problems which arise from the tension between the individual and the groups. We suggest, however, that the individual has at least the following obligations.

1. The individual ought to challenge the community or group to justify its position.

2. He ought to challenge his own motives for either accepting or rejecting the reasons of the community.

3. He should decide on the exact moral significance of his position and determine what he can tolerate even when he cannot approve.

4. He must commit himself one way or another on each issue.

If the individual refuses to follow these rules, he may find that he has become lost in the lonely crowd. If he follows these rules, he may find that he is unpopular. He has to choose, then, between his own basic integrity and full group acceptance.

Although a healthy suspicion of group standards is a necessary protection for personal integrity, we should not overlook the fact that group standards can and often do enshrine valid ethical judgments. The group generally has more experience than any one individual. The group may also be less selfish than some members. Moreover, where actions will affect the many, the many must have a say in judging them.

ENLARGING ETHICAL CATEGORIES

The mature adult who constantly reexamines his personal standards and the values of the community will soon face the need for new ethical categories. An adult with real ethical sensitivity will often be aware that something is wrong, even when he cannot put his finger on it. He lacks categories to use in communicating and analyzing his own reaction. As a result, he may not be able to justify his stand even to himself, let alone to those whose help he needs. To put it another way, we need theories and categories which will enable us to pass beyond our first vague reaction to a reasoned position and justified action.

Children are taught not to lie, but not taught the difference between a lie and a falsehood. As a result, they may think they are being unethical when they tell a falsehood in order to protect a legitimate secret. A more accurate notion of what constitutes the evil of a lie would enable them to lead lives that were both more tranquil and more ethical. A businessman knows he should treat human beings with respect but does not know how to reconcile this with his obligation to make his business prosper. As a result, he may feel guilty about doing the right thing and complacent about doing wrong. He needs some norms for assigning hierarchy and resolving conflicts of obligations. Many people speak of the golden rule, but few know what to do when their actions on behalf of one group are going to hurt another group.

Even experts in the field of ethics often find themselves embarrassed by lack of suitable categories and norms. The experts recognize the existence of social responsibilities, but they are hard put to it to tell us how to recognize them. Indeed, ethics is particularly weak when dealing with such new realities as the modern corporation, the large labor union, or big government.

Often people attempt to solve complicated problems by appealing to community norms. This can be a dangerous procedure, because not only does the community often lack technical knowledge but its moral categories also may be twisted or seriously incomplete.

There are, for example, laws which protect the businessman at the expense of the consumer. An appeal to such a law would enable a man to dodge his real responsibilities. Some communities may tolerate premarital intercourse, but this may be a result of blindness to the dignity both of sex and of the human persons involved. This blindness may be a result of ignorance of the psychological impacts of premarital sex. In short, the community may have overlooked crucial ethical factors because its ethical categories do not call for a consideration of these points.

Not only community categories but community judgment of facts may be defective. It is easy to assume that people can obtain equal justice in the courts. As a matter of fact, lack of money or organization, or the presence of prejudices can negate truly equal justice. Similarly, the community may assume that all its schools provide the same educational opportunities, whereas some are vastly inferior. If these assumptions are not questioned, even the mature adult may approve of situations that are truly unjust.

THE NEED FOR INFORMATION

Ethical judgments depend not only on the maturity of the individual and the adequacy of his moral categories but on the information he possesses. The more complicated the situation, the greater the need for information, including technical information from economics, sociology, political science, and psychology. As life becomes more complicated, the experience of the individual is no longer sufficient. He must rely on the experience and information gathered by others.

We cannot have personal experience of the good or bad effects of all medicines without running tremendous risks. We cannot have personal experience of the effects, good or bad, of all social arrangements, since sometimes it takes several lifetimes for the effects to be fully visible. Most human beings do not have the direct experience to make business decisions that are both ethical and economically sound. Ethical problems in these areas can be solved only by men who have data, experience, and adequate moral categories combined.

Even in the situations of everyday life, information is important. A teacher disciplining a student must look to the effects of his act on the child, the other members of the class, and the school as a whole. He should have some idea of what can be expected and how to minimize the undesirable effects of his activities. Since we will return to this problem in the chapter on the expression of love,

here we will merely summarize by saying that even the simplest
ethical judgments require some information.

IS IT BETTER TO BE IGNORANT?

The difficulty of preparing for the formation of conscience combined with the difficulty of passing judgment on concrete cases
makes many wonder if it is not better to be ignorant. Since knowledge creates obligations as well as freedoms, many people are
reluctant to obtain a knowledge of right or wrong. Why not remain
ignorant? But if we remain deliberately ignorant, we have obviously refused to take a necessary means to our growth as men.
Unless there is a proportionate reason for remaining ignorant at a
given time, I am guilty of a moral evil, since I have taken a more
or less serious risk of harming myself or others. Even indeliberate
ignorance, however, is an evil, and in ethics possibly a tragic and
definitive one.

Many evils affect me whether I know it or not. The man who
overindulges in food and drink harms himself no matter what he
thinks about it. The effects are not directly under the control of his
will. The same can be said of the man who abuses anything under
the illusion that no one is harmed. The objective evil is there no
matter what he believes. Of course, if the evil is willed or risked
without a proportionate reason, the wound is deeper. Unfortunately, even the unwilled and unknown evil can render a man less
capable of being a man; less capable of knowing and loving and
growing. Ignorance, then, is a tragedy even when indeliberate.

As we grow older, we should also become conscious of the
tragedy involved in ethical ignorance. We may discover that we
allowed the exploitation of certain groups of workers, the Negroes
or others among our fellow citizens, or the Vietnamese, because
we did not know or would not believe that any real evil was being
done. We may discover that we have spoiled a child and weakened
his character by what we mistakenly thought were acts of kindness.
While we may not be fully responsible for the evil we permitted
or caused (our ignorance may have been indeliberate), we must

fear that we are unknowingly involved in evil. At this point, ignorance no longer looks like a blessing or a handy excuse. With age we see ignorance as a primary cause of evil. We see ignorance as part of the human tragedy.

Our ignorance is tragic not only because it allows us to do evil unwittingly but also because it prevents us from seeing all the opportunities for good which are open to us. The individual who has never seen the value of love will cut himself off from full communion with other human beings. The individual who sees money, and not service, as the wellspring of human activity will not realize that much of the real creativity in the world has no monetary reward. In short, the failure to elaborate an ethical ideal which contains the highest values can stunt growth and leave a man on the level of the mediocre.

IGNORANCE AND PERSONAL RESPONSIBILITY

The consciousness of our own ignorance can paralyze our ability to make ethical decisions. It can create a climate of moral scepticism. College students, for example, can be quite vigorous in demanding more responsibility and yet dodge responsibility with the question, "Who am I to say what is right or wrong?" At first glance, the combination of a demand for responsibility and the refusal to take a stand may seem paradoxical. Actually, it points to the necessity of a redefinition of terms by people who have despaired of finding any ground for ethical decisions.

Responsibility has at least four dimensions, three of which demand some knowledge. The person who has responsibility for a certain activity must accept the praise or blame for his success or failure. In addition, he must be responsive to the objective situation, since responsible action is not arbitrary. A truly responsible agent, moreover, is capable of giving an account of what he has decided to do. Finally, a responsible person carries out the actions he has decided on or committed himself to.

Because responsibility has these manifold dimensions, it is not easy to achieve full responsibility. We can fail by refusing to face facts, by refusing to make decisions, or by failing to think out the reasons which support our actions. We act irresponsibly when we will not investigate, calculate, ponder, and attempt to control our lives. We are irresponsible when we let weariness, cowardice, or sloth stop us from completing the task begun.

How much knowledge does a man need before he can act responsibly and ethically? When is ignorance culpable and unethical? These are key questions in any ethics which gives prominence to the use of man's intelligence. They are not easy questions to answer, since the answer must cover millions of possible situations. Indeed the difficulty is such that many despair.

Traditionally, these questions have been answered by saying that a man is obliged to make reasonable efforts to get the knowledge necessary to act ethically. The word "reasonable," however, is rather vague. In practice, *reasonable* means proportionate. This is to say that the effort made has been reasonable when it is proportionate to the seriousness of the matter, to the talent and time of the person, and finally to his official position. More often than not, it is impossible to have absolute certitude about what to do in an entirely new type of situation, but this does not make a judgment unreasonable. In practical affairs, certitude is nearly always somewhat conditional. This is merely to say that we are not infallible or omniscient. When we have done our best and have as much certitude as men ordinarily have in practical matters, we must follow our judgments, even though there is some risk of being wrong.

Many writers sum this up by saying that we are obliged to use reasonable means to form our moral judgments and to follow them when they are certain for all practical purposes. The reason is simple: we have no other way in which we can responsibly run our own lives. The refusal to use reasonable means in searching for valid judgments and the refusal to follow judgments about which we are certain both involve the rejection of the only, and therefore the necessary, means of perfecting ourselves. The two refusals are, in short, a rejection of our own gifts and of control over our lives.

WHEN IN DOUBT

There are times when reasonable and even heroic efforts to make a moral decision leave us still in doubt. The mind, the whole being of the individual, wanders back and forth between the Yes and the No. There is some evidence to say that a thing is harmful and some that says it is good. There are some authorities who say the law is such and such; others who deny this. It is a state in which even practical certitude is lacking. At the same time, there are moments in which a man must act. He cannot treat his doubt as a purely theoretical problem which can be solved at a future date. Yet, because he is a man, he cannot simply choose and plunge ahead in doubt. In one way or another, he wants and needs some sort of indirect certitude; at the very least, the certitude that he is acting like a man—that is, reasonably, prudently, and with a sensitivity to the basic values which must be respected.

There are two methods for arriving at indirect certitude about the reasonableness of a decision. Both methods assume that an individual has already made an effort to get information, since the effort is a proof of sincerity and good will. The methods, however, do not promise a man that he will always be theoretically right, but only that he has acted reasonably and ethically in a perplexing situation.

The first method applies to those situations in which there is some risk of harming either oneself or others. Since we must always act so as to minimize the risk in such cases, it is practically certain that the man must take the safer course of action as he sees it, then and there. Reasonable conduct demands that we shall not take risks without a proportionate reason. A doctor who must choose between two modes of treatment and cannot be positive about the actual results must use this approach. Parents use such a method in punishing children. Indeed, all of us use it when we cross a dangerous street. We are not certain that we will make it to the other side, but we are acting ethically if we have a proportionate reason for taking the risk. The fact that on a given day we are actually hit by a car does not mean that we made a bad or unethical choice so long as we acted reasonably in the first place.

The American involvement in Vietnam is a question where even a man of good will may have serious doubts as to what is right or wrong. The ordinary educated citizen does not have access to all the facts. Experts line up on both sides of the question, and even the Churches appear to be split in their teaching on the subject. At the same time, the situation is such that a person has to take a stand—for silence and inactivity are themselves stands in favor of the government's policy. It seems to me, however, that either support or protest can be seen as a reasonable course of action for the large group who do not have the evidence for absolute certitude one way or another. Indeed, I would venture the opinion that the only demonstrably unreasonable position is mere drifting without making a conscious, even if conditional, choice.

The second method of changing doubt into a state of practical certitude can be applied in those cases where there is no known risk of harm to oneself or to others. It has important applications when the doubt concerns an obligation to obey a positive civil or ecclesiastical law. Like the first method, it assumes that the person in doubt has already tried to form his judgments by investigation and wants to do the right thing. Where the first method rests on the principle that forbids us to risk harm without a proportionate reason, the second is based on the idea that a doubtful obligation is no obligation at all.

An obligation, as we have defined it, is a moral necessity that arises from the knowledge of an objective necessity. If the mind does not see an objective necessity, no moral necessity can arise. A person who is sincerely in doubt does not see an objective necessity and so is free to choose the goods he does see. In short, liberty is to be favored in situations where there is no risk of harm to oneself or others. It should be noted that there is a general necessity of avoiding risks in the absence of a proportionate reason. It is for this reason that the safer course must be followed in some cases.

People ask, "What do you do when the risks themselves balance out?" The answer is simple: if you must choose, you are morally free to choose either course of action. This sort of situation occurs when not acting is certain to cause more harm than either of the courses open to you. A doctor, for example, cannot hesitate forever because he is not certain that one treatment is better than another.

All of this may seem very unsatisfactory to those who like a nice neat world. It is unsatisfactory, but then, being a fallible human being is a bit unsatisfactory. Because we are only men and not God, we can only do our best, even though that is far short of perfect. Indeed, the acceptance of our limitations along with our obligations is part of being a mature human being. There is really no way out for those who want to be more than machines or perpetual children.

TAKING A STAND

The human condition is not always a pleasant one. Most of us are all too aware of our frailty and fallibility. Often we are tempted to despair and to hand over our moral autonomy to the drift of events. Sooner or later most of us have to take stands if we are to remain men. We cannot remain forever neutral with regard to disputed questions of social and international justice without creating a vacuum which will be filled by men who may have no sense of justice, but who settle all issues by power. There is evidence that some of the greatest evils have occurred while good men stood by in indecision. The apathy of people who will not vote, or of men who will not take a stand, can be really evil.

While I shall return to this question in Chapter 11, The Expression of Love, here and now it should be said that our doubts do not excuse us from taking a stand forever. It can be unreasonable and unethical to do nothing because one is not sure. After all, the obligation to minimize risks and harms remains with us every day.

PREPARATION FOR ETHICAL KNOWLEDGE

Everything in the earlier part of this chapter has particular relevance for educators, clergymen, and parents. Those who are responsible for the formation of youth must recognize the need for both broad and specific ethical formation. Men must be prepared to make ethical decisions, for there are no automatic processes that guarantee even relatively sound ethical judgments.

Many things in our society are obstacles to this preparation. The dominance of the community, the diminishment of the individual, the stress on happiness and pleasure, all block the growth of the individual towards openness to the world and involvement with it. Since both openness and involvement are necessary for moral knowledge, these barriers are considerable. There are, however, other difficulties. The conflicting demands made on us make it more difficult to achieve a sense of identity, for we are torn this way and that, with no sense of direction. In many cases, the lack of even formal mechanical order leaves the individual with little control over the important details of his life. Such an individual has no peace and no chance to assess either himself or the world. A college student, for example, gets conflicting ideas from his home and friends, as well as from the mass media and the school. If he has not learned to make his own decisions and set up his own regime, he can drift for years, or be torn apart by the conflicting demands made on him.

Ideally, many of the barriers should be removed by growing up in a family where the child sees the model of both love and discipline in his parents. He should have experienced real involvement with a loved one even if he could not analyze it. At the same time, the good home should have helped him to free himself from petty attachments, taught him how to cope with his feelings, and given him confidence that he can grow on his own. If all these things had been done, the pressures of society would not prove decisive. All too often, however, the home produces an emotional cripple who is a bundle of aggressions and unresolved conflicts; whose emotional life is still one of infantile attachment and attention-getting devices.

When the child has not been helped to integrate his being, even the body of the adult may be an enemy. Lack of sleep and exercise leaves him languid and subject to what the Victorian novelists called the vapors. Sexual fantasy and reflex make continued insistent demands because energy has not been channeled into any activity which gives significance to life, whatever may be the sources of temporary satisfaction. The result is often greater weariness, loss of focus, and affective dispersal.

Many of these problems have been caused or reinforced by a belief in "magic" of one sort or another. The pill, the psychiatrist's couch, the thousand forms of escape, are used not as helps, but as *the thing* which will solve all problems. There is, in short, a world of illusion that keeps people from facing reality, which, though it may sometimes be frightening, is easier to cope with than a dream world which continuously escapes us.

In view of all these things, I do not believe that we can prepare for either moral knowledge or the moral life without taking a stand on some basic issues. First, I can control my life to a very large extent. Secondly, I must control it and form myself to some image. Thirdly, I need discipline and system, and possibly some friendly help. Fourthly, other people cannot solve my problem for me any more than they can really create most of them.

THE RIGHTS OF CONSCIENCE

A man must follow his certain conscience, since it is the only means he has for guiding his ethical life. If he refuses to form and follow his conscience, he has refused to be a man and to work toward his own human fulfillment. Yet devotion to conscience causes problems. Conscience forces us to make choices which involve forgoing many goods in view of higher human values. The commands of conscience can also bring us into conflict with other men. Indeed, the fact that different men arrive at different judgments of conscience can be a major cause of conflict.

The conflict of consciences should not surprise us. Not all men reach the same stage of ethical growth at the same time. Men are subject to different basic visions of the world and are influenced by different groups. Moreover, because our ethical judgments are concerned with the contingent, complex, and changing world of men endowed with freedom, they often heavy with calculated risk. Even an expert in ethics must note that in some cases he cannot tell another man what to do, even though the expert is quite clear as to what he himself would do. Such situations are common enough when the choice involves untested alternatives or once-in-a-lifetime decisions. It is not surprising, then, if even men of good will sometimes arrive at judgments which are in conflict.

If the judgment of conscience was not aimed at action or at the deliberate omission of action, there would be little problem. We ought to respect the consciences of others and refrain from trying to change them by force. We do not, after all, have to agree with others in order to respect them as persons. The problem, however, is different when the judgment of conscience is translated into action. The external acts which flow from conscience have consequences. If these consequences are harmful in the eyes of others, certain important questions must be asked. Do individuals and groups have a right or obligation to suppress those actions which we consider evil even though the agent performs them in good faith? Does the fact that a man's conscience obliges him to do something mean that he has a right to place an act which others condemn? May individuals or the state force a man to omit something commanded by his conscience or to perform an act forbidden by his conscience?

Obviously there is no problem if the acts commanded by conscience produce no harmful effects. We do not worry about people who think it immoral to drink, gamble, or dance, so long as they do not try to force their conscience on us. We may disagree with them, but we are hardly tempted to use force in stopping them from preaching and working peacefully for their ideals.

Let us suppose, however, that those who condemn drinking, dancing, and gambling tried to force us to omit these actions which our consciences consider as either good or ethically neutral. According to our consciences, these people are unreasonably interfering with our right to pursue useful goods. Are we obliged to submit our actions to their consciences? May we ethically defend ourselves against these efforts to limit us? The principles developed earlier in this book would justify us in defending ourselves, so long as due proportion is observed. This is to say that we should first use the tools of government and then use only as much force as is necessary to protect the right, granted that the resulting harm is not greater than the good to be protected. After all, even though the fanatics in question are trying to limit our liberty, they are not forcing us to do something unethical, unless we believe that we are obligated to drink, gamble, and dance.

The problem becomes more acute when we are dealing with people whose consciences cause them to do things which we see as seriously harmful to themselves, others, or the society as a whole. May we use force to prevent these people from following their consciences? The colonial powers were faced with this question when they met native cultures. Were the British ethical when they prevented Indian widows from fulfilling their obligation to immolate themselves on the funeral pyres of their husbands? Were the British right when they stopped the Thugs, who believed they had to kill in the name of their goddess? Is the government right when it orders a doctor to give a transfusion to a child whose parents' religion forbids such practices?

In all these cases, the government was fulfilling its obligation to protect the rights of citizens and to stop evils which harm the common good. If the principle of proportionality was observed, it is difficult to see how the government could be accused of violating the rights of the persons involved. At the same time, any ethical man must be uneasy about the use of force, since the government may be tempted to use it even when there is no clear question of an evil to be avoided. Does the government have the right to coerce or punish a college student who refuses to serve in Vietnam because he considers the war unjust? Do parents have a right to force an eighteen-year-old to go to church when he no longer accepts the religion of his parents? The boy argues that it is hypocritical to do something you don't believe in. The parents tell him to conform or get out.

The case of the conscientious objector and of the unbelieving son do not involve restraining someone from an act that is *clearly harmful* to himself, others, or the common good. They do involve forcing a person to do something which is against his conscience. In each case the person is being forced to commit an act he considers evil and not merely to omit an act he considers good. While there may be long, involved arguments about the justice of the war and the truth of the religion which the young man rejects, the fact remains that the consciences of these individuals forbid the acts which others command.

Although these issues cannot be fully settled without reference to Chapter 12, on society and its authority, we believe that force should not be used in cases where there is no clear proof that the individual's conscience has caused serious harm to himself, others, or society. This opinion rests on the assumption that the benefit of the doubt should always go to the individual. It is bolstered by a profound conviction that the use of coercion must always be a last resort, because it seldom offers enduring solutions to problems.

Those who are the victims of coercion must remember that we must follow our consciences, and we must be willing to pay the price. A person who believes it unethical to cooperate in the prosecution of a war should accept prison and death rather than violate his conscience. If there is nothing worth dying for, then there is nothing worth living for. If we are unwilling to pay the price for being ethical, we are not really ethical at all.

BY WAY OF SUMMARY

Though the present chapter poses many questions and then leaves them unanswered, it takes a very definite stand on a few key issues. Men do not automatically make good ethical judgments. It is necessary to use the intellect and to gather information before we can be said to have acted ethically. In order to use our intellect properly, we need to attend to our general human and emotional development so that we do not become victims of either our own feelings or the group norms which are constantly being pressed on us. If we refuse to fulfill these obligations, we shall have refused to be men.

NOTES

1. Clara Thompson, *Psychoanalysis: Evolution and Development* (Camden, N.J.: Thomas Nelson & Sons), p. 120. Copyright 1950 by Clara Thompson.
2. Roger W. Brown, *Social Psychology* (Glencoe, Ill.: Free Press, 1965). p. 407.
3. Erik Erikson, *Childhood and Society,* 2nd ed. (New York: W. W. Norton, 1950), pp. 247–274; especially p. 269.
4. Erik Erikson, *Insight and Responsibility* (New York: W. W. Norton, 1964).
5. Abraham H. Maslow, *Toward a Psychology of Being* (Princeton, N. J.: D. Van Nostrand, 1962), especially Chapters 6, 7, and 10.
6. Gordon W. Allport, *Pattern and Growth in Personality* (New York: Holt, Rinehart & Winston, 1961), p. 201.
7. *Cf.* Edward Joseph Shoben, Jr. "Towards a Concept of the Normal Personality," *The American Psychologist,* 12 (1957), April No. 4, p. 187.
8. Jean Piaget, *The Moral Judgment of the Child* (New York: Collier Books, 1962), p. 102.

POINTS FOR DISCUSSION

1. List some of the evils you have done out of ignorance. Was this ignorance deliberate? Could you have overcome it sooner if you had made greater effort?
2. Discuss the influence of general growth in maturity on your ideas of good and evil.
3. In what areas do emotions make ethical judgment and ethical action particularly difficult? Why?

4. What group standards do you mistrust? Why?
5. What group standards have you accepted uncritically?
6. List and discuss ethical problems where there is real doubt about what is to be done.
7. List and discuss situations in which individuals or groups force men to act against their consciences.

READINGS*

Eric D'ARCY, *Conscience and Its Right to Freedom* (New York: Sheed & Ward, 1961).

Harry K. GIRVETZ, *Contemporary Moral Issues* (Belmont, Cal.: Wadsworth, 1963), pp. 23–51. Readings on civil disobedience.

Louis MONDEN, S.J., *Sin, Liberty and Law* (New York: Sheed & Ward, 1965).

Gerard S. SLOYAN, *How Do I Know I'm Doing Right?* (Dayton, Ohio: George A. Pflaum, 1960). A short popular essay in the direction of a modern theology of conscience.

Allen WHEELIS, *The Quest for Identity* (New York: W. W. Norton, 1958).

* All the books listed in the notes to this chapter can be read with profit.

8/ LOVE
AND INTERPERSONAL
RELATIONSHIPS

INTRODUCTION

Man's knowledge is capable of uniting him, at least in part, with all things. Through knowledge man grows, as he sums up within himself more and more of created reality. Knowledge, however, does not satisfy completely. It may give greater satisfaction than eating and drinking and sleeping, but it does not slake our thirst for completion. The senses and the intellect bring reality into man, but his heart—his will—tends outward and roams the world, seeking to be filled. What will fill the heart of man, even partially, in the course of time? What will so fill his heart that he moves towards God, who alone can totally satisfy the hunger of his being?

Even a little reflection will show us that the beauty of the subrational world leaves man lonely. Whether we speak of food, drink, power, or even the beauty of sun-washed mountains, we recognize that these cannot fill the void, for they are less perfect than man himself. Only other men are equal to us in perfection, for only men are images of God, rather than faint footprints of the Infinite. So man turns to other men in order to escape his isolation and emptiness.

At this point, the means-end relationship leaves something to be desired. Other men are not means or things, they are other selves, other ends in themselves, other projects as worthy as I. Our relationship to them must be different from our relationship to things. We have already mentioned this in our treatment of rights. A mere respect for rights does not save us from our isolation. Neither does mere physical contact. I can be lonely in a crowded room. Men find themselves isolated even in the act of intimate sexual union. They may lose themselves for a moment, but the physical union itself does not end the loneliness or its cause. Neither touch nor taste—nor intelligence, for that matter—can reach the loneliness in any significant manner when such contacts are isolated from experience on a deeper level.

For centuries thinkers have tried to find the means of union in love. But the word love is so vague and so deceptive that it needs investigation and analysis. In our own culture, the Judeo-Christian tradition has made us conscious of the need for love. One does not, however, need to be committed to this tradition in order to realize love's importance and value. Maslow's studies of self-realization[1] and Bowlby's work on child care[2] indicate the value of and need for altruism. The observations of Erich Fromm[3] or Erik Erikson[4] point emphatically in the same direction. Karl Menninger and numerous others might be added to the list of psychologists and psychiatrists who point up the need to love unselfishly if one is to be fully human.[5]

SARTRE: THE OTHER AS ENEMY

For some thinkers, the drive towards the other, the search for love as a means of union and completion, is a dream. Sartre, for example, sees all persons as being essentially in conflict. The stare of the other turns me into an object. I, in my turn, defend myself only by turning him into an object. This, despite the fact that men will forever tend to intersubjectivity.[6]

We would be foolish to deny the fact that many men do attempt to turn us into objects. The hateful stare is common enough in our world. Worse yet, there is the stare of indifference which looks through us as if we were not there. Anyone who has ever ridden the New York Subway will have experienced the horror of the vacant eyes and the terrible isolation in a crowd. Increasingly, too, many of our relationships are impersonal or superficial, so that we never meet the person who lives behind his public mask. Often, we even find it difficult to deal with those who are close to us because we fear them or they fear us. Yet love and interpersonal relations of a deeper sort do exist. Love is a possibility, but it is not necessarily present in all lives. There are men who remain forever alone and isolated.

Our loneliness and isolation are the result of many factors. We may be lonely because we have a sense of incompleteness and know that nothing short of the infinite can fill us. At the same time, much of our loneliness is recognized as resulting from factors which can be overcome. How often we are lonely because we see others as hostile, threatening, and unpredictable. Having been hurt in the past, we are afraid of being hurt in the future and no longer attempt to make contact with others. Often, too, we see ourselves as un-lovable and having nothing to give. We hide our supposed poverty by staying away from people or by reducing our relations to rituals. The hostile stare of the other person may be only in our own mind, but it cuts us off and leaves us lonely.

Others may see us as hostile, threatening, and unpredictable, and so be afraid to approach or reveal themselves. This may be especially true if the other is timid, insecure, or filled with anxiety. He may be reading our signals incorrectly, but the result is still isolation. There has been a failure of basic communication, and both love and sharing are blocked.

The inability to communicate, or at least the inability to communicate accurately, lies at the root of much isolation. In some cases, this is due to the psychological blocks we have already mentioned. In other cases, the problem arises from lack of a suitable idiom. Words and gestures and postures have different meanings to different people, so that often we have to learn a whole new language in order to communicate with a single individual. If we fail to recognize this, we may find that our very effort to communicate creates misunderstandings and increases loneliness.

In the last analysis, the greatest block to union and to love is found in the fact that some people have never experienced love. Such individuals may have little reason to believe that life can be more than a series of casual, indifferent encounters. Lacking the experience, they must see love and union as words for nonexistent realities. They may even be resigned to deep inner isolation, or a life of surface relationships. No amount of intellectual argument will really convince an inexperienced person that love and union are possible. He has to experience love to believe in it, and often he has to believe in its possibility in order to experience it. Indeed this is one of those areas where basic commitments are called for if the realities we are discussing are to be meaningful.

LOVE AND LOVE

In our culture love is recognized as the means of overcoming isolation and/or finding ourselves. There is, unfortunately, considerable confusion as to what love is and how it works. While no one seems capable of removing all confusion in this area, we can at least reduce the confusion by trying to delimit the area of discussion. In the present chapter, we are not going to talk of sexual or erotic love, though this form is of unquestioned importance. Neither are we going to concentrate on the emotional side of love, though love can hardly exist without emotional support. We want to concentrate on love as an attitude or a psychological posture. In subsequent chapters we will return to the emotions and the expression of love, and in particular to the problems connected with human sexuality.

Nearly every thinker who has ever written on love distinguishes at least two types: selfish and unselfish. A selfish love may be called the love of desire, the love of concupiscence, the love of the earthly city or eros. But the essential concept remains the same. So too, unselfish love is given a variety of titles: altruistic love, benevolent love, the love of the heavenly city and agape. In this chapter we shall use the terms "love of desire" and "love of benevolence."

The love of desire is directed to an object precisely insofar as the object is perfective of the lover. Love of benevolence, however, looks to its object as being good in itself. It is a love for the sake of the beloved. The difference is a question of intention and direction. As a result, the term love is best reserved for the free acts of man. Although his unconscious and spontaneous tendencies also move him toward the good, these spontaneous tendencies may be either selfish or unselfish. However, since they have their full moral meaning only when consciously directed, we shall confine our study to love as a free act of the will by which man tends to, or is united with, a good. In the love of desire, the tendency and the union are selfish; in the love of benevolence, altruistic.

The love of desire is a taking, or at least an attempt to use, someone or something as a means. Obviously such a love is legitimate when directed towards objects which are, by nature, means. The act will be ethical if the object is used in accord with the principle of proportionality. Persons precisely as persons are not objects, or not means. To attempt to possess a person with a love of desire does violence both to the other and to oneself. Such love cannot unite one man to another, for a variety of reasons. In the first place, desire, by making a person an object, prescinds from the center of human goodness which alone can fill up human emptiness. In the second place, if the other person detects selfishness, he will mask his inner self so that the exploiter cannot come near the secret of his being. In many cases he will even retaliate by exploiting the exploiter. Desire, then, is doomed to frustration, for in intention it destroys the thing it claims to love by turning it into an object.

The inability of the love of desire to unite persons points to the paradox of love. We can find union and completion only by transcending desire and refusing to treat others as objects. We must see persons as persons and not as things or means. We must, in short, forget ourselves in some respects if we are to find ourselves on the deepest levels.

In most of our relationships with persons, there is some taint of self-interest. This need not surprise us. We ourselves do not reach full perfection in the twinkling of an eye. We can be confused about our proper stance towards others. In addition, there are relationships with persons which are not, and possibly should not be, truly personal. When I purchase something from a clerk in a store, I must recognize that the clerk is a person, but I must recognize the fact that our transaction is largely impersonal. When I hire an employee, I am not buying a man, I am buying some of his services. A certain amount of impersonality may even protect our personalities from exploitation. At the same time, we must recognize the fact that if we treat everybody impersonally, and as if they were mere objects, we will never find our fulfillment.

Benevolent love recognizes the other person as a person worthy of love *because he is,* and not because he is rich or strong or beautiful or patient or charming. This love cuts through the superficial, the accidental, the transitory, and acknowledges the unique and permanent goodness of the other. Even if the love is not returned, it transforms the lover. It turns the lover's whole being to the inner goodness of the beloved; then, having discovered the secret of the beloved, the lover discovers more of his own goodness. It is as if he had come to a new possession of himself. So too, because benevolence by-passes the superficial, it frees the lover from slavery to the relatively meaningless.

Benevolent love not only starts with a recognition of the essential goodness of the other, it looks to the promotion of the other. The benevolent lover wants the other to grow, to be himself, to arrive at the ideal. Benevolence aims to protect the beloved from harm and to endow him or her with the good things the lover possesses. It is a giving love, not a grasping desire. We see this love in parents who worry more about their children than about themselves. It manifests itself in the parents' willingness to let the child develop and even separate himself from the home. In an ideal marriage, benevolence shows itself in concern for one another's needs and in a willingness to endure the day-by-day strains necessary to help one another.

This truly unselfish love can even exist without the heady intoxication that we associate with falling in love. It resists the possessiveness of being in love which is so strongly tinged with desire. It may or may not involve delight in the presence of the beloved. It can tolerate long separation because it is not based on the surface characteristics of a person, but on the recognition that the other is good as person. Benevolence is strong and enduring, for it goes to the very root of being.

MUTUALITY

Benevolent love can be one-sided. Because it looks to the good of the other considered as an end in himself, it is not motivated by hope of gain. If the benevolence is genuine, it can even continue in the face of hatred and rejection. This is, obviously, very difficult, since desire is forever dragging man back to a lower level. How much rejection can be ethically tolerated we will deal with when we come to self-love and its limits. It should be obvious, however, that the lover cannot turn himself into a thing, even for the sake of the beloved.

Although benevolence can be one-sided, it tends to call for mutuality and reciprocity. The healthy personality answers love almost spontaneously. When people have recognized us as persons, we tend to recognize them in the same way. The response, however, is not automatic. As we noted earlier, fear, the inability to communicate, or a false perception of the other's intention can drive us into our shell. Similarly, when others do not recognize our benevolence, we may be tempted to become indifferent or even to hate them. This may, indeed, be a sign that our own love is not disinterested and is far from perfect.

There are grave problems concerned with the expression and modality of the response to love, but the fact itself is common. This return of love has powerful effects. It can convince the other of his value and open up new possibilities. It can ease the loneliness of life and move one towards greater generosity. It can create a "we" or community in which men can exist for their own sake and for the sake of the other, and not for some purely utilitarian and pragmatic purpose. In short, a truly personal and human sphere is created where two or more persons meet as persons in mutual love. The importance of this for mental health, clarity of vision, and sensitivity to values cannot be overemphasized. Within such a community, the person not only has value, he is sure of it and has a solid base from which to resist the encroachments and pressures that tend to depersonalize him. We can feel the effects of mutual benevolence when we walk into a home where there is deep respect for each member mingled with a sense of security. It manifests itself in those friendships where there is no need for words.

Mutual benevolence should be carefully distinguished from its counterfeit, mutual exploitation. The attitude on each side in such a relationship is like this: "I will love you if, and only if, you will love me"; and, "If you don't give me what I want, I will withdraw my love from you." Jealousy is often a sign that one or both parties want to possess and exploit. It can hardly coexist with deep concern for the good of the other. While we have no careful statistics on the incidence of mutual exploitation, it is probably common. How many friends become strangers when we lose our money, our power, or our beauty? How many friends become strangers when they have taken what they want, and then wander off to despoil someone else?

Because mutual exploitation is a common danger, the mature person who really wants to love benevolently will often question his own motives, lest he be exploiting. The mature person will also be on his guard against exploitation at the hands of others, not merely because he fears for himself, but because he does not want others to fall into selfish postures. This does not mean that every relationship must be dissected and torn to shreds. It does mean, however, that men must make a calm effort to distinguish between real and counterfeit relationships.

LOVING AND LIKING

Unselfish loving and liking are not identical. Unselfish love can and does coexist with an intense dislike for some characteristics of another person. The dislike can even be a sign of love if it springs from sorrow over the real defects of a beloved. After all, we want those we love to be perfect and to enjoy all possible goods. My closest friend has a bad habit of giving in to gloomy thoughts and making everyone around him miserable. I dislike this and do not enjoy his company when he is in these moods. At the same time, he needs me around when he is depressed, and I show my love by supporting him when I least enjoy it. Some of the people we love deeply may have bad breath, body odor, no manners, little sense of humor, and very little sensitivity to our feelings. This, however, need not destroy our love, and indeed cannot destroy our love if we focus on the basic goodness, need, and ability.

Unfortunately, dislikes can block love if we let them. If we are concerned with the superficial characteristics of others, our likes and dislikes may rule our relationships. The person who is not used to looking beneath the surface characteristics of human beings can be scared off by the gruff or blunt individual. A person who looks only for a pretty face can overlook the solid characteristics which make a person really lovable. For these reasons, we do well to block our likes and dislikes and look for the real person who may be hiding behind an unattractive façade.

Without a doubt, the fact that we like a person can help us to love him unselfishly. A powerful attraction can help to overcome our fears and remove the distance which prevents us from knowing the other person as a person. Our likes can reinforce our decision to love and serve the other person. They are not, however, a sufficient basis for a lasting relationship. Beauty vanishes, the gay person may become morose and gloomy, the vibrant, healthy person can fall ill. If the relationship was founded completely on such superficial qualities, it will collapse, and the person we pretended to love will feel that he has been rejected. He will realize that he was not loved for himself, but for the pleasure he gave others.

FORMS OF BENEVOLENCE

Benevolence is not a completely homogeneous act or attitude. It can take various forms and vary in both inner intensity and outer expression. At the very least, benevolence involves respect for and concern about other human beings. At a higher level, it involves a willingness to serve others just because they need help. Finally, it can rise to an effort of self-donation to another human being.

Respect for others as persons is a minimal level of benevolence which is probably not distinguishable from a sense of justice. Respect leads us to give others what is due to them and keeps us from injuring them or using them as mere objects. Respect, however, does not necessarily lead to deep personal involvement or extensive service to others. Although respect for others is a minimal form of benevolence, it should not be despised. Respect for and concern about the needs of others is a necessary prelude to any higher form of love. If every man had respect for every other man, we would already have made great advances in the ethical life. To the extent that we exclude anybody from our concern, to the extent that we are indifferent to the needs of others, we will find ourselves less capable of serving and loving even limited groups of human beings.

As our concern for others grows, we should be led to the service of others. At this higher level, we are no longer content to give others the minimum which is their due. We want to be actively engaged in promoting the good of other men. We want to serve, not because the other has a specified claim against us, but because he is a person capable of growth. This love of service is not without its price. When we start to help others, we become more and more sensitive both to needs and to the limits of our talents. We are forced to make choices because we cannot help everyone. Each choice hurts because the good we cannot do keeps beckoning. The young, the sick, the crippled, the alcoholic, the poor, the confused, all need our help, but our time and talents can only go so far. The infinite needs of men call, but only a few seem to answer, and we grieve over the good that will never be.

Although there is great joy and satisfaction in the love of service, the person who opens his heart and gives of his time and energy will feel the agony we have described above. The agony is not an evil. It is a sign that we are growing in sensitivity. It can also cause us to develop ourselves and to make fuller use of our talents. The agony can also tempt us to run away, to hide our head in the sand and pretend that the needs of others are no concern of ours. This means that the agony calls for a decision and a commitment if we are to realize the full potential of the human condition.

The love of self-donation has a more limited scope than the love of service. Where I can share my time and activity with many people, I can share myself with only a few. Self-donation involves more than time and energy. It leads to a revelation of ourselves to others. It puts us in the power of the beloved when we let him know our secret fears, longings, ambitions, and ideals. Because self-donation gives the other power over us, it is dangerous. Not everyone will keep our secret or respect our weakness. Some will try to use us as a thing or to exploit us. In conscience we cannot permit this, for we cannot become an occasion of evil for others whom we claim to love. We want to give ourselves as persons, not as playthings. Our respect for others must cause us to fight anyone who abuses a person.

Because self-donation is dangerous, we approach it tentatively. We want to give ourselves to the other, but we do not want to harm them by allowing them to harm us. For this reason, if no other, we cannot give ourselves to many people. For this reason, too, self-donation takes a long time and requires growth in both our knowledge of the other and our trust. Some people, it would seem, never arrive at self-donation with even one person. They are so riddled with wounds and filled with fears that they cannot or will not take any risks. Sometimes youthful efforts to love another have brought heartache or exploitation. The person may feel he has so little to give that he avoids any relationship which would expose his imagined poverty to another. No matter what the reason, the person who never succeeds in giving himself to another lives a diminished life, for we never really find ourselves until we lose ourselves in the highest form of benevolent love.

Fully expressed sexual love in marriage is supposed to be one way in which self-donation occurs. It is also one of the more dangerous forms of love, for it can lead to egoism as well as to the highest form of self-donation. Sexually expressed love can create mutual exploitation as well as it can support and cause a beautiful union of two persons. Because sexual love is so ambiguous, we have left it for a separate chapter.

GROWTH IN LOVE

Nearly everything we have written thus far should indicate that benevolent love is subject to the laws of growth. While the process may seem to start with the experience of *falling in love,* the beginning of love, or at least the ability to love, generally antedates adolescent crushes. In order to love benevolently, we must learn the value of others and be open to their goodness. Somewhere along the line we must also have transcended our fears and come to trust others. At every stage we must fight our petty likes and dislikes and penetrate beyond the superficial. In most cases, we have to witness love in others in order to see the meaning of dedication, commitment, sacrifice, and mature self-donation.

Even the painful experience of falling out of love contributes to our growth. The disappearance of ecstasy and the evanescence of the intoxication with another person force us to distinguish between our emotional reactions and our deliberate dedication to others. A broken heart can even force us to deepen our sense of values and cause us to love more freely and more profoundly, because we now know that love is something we do and not merely something that happens to us.

Each time we open our hearts and give, we realize that we are capable of giving something more. Love opens up new possibilities for love and finally reveals the almost infinite scope of the human person. For this reason, we need never stop growing unless we choose to do so. At the same time, because love opens up possibilities, it does not take away all of our loneliness and emptiness. The more we give, the more we have to give; but the more we have to give, the more conscious we become of the fact that we want to give more than we have.

In the last analysis, no purely human love can satisfy man or complete him, for the human person is still finite; an image of God, but not God himself. To ask completion in human love in time is to ask for frustration. On the other hand, human love can open man to the infinite in a way that no mere reasoning can. It increases not only man's being but his openness. It alleviates his thirst in one respect, but at the same time it creates a deeper longing for infinity. This sense of need, however, is not like that emptiness left when sense pleasure, power, and prestige have failed to bring fulfillment. The emptiness now is seen as a driving force to what is worthwhile. Man's mind knows the secret, even if it cannot use it at once.

BENEVOLENT LOVE AND INTERPERSONAL RELATIONS

Without benevolent love, there can be no true interpersonal relations. If we do not acknowledge others as persons worthy of respect, we will treat them as things, not as persons. At best the relationship will be impersonal, pragmatic, and functional; at worst, it will be hostile, exploitive, and destructive.

Even when we respect others and want to serve them, many of our relationships are impersonal rather than interpersonal. Teachers often deal with students only as students and not as human persons. We go through endless rituals of courtesy with people we meet but seldom deal with them as persons. At times courtesy and ritual even seem designed to regulate relations in such a way that there is no need for real personal interaction. The impersonality of much modern life appears in the methods we use for judging and rating people. Students are classified on the basis of marks, rank in class, college board scores, and check lists of personality traits. Neighbors are judged on the basis of income and occupational status. Employees are rated on productivity and professors on the number of books they have published. At times we almost seem to consider the individual as the sum of the various ratings given.

Some of this impersonality is a result of the complexity of the world and the necessity of dealing with large numbers of people whom we can never really get to know. At times, impersonality seems to be a defense against involvement and concern. If we do not know a person as a person, he can make only limited demands on our time and energy. If I know little about a person beyond his job qualifications, I need not feel guilty when I fire him, even though—conveniently unknown to me—his family will be impoverished.

There can be little doubt that some impersonality is necessary if we are to survive in a mass society. We must ask, however, if impersonality has not gotten out of hand. We must ask if increasing impersonality does not threaten our ability to respect and love all men. These are not easy questions to answer, for they challenge our ordinary way of doing things. Yet we must answer them if we are to deal honestly with those young people who want to escape the cold world about us and reestablish human contacts with more than a few intimate friends. Were the students at Berkeley wrong when they protested against being treated as numbers? Are the Hippies completely stupid when they withdraw from the world of impersonal job classifications and the routine of earning a living? Have we impoverished ourselves by retreating from personal involvement and playing games in which people are just so many checkers on the board?

Self-love, or selfishness, has been constantly condemned in western thought. Yet a man cannot love others unless he loves himself. The appreciation of one's own dignity is a necessary condition for the appreciation of value in general. This seeming contradiction between the need for and the condemnation of self-love can be resolved if we realize that distinctions must be made between the ways in which the self is loved and between the various selves which can be loved. When these distinctions have been made, it is possible to condemn one form of self-love and praise the other.

The self-love which is almost universally condemned is self-centered, egotistical, exploitive, and rapacious. It excludes love for others and treats both persons and things as mere means to be used for the pleasure of the individual. This form of self-love will not recognize the value of others, the obligation to cooperate, or the need to serve. It is purely and simply a love of desire extended to all possible beings. People who are afflicted with this form of selfishness even try to manipulate God to their own advantage. A proper love of self need not be selfish and exploitive. It recognizes the value of the true self and is dedicated to the growth of the individual; at the same time it includes respect for others and a recognition of their rights and essential goodness. The person who loves himself properly knows that he cannot serve unless he takes care of his own health and develops his talents. His self-respect is at the root of his respect for others, since he recognizes that others have the same basic value.

Proper self-love centers on the true self and the ideal self, while improper self-love, which men despise, is generally focused on what we will call the false self. The true self is not merely a collection of attributes and characteristics unified by a name. The dignity of man is something more than this. It involves the very value of the person, as well as the value of what he has done and can do. Moreover, because the human person is essentially open to all goodness, the true self has much of its value by relation to the ideal it can achieve. Now since this ideal can only be realized in cooperation with other men, the love of the true and ideal self is not selfish. Indeed, in loving this self, we already love others in some way. It is for this reason that we cannot love others properly without loving ourselves. For this reason too, we ought to love our true and ideal selves. To put it another way, our love for the goodness that is in us, and the goodness that can be, is a precondition for all love of others.

The false self, or perhaps we should call it the inauthentic self, is superficial and incomplete, a construction of the imagination which omits the ideal and our relationship to others. In the false self, the dominant places are given to such accidentals as pleasure, physical beauty, strength, particular talents, power, or possession. These accidentals, which should be means at the service of the ideal self, are turned into ends and worshiped for their own sake. Not only other human beings but the essential energies of the person himself are subverted and put in the service of this false self. As a result, the person grows only in accidentals and gradually loses sight of the value of persons. Love of such a self is to be condemned, for it does violence to reality.

In some cases, the false self is extremely negative in form. The person identifies with his faults and weaknesses, real or imagined, and denies the possibility of attaining even such superficial goods as pleasure or possessions. Persons with such a negative view of their being run from responsibility by pretending to be incapable of any real good. They hide both from their own potential and from other men. Often they see all other men as being equally small and evil, so that self-defense becomes a cardinal rule of life. Love for such a false self is obviously to be condemned. It is a distortion of reality and a denial of human potential and value.

There is no opposition between proper self-love and benevolence, since both are focused on the same values. There can be, and often is, tension between the expressions of the two. The lover wants to give himself to the other, but he cannot make himself a thing or allow himself to be treated as a thing without harming the other and losing his own power to love as a person. Because all human loves are mixed with desire and benevolence in unequal proportions, there is always a danger of falling into false expressions. The true lover must guard his essential value if he is to love and help the other, and this means that he must be careful of the way he gives himself.

The lover, of course, wants his love to be accepted, since this promotes the good of the beloved. He does not necessarily ask to be loved in return, though he cannot be indifferent to that minimum of love which is respect, since he cannot be indifferent to his own value. There is a tension here, for since we are in the process of growth, we are never sure when false self-love is speaking, or at least whispering, beneath the surface of benevolence. There is need, then, for self-examination and for continual efforts to eliminate narrow selfishness.

PARADOX OF LOVE

Benevolent love is paradoxical. The more one thinks of the good of others, the more he himself grows. The free act of being unselfish is more profitable than any attempt to use the other as a means. Because this paradox exists, many people view benevolent love as an illusion, a rationalization, or a bit of pious hypocrisy.

This paradox does not exist in God, for being all-perfect, he can gain nothing by his love. Man, however, being imperfect and limited, is necessarily affected by everything he does. Furthermore, since many of the effects are automatic, he cannot control them by mere choice. In benevolence, his conscious, deliberate intention is unselfish, and so the act itself is directly altruistic. This is on the level of the person. On the level of nature, however, the act automatically enlarges his being and fills up his emptiness. We may speak of self-perfection resulting from love, but it is not selfishness, for the perfection itself opens man even more fully to others. What really determines the quality of the act in this case is the intention, and not the results. In the last analysis, then, the paradox of love is really the paradox of the human being who is at one and the same time a person and a nature—free and determined.

The paradox of love also includes a social dimension. Though the individual is an end in himself, and not a means to anyone or anything else, he cannot realize himself without unselfish relations with others. The individual, in short, has to escape part of the means-end mentality in order to achieve his own perfection. This creates tensions, for it is easier to make ethics an either/or science. The tension, however, is part of the individual's being. He must accept it if he is to be fully a man.

IS MAN OBLIGED TO LOVE BENEVOLENTLY?

Few people would deny that benevolent love is a great good. Joseph Fletcher would even make it *the good*.[7] If Fletcher is correct, love is a necessary good, obligatory for those who admit this fact. Those who follow the Judeo-Christian religious tradition will also see love as necessary in virtue of the divine command to love one's neighbor as oneself. We may still ask, however, whether benevolent love is necessary and obligatory in a philosophic ethics which admits of a plurality of goods on the level of means.

When we ask if man is obliged to love benevolently, we are asking several questions. Is man obliged to love *anyone* benevolently? Is man obliged to love *everybody* benevolently? What form of benevolence is obligatory?

Benevolent love is not necessary for mere biological survival. Indeed there are situations in which the selfish and brutal exploiter seems to have the best chance of staying alive. Even in more ordinary circumstances, many people survive biologically on the basis of mutual exploitation. Biological survival, however, is not the goal of human life. We want to know whether benevolent love is a necessary means to the full development of the person and to his ultimate perfection beyond time.

If the ultimate perfection of the person involves union with God, benevolent love of God appears to be a necessity. This would seem to be true if man's acts and perfection in time are only conditions for union with God. In the first place, God cannot permit himself to be used as a means, since this would do violence to his nature. Indeed the man who treated God as a mere object of desire would be creating a false God and an illusion which could never fill man's emptiness. The final union with God will have to take place through benevolent love, for any other relationship would involve making God into an object.

Must we love God benevolently while still in the world of time and change? To the extent that we know God, man's ordination to the infinite, and the impossibility of reaching God by way of mere desire, we will see benevolent love of God as necessary even in time. As man's knowledge of all these points increases, he will see that the love of self-donation is the only form of love that is really suitable. God may be willing to accept respect as a condition for union, but only self-donation manifests our own seriousness and commitment. To choose less than self-donation is almost to be indifferent to both God and ourselves. It is to reduce the search for God and fulfillment to a sort of part-time job.

Everything we have said about the nature and effects of benevolent love for men points to its necessity as a means to human perfection. It is indeed difficult to see how a man can learn to love the hidden God unless he loves men. If we never see the goodness in the human person, we will hardly be able to envisage even the shadow of divine goodness. If we cannot give ourselves to the service of at least some men, how will we be able to give ourselves to the God we cannot see while we are in the world of time?

At the very least, we owe the benevolent love of respect to all men. If we refuse this love, we are rejecting the value of the person, or at least we are indifferent to it. In the concrete, respect, justice, and rights are so bound together that a lack of respect for any man will lead us to unethical conduct. We fail in respect when we penalize others because they lack some accidental characteristic. We fail in respect whenever we forget that we are dealing with men and treat others as mere ciphers. Each failure of this type prepares the way for exploitation. For this reason, we must strive to develop a real respect which acknowledges the value of the other. If we do not make such an effort, we will soon fail to attain even a minimal level in our ethical life.

We cannot be obliged to serve all men for the simple reason that we do not have either the time or the talent to do so. We are not God. On the other hand, there can be little doubt that most of us do not serve as much as is possible. Are we obliged to serve others insofar as we can?

In practice, we must probably direct the love of service to at least some individuals, lest our respect be merely a theory or a series of conventional gestures. This is to say that the practice of unselfish service is a necessary means to guarantee the genuineness of our respect and to break the mold of our own narrowness, which is so often protected by laziness. The scope and shape of service cannot be determined before the fact, since each life is unique, and the individual must constantly adjust to the changing needs of those around him. In some cases, it might even become necessary to devote nearly all one's time and efforts to others. We will return to the problem of service in the next chapter.

The love of self-donation is limited in scope, for we cannot give ourselves fully to many people. Moreover, it would be difficult to establish a necessity of giving oneself to this or that particular person. We are completely free in choosing the individuals we will love on this deepest level. We may still ask, however, if we must give ourselves completely to someone.

In the concrete, it is difficult to see how an individual can find himself unless he escapes from himself by self-donation. The man who cannot give himself either to God or a single human being is almost necessarily choked by fears and delusions which narrow his personality and his perspective. He will never discover the infinite range of his own potential for good nor experience that freedom which enables us to know the fullness of being. In short, it is difficult to see how a man can love himself properly if he cannot love at least one other person completely. We need to give ourselves to someone.

Our need for self-donation, however, is conditioned by our other obligations. We may not in good conscience make ourselves into mere things to be used and abused by others. We may not use the love of self-donation as an excuse for avoiding our responsibilities to others. Even the highest form of love must be harmonized with all the other demands of the ideal.

LOVE AND THE IDEAL

Benevolent love occupies a prominent place in the ideal. The experience of benevolence, both in ourselves and in others, is one of the chief factors in forming the ideal itself. Benevolence reveals to us the scope of our own capabilities. It shows us how everything in life can be endowed with a new meaning. It challenges us to develop all those habits, attitudes, and virtues which are necessary for the support of love. Justice, patience, temperance, fortitude, and truthfulness all take on a new significance in the light of love. Without them we cannot maintain a constant posture of respect, service, and self-donation. Without them we will not be able to express our love properly.

When love seeks to express itself, to make itself felt, we meet both new problems and new possibilities. The chapter which follows, on the expression of love, will help to put flesh on the skeleton we have developed. In addition it should indicate some of the ways in which we can start to make the ideal a concrete reality.

NOTES

1. Abraham H. Maslow, *Toward a Psychology of Being* (Princeton, N.J.: D. Van Nostrand, 1962) and *Motivation and Personality* (New York: Harper & Brothers, 1954).
2. John Bowlby, *Child Care and the Growth of Love* (Baltimore: Penguin, 1953).
3. Erich Fromm, *The Art of Loving* (New York: Harper & Row, 1956).
4. Erik H. Erikson, *Childhood and Society* (New York: W. W. Norton, 1963).
5. Karl A. Menninger, *Love Against Hate* (New York: Harcourt, Brace and Co., 1943).

6. *Cf.* The description and critique of this position in William A. Luijpen, *Existential Phenomenology* (Pittsburgh: Duquesne University Press, 1963), pp. 195–230.
7. Joseph Fletcher, *Situation Ethics* (Philadelphia: The Westminster Press, 1966), Chapters III and IV.

POINTS FOR DISCUSSION

1. How is the Christian concept of love different from and higher than the philosophic concept developed in this chapter?
2. Discuss the blocks to benevolent love which arise from our culture and economic organization.
3. What must be done to develop benevolent love in ourselves and others?
4. Develop norms for determining when benevolent love is genuine and when counterfeit.
5. If love is free, can we speak of an obligation to love?
6. Why must benevolent love prevent the beloved from exploiting the lover?

READINGS*

Jean GUITTON, *Human Love* (Chicago: Franciscan Herald Press, 1960).

Robert JOHANN, *The Meaning of Love*. (Westminster, Md.: Newman Press, 1955).

Maurice NEDONCELLE, *Vers une philosophie de l'amour et de la personne* (Paris: Aubier, 1957).

——— *Love and the Person* (New York: Sheed & Ward, 1966).

Rudolph SCHNACKENBURG, *Moral Teaching of the New Testament* (New York: Herder and Herder, 1965).

Pitirim A. SOROKIN, "The Powers of Creative Unselfish Love" in Abraham H. MASLOW (ed.), *New Knowledge in Human Values* (New York: Harper & Row, 1959), pp. 3–12.

——— *Studies of Harvard Research Center in Creative Altruism* (Boston: Beacon Press, 1956).

* *All the books mentioned in the notes should be added to this list.*

———— *The Ways and Power of Love* (Boston: Beacon Press, 1954).

———— (ed.), *Symposium: Forms and Techniques of Altruistic and Spiritual Growth* (Boston: Beacon Press, 1954).

———— *Explorations in Altruistic Love and Behavior* (Boston: Beacon Press, 1950).

Vladimir S. SOLOVIEV, *The Meaning of Love* (New York: International Universities Press, 1947).

9/ THE EXPRESSION OF LOVE

THE PROBLEM

Love is not complete until it finds its expression in action which effectively promotes the good of both the lover and the beloved. The inner attitude, whether it be respect, a desire to serve, or a determination to give oneself to the other, needs to be translated not only into words and gestures but into concrete actions which enable the beloved to find himself and grow. This is easier said than done.

A mother who loves her child can stunt his development by keeping him tied to her apron strings. Her love may be genuine, but her expression of love can hurt rather than help. On the other hand, the woman who throws a drunken husband out of the house in order to protect her children and bring the husband to his senses may be giving valid expression to love, even though her action may appear harsh. Similarly, the young man who breaks off his relationship with a girl he loves because it is harmful to her expresses real love. He is really concerned about the good of the beloved.

The expression of love is difficult, because it is not merely the communication of the idea "I love you," but it must also promote the good of the other person. While words may be cheap, the promotion of the good is often very expensive. At times, the things we do to help others may make them dislike us. A teacher often has to reprimand students. This is a genuine expression of concern, but it does not win many friends. A parent may have to punish a child for his own good, even though the child may dislike the parent for the moment. The punishment, however, is still a real expression of love.

Experience teaches us that love can be expressed in many ways, some of them a bit harsh. Experience also teaches us that many of our expressions of love are very defective. What was meant to help actually hurts. Our affection for someone may blind us to the real needs of others. We may think that the other needs sympathy when he really needs stimulation. We may think that the other needs a pat on the head when he really needs a good push. When we make mistakes like this, our effort to express love—that is, to promote the good of the other—can backfire. Indeed, as we grow older and more mature, we realize that the effective expression of love demands both perception of the needs of others and knowledge of the means that will actually help them.

EMOTION AND THE EXPRESSION OF LOVE

Our perception of need and our knowledge of means are influenced by our emotions. Just as hatred can cause us to overlook the virtues of an enemy, love can cause us to overlook the defects of a friend. When we do not see the defects of others, we fail to see their needs and so do not aim our actions towards the promotion of their growth. Our emotions can so focus our attention on our own needs that we see others as a means of perfecting ourselves and overlook their problems. The bleeding heart, for example, may be enjoying a good cry rather than expressing real sympathy. The merely effusive person may be expressing his emotions, but he does not necessarily help the other.

Emotion can blind us not only to the needs of others but also to the means available for helping them. Most of us become upset when we see a child cry, yet love may demand that we make the child cry when he has been naughty or wants something that is not good for him. If our fear of tears keeps us from seeing this, emotion has crippled the effective expression of real love. The joy and satisfaction we get from helping others may cause us to overlook the fact that too much help may keep the other unduly dependent and immature. Even our tenderness can make us shy away from administering the strong medicine that may be the only cure for certain ailments.

All of this does not mean that affectivity has no part to play in the expression of love. On the contrary, deep emotions are not only useful but often necessary. Schneiders notes:

Feelings are needed to enrich our lives and add depth to the meaning of our existence. Emotions like anger, fear, and anxiety are necessary to security, safety and getting things done. The emotion of love is as necessary to the health of the mind as food is to the body. . . . The dull, unresponsible, apathetic person is unable to respond to the world in which he lives.[1]

Emotion, however, is not enough. Reason must intervene and distinguish sentiment and disguised egoism from deep emotion. Reason must search out the means to be used, lest emotion act without a guide. Love is best expressed when all parts of man work together for the true good of those who are loved. This is to say that the full and effective expression of love demands maturity and the integration of mind and will and feelings. While we may admire the simple way in which a child expresses its love, we must remember that the child's world is fairly simple. The adult's world is complicated, so that the adult's expression of love demands a greater maturity.

Because the expression of love demands maturity and control over both emotions and the external world, it is subject to the laws of growth. In most cases we learn to express our love only gradually. While we can learn from the experience of others, much of our learning is still a question of trial and error. There is risk and uncertainty here as elsewhere in human life. Though we are seldom absolutely sure of our position or the effects of our actions, we must still make decisions and take the consequences. Ethics, of course, aims to reduce the risks and to increase the chances that the consequences are favorable to both the lover and the beloved. In order to achieve these goals, it is necessary to take a deeper look at the problems connected with growth in both emotional maturity and understanding.

GROWTH IN EMOTIONAL MATURITY

The emotionally mature person appears to act with a certain sure spontaneity in his expression of love. In many cases, he does not need to calculate the ins and outs of all the possibilities. He knows and acts with his entire being. The test of his maturity is found in the consequences of his acts, and not merely in his spontaneity. As a general rule, his actions promote the good of others and his own growth. On those occasions when he fails, the mature person reflects on the causes and plans for the future. He is constantly seeking for greater mastery of his activity so that he may operate with greater ease.

The emotionally mature man did not become what he is automatically. In most cases, he was fortunate enough to come from a home that taught him to control himself and gave him room for the healthy expression of his feelings. In addition, he has learned to distinguish between superficial feeling and deep affectivity. This can best be seen by comparing him with the immature. The immature become emotional about the latest fashion; what the gang wants to do; or even about the last pleasant thing that occurred to them. The mature man generally reserves his deepest feelings for what touches the well-being of people or his basic values. The immature becomes upset when the slightest thing goes wrong or when a whim is frustrated. The mature man can smile at the petty annoyances of life and yet become deeply involved with people and issues. Where the young fall in and out of love with amazing regularity, the mature person's love is constant, capable of weathering storms and offenses.

Emotional maturity is not an accident but a result of constantly directing emotions to the right objects until the direction becomes fixed and the proper reaction spontaneous. The deeply affective man does not suffer from childish tantrums, the uncontrolled anger of the middle-aged adolescent, or the infatuations of the teenager. He may become truly angry or be transported into high exaltation, but both feelings are directed towards what is real and important.

In the mature man, emotion supports basic commitments, enriches relationships, and humanizes actions. This is to say that the mature man has integrated his personality so that he need not calculate every move but can rely on the accumulated wisdom and discipline of the past. Children and young people have strong emotions, but as often as not they are undisciplined, confused, and even at odds with the demands of the situation. This should neither surprise nor disturb us. It takes time to distinguish chemical reactions from love. It takes effort to learn what reactions are appropriate and what feelings are dangerous. Even those who in theory should have reached maturity find that feelings can block effective loving. Timidity, anger, distrust, disgust, fear of being misunderstood, can cut us off from other human beings. The same feelings can also stop us from helping other men and so render our love sterile.

A realistic view of our emotions should lead us neither to a policy of rationalistic suppression of feeling nor to an exaltation of pure spontaneity. We need to cultivate our emotions and to direct them to the accomplishment of the goals we have set for ourselves. Indeed we must recognize the fact that we can grow only if we learn to integrate our feelings and our ideals.

THE NEED FOR UNDERSTANDING

The effective expression of love, the expression that truly promotes the good of the other, depends not only on our affective life but on our understanding of the means which can serve others. We need not only self-knowledge but knowledge of all the things which can heal and help and cause others to grow. In order to help the poor, we must know something about practical economics. In order to help the sick, we must have at least minimal medical knowledge. In order to teach, we must first learn.

The need for understanding, knowledge, and competence cannot be overstressed. The expression of love is concerned with getting things done. Getting things done demands know-how. Even if everyone were filled with good will and deep love, many of the world's problems would still be with us. Our sympathy for the starving millions in India will not put bread in their mouths. Our sympathy must be reinforced with the services of experts in agriculture, transportation and finance before it can have any real effects. Our love for the poor and the unemployed will remain locked within us until experts in economics, sociology, politics, and psychology find ways to translate wish into fulfillment.

Because our world is complex and the competence of any one man is limited, we must often express our love by supporting those experts who can do the job. Much of our love is not expressed in face to face relationships, but through vast organizations which are equipped to satisfy the needs of men. Often our obligation can only be fulfilled by contributing either our competence or our money to the groups which can do the job. In short, the expression of love involves social organization as well as sound interpersonal relations.

A short introductory book cannot go into all the areas of competence needed for the effective expression of love. It can, however, point up some of the general considerations which enter into nearly all situations. In particular, it can make the reader aware of certain factors which are often overlooked.

THE PROBLEM OF LOVE AND JUSTICE

In the preceding chapter we noted that love has degrees and that the lowest degree, basic respect for others, is also a matter of justice. This is to say that we owe a basic respect to every man, for justice seeks to give the other what is his due. In the concrete, this involves not merely basic respect but respect for the concrete rights of others. Love in its higher degrees transcends mere questions of rights. Love can and does and ought to go beyond strict rights. Indeed, unless we are striving to give the other more than his strict due, we will often fall short of the minimum. Justice cannot long exist without deep love.

The higher degrees of love may transcend justice, but they are not necessarily a substitute for it. As a result, the expression of love must be examined to make sure that it does not by-pass the demands of justice and rights in the name of transcendence. Love cannot be genuine unless it also fulfills the demands of justice. A few examples may help to illustrate this point.

Many Southerners were sincere when they claimed that they treated their Negro servants as members of the family. They had real compassion and took tender care of many Negroes. Unfortunately, however, they often treated the Negro as a perennial child and denied his right to be treated as an adult. The love may have been real, but its expression was vitiated by the failure to see that justice has to be served before love has its full effects.

In the past the paternalism of the industrial giants often provided workers with many blessings, but it also deprived them of a mature man's control over his own life. Today the paternalism of college professors and ministers of religion may be well-intentioned and motivated by love, but it can violate the rights of students and laymen. Of what use is a passing grade to the student if the student has not earned it? Of what use is moral instruction if the listener has not been helped to work out answers for himself?

At the present time, our juvenile courts are under investigation because, while seeking to help the young offender, they appear to have deprived him of his right to due process and fair trial. It may be another case where kindness has caused justice to be neglected.

How often are the rights of children and of an innocent marriage partner violated by those who break up a family in the name of a love that is "bigger than both of us"? How often has a husband tried to get out of his basic obligations on the ground that he no longer loves his wife? How often has a child been denied the right to live with his parents because they loved him so much that they kept him in boarding schools all year?

Love without justice can be a flimsy structure, but justice without love does not build at all; it can be cruel and self-satisfied. Selfishness tempts us to limit our idea of what is due to the other. Love is needed to go beyond the narrow view and to increase the chances that at least real justice will be done. A rule may require that a student hand in a paper on such and such a day. Strict justice may give the teacher the right to reject papers which are late. If the teacher wants to avoid complications, he may enforce the rule to the letter in the name of justice. Justice, however, should look at the reasons for lateness and also at the reasons for the rule itself. In practice, justice may not bring the teacher to this. A loving attitude, a deep compassion, and a real interest in his students may serve to motivate the teacher when his sense of justice is stifled by laziness or a desire to keep things neat.

Juridical forms of justice are useful and even necessary. They can, however, become façades which conceal injustice. Contracts with their obligations nicely spelled out should never be despised, but not all rights can be compressed into a few pieces of paper. Once again, examples may help to make the point clear.

According to the letter of the work contract, a veteran employee has no right to a pension, even though he has spent thirty years with the firm. The contract, however, does not recognize or in any way compensate for the fact that he worked for years at reduced pay because the company was in a poor financial condition. Quite apart from the question of a pension, then, to insist on the letter of the contract may be to deny a real right of the employee.

A property owner who has placed his house on the market is not obliged to sell to any particular individual. If three potential buyers make identical offers, he is free to select whom he will. Let us suppose, however, that one of them, a well-educated Negro, will not be able to get suitable housing if his offer is rejected. Is strict justice enough, or must love weigh in the balance in making the decision?

Perhaps the tension between justice and love is semantic, a matter of words and not of reality. No matter what the root of the difficulty, the fact remains that the ethical man must consult the demands both of justice and of love. The reason is simply that in practice all of us are liable to overlook some important factor unless we look at the situation from several points of view. We must be sure that a person has received his due before we shower him with gifts. In practice, we will seldom give a man his due unless we are ready to give something more.

EXPRESSION BY OMISSION

The most effective expressions of love are often found in the things we do not do or do not say. At times, the things we omit saying or doing may be trivial, but the omission can be a very real act of benevolence. For example, I never use the word blood in the presence of Mr. Smith, since even the word conjures up such images that he gets sick to his stomach. Obviously, the more sensitive we become to the needs and feelings of others, the more often we will omit things which are perfectly legitimate in themselves. There are, however, two ways in which we can harm others that require particular attention: bad example and cooperation in evil.

Human beings are strongly and often unconsciously influenced by the behavior of others. Sometimes we use the actions of others as an excuse for doing what we wanted to do all along. More often, however, we take subtle clues from what others do. This is particularly true when we do not know how to act in a given situation, either because it is unfamiliar or because we have no principles covering the case. Children, of course, are like little monkeys and learn more by example than by precept or formal instruction. Just listen to the way a child apes not only the accent but the inflections and the gestures of those around him. Observe young people who are forever trying to find out how their peers will act before they dare to take a step themselves.

Because people are influenced by our behavior, *we must not only be good but appear to be good,* lest we lead others astray. At times this is extremely difficult, for our good acts may appear evil and weaken the resolutions of others. Love, however, will not permit us to remain indifferent to the errors of others, since love wants to promote the good of everyone.

In problems involving bad example, as in nearly all ethical problems, we must distinguish between cases where we are directly responsible for the evil and cases where we are only risking or permitting an evil for a proportionate reason. If we deliberately do wrong in order to weaken the moral resolve of another man, we are unethical. More often than not, there is no such deliberate intent, but only a situation in which even a good act may cause the wrong impression. For example, there is nothing ethically wrong with the use of the word "hell" as an exclamation. Children, however, may take the word as a form of cursing and conclude that cursing is allowable. A man who is sensitive to the good of children would avoid using the word in the presence of children because he wants to promote their good.

A business executive may legitimately accept certain small gifts from customers. Unfortunately, employees might see these as bribes and conclude that they may imitate their superior. In the concrete, then, the executive who is concerned with both the good of his company and the conscience of his employees may have to refuse all gifts.

In the case of both the children and the employees, the harm is not a result of the act itself, but of the ignorance or weakness of others. There may be cases where a proportionate good would justify running the risk of bad example. The loving man, however, will not always want to use the excusing causes, for as he grows, he becomes willing to pay a high price in personal inconvenience in order to help others.

The simple cases given above all involve the omission of an act that might lead someone else into trouble. In real life, it is often the omission of an act that gives bad example by appearing to bestow tacit approval on an evil. What is to be said of the man who remains silent in the face of political corruption, racial prejudice, economic exploitation, and war mongering? What is to be said if the man in question is a leader—a clergyman, an educator, or a prominent political figure? Has his silence lulled others into the acceptance of the existing situation, no matter how evil? Has he led men into inaction and left the field open for the forces of evil?

While the rhetorical questions may seem to condemn the silent man, they really only point up the problem. In the concrete, there is a price to pay for protest. If the price is greater than the return, a man may be excused for remaining silent. How do we calculate the risks and rewards so that our voice accomplishes the good? Are we to praise the emotional protest that consoles the speaker but does not free the oppressed? These questions must be answered before we can condemn the man who remains silent or praise the man who speaks out.

Even when all the questions are answered, we may not be able to bestow praise or blame. Often the situation is so ambiguous, the potential results so uncertain, the balance of goods and evils so delicate, that no course of action appears either completely laudable or completely damnable. Ambiguous, uncertain situations of this sort are the torture of the loving man who is sensitive to all the dimensions of a problem. It is in situations like this that a man realizes how difficult it is to maximize the good in a world which has much evil built into the structures of everyday life.

INVOLVEMENT IN EVIL

Sooner or later, everyone finds himself involved in a situation tainted by evil. A printer can discover that he is setting type for fraudulent stock reports. A home owner may find himself part of a neighborhood which is fighting integration. A man may fail to vote in a crucial election, thus allowing the less suitable candidates to take office. A citizen may believe that the nation is engaged in an unjust war. A taxpayer may see government monies going to support activities he thinks immoral. A teacher may fail to proctor an examination carefully and thus facilitate cheating, even if his carelessness is not taken as tacit approval. The list of possible cases is almost endless.

If the individual has helped to create the situation of evil or actually wills the evils as means to his own ends, the ethical quality of his acts may be judged by the method given in earlier chapters. Often, however, individuals find themselves in evil situations which are *not of their own making and not to their liking*. Despite the fact that responsibility for these situations belongs elsewhere, such individuals must take into consideration that others are being hurt. Love is not being served.

Sometimes the temptation is to say simply, "Get out of the situation." But there are two problems here. In the first place, the individual may not be able to get out of the situation. If your country is waging an unjust war, it is difficult to resign your citizenship. In the second place, getting out may only make the situation worse. If every honest man left a government because there was some corruption in it, the criminal type would have a field day. Indeed there are times when a man has to risk involvement in evil in order to express his love for others. Here as elsewhere in ethics, then, we are faced with the problem of the proportionate reason for risking or permitting evil.

Sometimes it is possible to withdraw from a situation. It may even be wise to withdraw if there is no possibility of stopping the evil. Escape, however, has a price in many of these cases. The printer may stop setting type for fraudulent stock reports, but it can be difficult to find another job. A taxpayer might decide not to support the government's unjust war, but he may go to jail for it. In such cases, there is room for the judgment of proportionality, but the judgment is not without its dangers. Men being men, narrow views and fear and selfishness can lead to a minimizing of our duty to love others and a maximizing of the duty to love ourselves. Worse yet, the use of proportionality within narrow limits can lead to situations where evil is allowed to grow un-checked.

A guard in a Nazi concentration camp was involved in evil of the worst sort. His withdrawal would have cost him his life and not saved one person. Unfortunately, because all the guards could invoke the same excuse, the evil continued. An individual who knows the inner workings of a large criminal organization wants to destroy it, but he knows that he will pay with his life if he gives testimony.

We must ask if there are not times when the evil is so great that martyrdom is necessary to dramatize it and shake up a society so that it will act. Are there times when the good demands that we transcend all calculations and risk losing all, in order to break the system which perpetuates evil? I believe that there are, but I am hard put to it to formulate the rules for making such a judgment. Perhaps this is part of the tragedy of man who must take risks beyond reason in order to fulfill the highest that is in him.

Many of the dilemmas mentioned above arise from the fact that the isolated individual can be relatively powerless in the face of organized evil. If every individual is excused on the grounds that he can do nothing, the evil will continue. This comes down to saying that no one is responsible for the destruction of such evils. The loving man, obviously, cannot accept such a conclusion, for it involves a sort of moral despair, a surrender to the forces of evil. The conclusion need not in fact be accepted, for what a man can-not do as an individual he can do as a member of a group. Indeed love demands that we form groups to fight the evils created by other groups. If we fail to cooperate with others and to organize for the good, we have made a mockery of love, for we have neglected one of the greatest instruments for the expression of love. Alone we can do little against unjust wars, political corruption, organized crime, and widespread prejudices. Alone, our love is rather helpless. In union with others, we can give effective expres-sion to our desire to promote the good of others.

There are, however, moral and human dangers in the socialized expression of love. Institutions can and do become impersonal.

The giver seldom sees the need he is satisfying. The expression of love is not fed by a love which grows more sensitive by direct exposure to need. The expression can be so divorced from the person that there is no longer a vital and mutual reinforcement between expression and love. The need may be satisfied, but the bonds between men may not have grown in real human intimacy. For this reason, social expressions should be balanced by those in which we are personally involved.

THE COMPARTMENTALIZED CONSCIENCE

Evil can continue to exist not only because good men do not organize to prevent it but also because good men do not even see it. As we have mentioned earlier, there are men who compartmentalize their conscience so that they see evil only in a limited number of cases. Members of some religious sects are sensitive to anything involving sex, but blind to many forms of dishonesty and social injustice. I have known refined individuals who would rather die than say an unkind word to anyone, but still defend racial segregation. On occasion you meet businessmen who would not steal even a ten cent piece, but see nothing wrong in taking millions through price fixing.

When the conscience is compartmentalized and evils overlooked, much good remains undone and a great deal of evil goes un-opposed. The loving man, then, strives constantly to sensitize him-self to reality and to enlarge his conscience. If our conscience is narrow, we may in effect be indifferent to the good of others, even though our heart is filled with compassion.

SOME LIMITS

We must express our love positively whenever the failure to do so would be equivalent to an act of *indifference* to the welfare of others. By the very nature of the case, we cannot express our love to all men at all times in the way we would like to. Means, in-cluding time and talent, are limited. Moreover, there are obligations of justice to oneself or to others which may take priority over the need of the stranger before us.

The first limit on our obligation to express our love positively can be phrased as follows: I am not obliged if the expression would cause as much harm as good. If a given activity will produce more harm than good, I am obliged not to use it, since such an act cannot be an expression of love no matter how good my intention. Thus, giving money to an alcoholic is often not an act of charity but the creation of a temptation. Giving away everything to the poor may be a grave injustice to your own family, which has a right to decent living conditions. The mother who rushes about doing good but neglects her own family is not expressing love, but only escaping from a basic obligation.

In the second place, I am not obliged to help those who will not help themselves. The reason is simple. Help in these cases can only cripple a person or lead him to believe that the world owes him a living. Love which cripples or stultifies the recipient is not true love. It may be a disguised desire to feel superior or to assuage some feeling of guilt.

This second principle can be abused. When we are looking for an excuse, we tend to exaggerate the ability of the needy to help themselves. In the past, many refused to help the Negro because they claimed that his problem was no different from that of the Italian, the Pole, and the Irishman. Self-love or a narrow conscience blinded them to the fact that the Negro suffered special disabilities. It is easy to say that a man could find work if he wanted to. In practice technological advances have so often obsoleted some skills that the most willing workers lack salable talents. Because selfishness can block our perception of need and ability, love requires that we investigate cases before we invoke excuses.

Finally, our obligation to express our love may be limited by the fact that others have the primary obligation, whether in love or justice. I am not obliged to feed the children next door when their parents are living and able to do the job. If the children are going hungry, this would be a case which might involve going to the authorities, but it need not involve direct help, which might only increase the evil. This, of course, is in line with the idea that love should seek to be truly effective and to protect the goods involved, rather than merely to appear loving.

TACTICS AND PITFALLS

Because the expression of love is a function of what the other needs and not merely what I would like to give, love must sometimes use unconventional tactics. Often it must resist rather than give in, not only when it is a question of principle but when it is a matter of regulating the expectations of others, or providing them with the assurance that there is someone decisive and strong on whom they can depend. Sometimes the lover must laugh when the beloved wants him to cry. Sometimes he must turn a deaf ear to complaints lest sympathy weaken the beloved. Often love must even strip the beloved of illusions so that he can discover his real self. Much of this flows from the fact that the effective expression of love must help the other to see and face reality rather than hide from it in a cloud of sentimentality or in any other inane form of acceptance.

There may be times when a husband should beat his wife and times when a wife should leave her husband. There are moments when anger can be used to good effect and moments when silence is in order.

Nearly everything said so far should indicate that it is a difficult thing to express love effectively. There are, however, a few special difficulties which should be mentioned, since they bring together many of the key points made thus far. In particular, we must mention emotional blackmail and trading.

Although emotional blackmail is as ugly as its name, it is not always easily identifiable. It is practised by the mother who threatens to commit suicide if a daughter marries anyone at all. It appears in the child who falls violently ill whenever he is not given what he wants. The seducer practices it when he unveils his "bleeding wounds" to the innocent girl and says that he cannot live without her. Students use it when they try to talk a teacher into passing them because a failure will give their father a heart attack. In minor forms, it uses the tantrum, the cold shoulder, or the scene to force others to give up what the blackmailer wants, whether or not he needs it or has a right to it.

The lover who is emotionally involved with the other cannot but feel torn by any and all of these stratagems. If he felt nothing, we would suspect his humanity. He must, however, look on them as stratagems which are largely irrelevant to his effective loving. He must refuse to give in, lest he betray his love and the person he loves. This may exact a large emotional price. The immature who have not grown in love may lose ground in the face of such pressure.

The expression of love should promote the good of the beloved. Unfortunately, most lovers have not arrived at complete unselfishness, so that in practice the love gift is used to buy a return. What should be a sharing becomes a form of barter, or "horse-trading." "I will buy you a new fur coat if you will promise to keep out of my way on the week ends." "I'll stop nagging if you'll come home on time." The dialogue might be expanded, but the idea should be clear. The gift is conditional in these cases. It is not given for the benefit of the other, but to buy something for the giver.

Realistically, a certain amount of trading enters into all relationships, since no man has reached the perfection of love. Things have to be done, and sometimes trading is the only way to get them done. The danger arises when trading is made into *the* relationship either deliberately or by force of habit. If extensive and long-continued trading eliminates a response to the real value of the other, and makes us concentrate on the superficial things which can be traded, it leads not to sharing but to mutual egoism, not to growth of love but to the dominance of petty desires.

There are more suble pitfalls to be avoided if love is to be effective. In our society, for example, we are taught that it is necessary to respect the feelings, opinions, and desires of others. While this is not a false principle, it can lead to indifference if applied without thought. There are times when the expression of love may involve hurting the feelings of others, contradicting their opinions and frustrating their desires. Parents must do this constantly with children, and a sensitive adult will discover many cases where he ought to step on the other's feelings in order to help him. If we do not have the wisdom and courage to do this, our silence can often encourage others to continue in illusions that hurt them. It is as bad as praising people for the wrong things and so enforcing unsound attitudes or activities.

In a similar way we must be on our guard against the dangers of giving sympathy when strength may be the appropriate gift. Sympathizing with people in misfortune can rob them of the strength to start again and convince them that their case is hopeless. Often our effort to help others will require us to act as if the sorrow or hurt of others were small and insignificant, so that we can get them back on their feet.

THE SUBTLETY OF LOVE

Because love wants to help the other, it must be sensitive to the other's moods and needs and language. Love cannot just blunder in or rely on native good will for the effective expression of love. There is a time for silence and a time for talking. There are times when demands should be made and times when gifts should be given. Experience and sensitivity are needed to detect the opportune moment and to select the right means of helping the other.

Sometimes we can help others by allowing them to help us. This requires humility, but often the fact that the other no longer feels like an inferior enables him to accept the help we want to give. The need for accepting gracefully often means that we reveal a little of our own humanity to others. We overcome some of our own fear and dare to enter into a more intimate relationship which can itself be supportive of the other. We have abandoned some of the pride which, as we have noted, can turn our gifts into selfish tools designed to make us feel good rather than to help someone else.

All this comes down to saying that loving demands maturity, self-knowledge, and skill and not merely good will. It means that though love is interior, the expression of love demands a competence which turns good intentions into the effective promotion of those we love.

PRIORITIES IN LOVING

The loving man will always want to do more than he can. The needs that call out for satisfaction are almost infinite in number, but time and talent and energy are limited. Even the superior individual must allocate his time and energies if he is to maximize the good. In view of what we have said about the obligation to maximize, we may say that we are obliged to set up priorities. A system of priorities is also a check against the temptation to give until one collapses.

Any system of priorities must start with the basic obligations that are clear and cannot be by-passed without denying the claims of justice and the obligation to love one's true self properly. In the second place, the system must recognize the fact that our lives have committed us to giving some individuals a special claim on our time. We owe more to those who have already come to depend on us than to those who as yet may be unknown, or only faces in the crowd. A married man, for example, cannot neglect his own children merely because other children are in extreme need. Only when he has filled his basic obligation to his own sons and daughters is he really free to allot time elsewhere.

After we have given the first places to the things we clearly must do, it is necessary to make decisions about the good that beckons to us. We must decide where the need is greatest and most urgent, as well as where our efforts promise to produce the best results. We may be unable to help those in greatest need, but capable of doing a great deal for those with lesser problems. On the other hand, it may be that the urgency of some needs leads us to concentrate on the here and now rather than on long-term results. There are really no hard-and-fast rules that will cover all situations.

Although we do not have a set of handy rules which will settle all questions of priority with ease, one rule of thumb should be observed. It is better to make a decision and act on it than to worry about the theoretical perfection of choice. Love should make us act once we have made reasonable efforts to investigate a situation. Reason should serve love, not paralyze it.

NOTES

1. Alexander A. Schneiders, *The Anarchy of Feelings* (New York: Sheed & Ward, 1963), p. 179.

POINTS FOR DISCUSSION

1. Make a list of actions that are meant to be expressions of love but actually harm others. Why was the mistake made?
2. When has experience taught us to be particularly wary of our emotions?
3. Discuss the ethics of silence in the face of the serious injustices of our times. What are your personal obligations?
4. Draw up a personal table of your activities and assign reasoned priorities.
5. Analyze the reasons you give for omitting various activities which might help others.
6. How did the saints and great humanitarians express their love?
7. Does the literature on human relations, motivations, and small group activities provide us with help in expressing our love?

10/ THE BODY AND LIFE IN TIME

INTRODUCTION

Every ethical system must take a stand on the value of human life and ultimately on the rights and obligations of individuals with regard to their own life as well as the lives of others. The stand is crucial, for it affects the position adopted with regard to all other activities and reveals the values which man places above life, as well as his attitude towards his fellow men.

The ethics of life and death are not purely theoretical. Both the daily press and the great popular magazines run articles on abortion, capital punishment, self-defense, war, and mercy killing. People discuss the rights and obligations of a spy who may reveal information that will harm others unless he kills himself first. Groups are formed to promote euthanasia or to change our laws on abortion. The debate on the ethics of war embroils all levels of the population and influences matters of national policy and survival. The doctor who struggles to save life and the soldier who takes life both have an ethic of life and death. As a result, no one who is touched by their work can remain indifferent to the basic questions: Of what value is human life? What right do I have to my own life? What obligations do I have with regard to the lives of others?

METHOD

Most of our ethics of life and death are a legacy of Christianity. Our treatment, however, is philosophical and not theological. As a result, we must seek to discover the answer to our questions without recourse to revelation. This means that our treatment is limited and incomplete. At the same time, a philosophic treatment may be of service to the theologian, who, after all, uses some philosophic framework in interpreting the meaning of God's words to men. If nothing else, a philosophic treatment can help the theologian to appreciate the difficulties of those who do not share his faith. Such appreciation, as we pointed out earlier, is necessary if men of all faiths are to arrive at some minimal consensuses in the public order.

A philosophic ethics of life and death ought to be consistent and coherent. It should not make absolute statements which then require numerous unjustified exceptions in order to make the theory cohere with common sense. On the other hand, if philosophic ethics is to be of any use to man, it cannot treat reality as if there were no generalizations which a man can use in making choices. In short, the theory of life and death must seek to establish a balance between the permanent, or relatively permanent, in human life and the contingent and changeable, which escapes all forms of generalization. While no theory can cover all the millions of cases which arise, a good theory ought to guide us in the vast majority of them.

In the present chapter we have not attempted to cover all of the cases which involve problems of life and death. Rather, we have chosen to concentrate on basic issues. As in previous chapters, we have raised more questions than we can answer. It is hoped, however, that the questions will at least enlarge the framework of consideration and help people to appreciate the values at stake.

THE VALUE OF LIFE

Man expresses his love through his body and in the world of temporal existence. So far as we know, man grows and becomes himself only in time and through the activity of his body. We have neither evidence nor arguments for the existence of human activity which makes men grow after death. The body not only places us in the world of time, but it is necessary for life, and so for growth in time. Within limits, then, both life in time and the body are necessary means to man's perfection. This is to say that they have a very high instrumental value. They are not ultimate ends, however, for both cease to exist with death. Nor are they purely means, for the body is the body of a man; more than an instrument of the individual, though not identical with him. So too, life in time is the peculiarly human way of existing, even though it is not the ultimate human state. We must admit, then, that both the body and life in time escape our ordinary categories. They are means, but more than means. They are specifically human, but they do not represent the only human way of existing.

We are not Manicheans who see the body and all matter as evil. Neither are we crude hedonists who sing, eat, drink, and are merry, for tomorrow we die. We are not Platonists who see the body as the prison of the spirit; nor are we followers of Spinoza who view the body as the source of illusions to be escaped. The body demands respect because it is the body of a man, but it cannot be accorded the reverence due to the human person himself. We are, then, balanced obscurely between our ordinary ways of looking at things.

Perhaps we can best place the body by saying that the union of body and soul is real but incomplete. It is not an identity, but neither is it a harmonious integration already achieved. Thus, under one aspect, it is an instrument to a more perfectly integrated whole, while under another aspect it is a sacred thing as already united to man. The tension between the two aspects must be watched, for the ethical problems of the body revolve around the shifting balance between the two.

Similarly, life in time, which is a dimension of man mediated by the body, involves man in a tension between what he is in time, what he ought to be in time, and what he can be beyond time. We do not know exactly how to evaluate life in time because we do not know from philosophy exactly how God evaluates it. We do not know how much time we need to reach a state acceptable to God. We do not know at what point we cease to need the body for minimum necessary growth. We lack the information to make choices based on a knowledge of all the facts. As a result, we are certainly involved deeply in risk. Not merely life in time, but my ultimate perfection, is at stake. This is true not only of ourselves but of all other men. For this reason, not only the ethics of our own life but those of others' lives are shrouded in ambiguity.

Certain facts, however, are clear for those who believe in God. Man does not have complete control over life in time. He depends for his existence on God and on the world around him. God can withdraw his gift when man wants to keep on living, and God can continue to give life when man finds it a burden. Advances in medical science give us new control of this or that part or function of the body, but they also deepen the mystery. Why does one man die and another live, contrary to all we know of the body? Some cases we can explain by the will to live or its absence, but in many instances the mystery remains.

Life in time is a *value,* but it is not *the* value. Man has some control of his life, but this is not absolute. Moreover, life in time is shrouded in mystery and is heavy with risk, for we do not know when we are ready to go. At times, however, it appears that life in time is not even *a value.* We have the patient in a coma who will never awake: the delirious sufferer whose body is so badly torn that he will never recover; the incurable madman whose good health seems a mockery; the malformed child who seems no more than a vegetable. Of what value are their lives?

It is clear that life for some people lacks all instrumental value for their own perfection. They exist, but cannot operate as men. Yet, because we are talking about men, we recognize the fact that often their existence has a high instrumental value for others. Paradoxically, it is often the suffering and helplessness of others which brings out the finest in us. Our most unselfish expressions of love are often directed to those who not only cannot help themselves but cannot help anyone else. Indeed it is suffering that makes us see that we value others because they are men, and not because they can help us or serve some narrow utilitarian purpose. The seeming uselessness of some life brings us back to the mystery of life and death and to the paradoxes of human existence.

All this should not blind us to the fact that there are situations where life in time is not only useless to its possessor but a threat to the lives of others. The aged Eskimo who can no longer hunt or work becomes an intolerable burden in the harsh conditions of Arctic life. The comatose patient who takes the attention of doctors and nurses away from those who can recover; the incurable cancer patient whose care is eating up the small resources of his family—such cases as these pose the question, Are there not instances in which death would be better than life?

Certainly there appear to be cases where continued existence is no longer a good. There are cases where life is no longer human, as far as we can see. Since the meaning of continued existence is ambiguous, we ask whether there are not instances in which a man may take his own life, or legitimately delegate another to take it for him?

SUICIDE

Catholic moral theologians say that a man may not deliberately cause his own death on his own authority. They argue that only God has direct dominion over human life. At the same time, these thinkers will allow a man to risk his life or permit his own death for a proportionate reason. This means that I may not put a bullet through my head in order to escape the sufferings of terminal cancer, but I may stop using blood transfusions which are prolonging my life and my sufferings from cancer. A soldier may throw himself on top of a grenade in order to save the lives of his companions, but he may not shoot himself in order to avoid revealing secrets.

Behind these opinions, we find two basic ideas. First, the obligation to use positive means of preserving life is conditional, but the negative obligation not to take one's life is absolute. As we saw earlier, I am not obliged to do something good if this will produce as much harm as good, or more harm than good. On the other hand, I may not will something which is against the end. We may sum this up by saying that there is an absolute prohibition of direct suicide but only a prudential ethic of indirect suicide. To put it another way, I may not deliberately cause my death as a means or an end, but I can risk or permit death for a proportionate reason. While this seems clear-cut, a more careful examination of the definition of direct suicide indicates that it, too, may involve a prudential ethics—that is, a calculation of proportions.

Direct suicide is unethical if done on *one's own authority*. It would not be unethical if done on *divine authority*. God, after all, can delegate his rights. The crucial question remains to be answered: How do we know when God has delegated this right to us?

This question is generally answered by assuming that we never have divine authority to kill ourselves. If God never delegates direct dominion over human life, then we cannot know when he delegates it. We may ask, however, how these thinkers know that God never delegates direct dominion over life. Even Catholic moral theologians who uphold the definition of suicide we have given admit that God can and does grant the state the right to inflict capital punishment. In ethics this right would be justified on the ground that God, having created man in such a way that the state is a necessary means in human society, must also grant the state those means necessary for its end.

We may hesitate to admit that God can delegate his right to the individual as well as to the state, but it is difficult to show that he cannot and does not. Because we fear that the admission of divinely granted exceptions would lead to abuses, the tendency is to make an absolute rule. In theory, however, only a general rule may be justified. Those who define suicide as the direct—i.e., deliberate—killing of oneself on one's own authority implicitly admit that not all direct killing of oneself is an ethical evil. The rule is made absolute only by assuming that divine authority is never given.

In ethics we can argue to divine delegation only from the nature of things and from the situation in which a man finds himself. This is a dangerous business, as we shall point out a little later, but ethics rests on the assumption that we can learn something about the relationship of our acts to God by considering the relation of acts to our perfection in time. It may be argued, then, that we have a reasonable assumption of a divine delegation of the right to kill oneself in those cases where an objective examination indicates that continued life will produce more harm than good. Such situations are rare, but we cannot deny their existence.

Continuing studies of suicide indicate that the motives of suicide are not exactly rational. In addition, some of the factors associated with higher suicide rates seem to imply that many people who become suicides are running away from the challenge of life or have failed to grow. Divorced people are more likely to commit suicide than married people. Members of dominant majorities commit suicide more often than do members of suppressed minorities. Suicides are more common in time of peace than during wars. Strangely enough, suicides are liable to occur more frequently in times of economic change even when the change is for the better.[1]

Because men can be very poor judges of the meaning of their own lives, we hesitate to say that there are times when a man has the right to make a judgment of proportionality about the value of life. We fear that any weakening of the prohibition of the deliberate killing of oneself, as a means or an end, will open the floodgates.

Particular situations exist in the total human context and have broader meanings. Exceptions to general rules are dangerous if they weaken the general rule itself. As a result, our situation includes the impact of our act on others who are not immediately involved.

It involves a consideration of whether or not this exception will be falsely generalized by others to justify what is clearly wrong. When we are dealing with things so basic as life and death, prudence must be very great, lest narrow views or narrow values erode the lives of others. A look at the larger context of the terminal cancer patient and the spy will illustrate the dangers which must be taken into consideration.

The terminal cancer patient who asks the doctor for an overdose of sleeping pills is really only speeding up his death a little, yet he must realize that his act can be an example for those whose lives have become tedious, joyless, and agonizing because they have not used their powers to face life. In short, he may encourage others to take the easy way out. Indeed the cancer patient may be refusing to use his suffering to strengthen others and to point up the transcendent importance of the inner life. To put it another way, he may be encouraging the idea that man alone decides the meaning of life and that pain is the greatest evil. He may not want to say these things, but the fact that he does, or may, must enter into the calculation of proportionality.

These may seem like minor points, but we live in a society where so many want to propose eugenic mercy killing, and even mercy killing without the sufferer's permission, that our obligation to love others and to affirm basic values forces us to consider these impacts. In particular, we must beware of strengthening the position of those who want to make self-destruction obligatory for people like the captured spy.

The case of the captured spy, whose secrets may harm many people, tempts us to make a quick judgment of proportionality. We must, however, take a long look at the hidden dangers in such a judgment. There is a temptation to pass from the judgment that the spy *may* take his life to the idea that he *must* take his life, or that others may take his life. If we say that an innocent man must kill himself or be ethically killed in order to protect others, we have opened the door for the killing of all who are in some way a drain on society—the insane, the aged, the crippled, and the lazy.

Even if the judgment remains at the level of *may* rather than *must,* there are difficulties. The death of the spy may prevent the revelation of secrets and save the lives of others for a time. Does it really produce any long-range good? Does it, perhaps, merely put the seal of approval on a system which itself may produce more harm than good?

Because so much is at stake in these cases, even a prudential ethic must demand a broad consideration of what is involved, lest human life be held cheap. Indeed the prudential ethic demands a greater effort to form one's conscience and imposes greater responsibility on the man who would debate the question of whether or not he has the right to take his life here and now. It is for this reason, if for no other, that many thinkers will admit no exceptions either in theory or practice. They fear that exceptions could be used by a Hitler in justifying the right to kill millions in the interest of the state. They fear the effect of exceptions on all those physically healthy people who want to escape the human condition because life seems intolerable or is not played the way they like. Perhaps they also fear that any exception will justify abortions and executions in all kinds of circumstances in which these procedures seem the easy way out.

SUMMARY

Despite the dangers of misunderstanding and abuse, dangers which must be calculated even by the individual, we must admit that in theory at least there may be cases where a man can ethically take his own life on the basis of a divine delegation. This, however, should not weaken the general rule, nor give the impression that the individual may do what he likes with his life, with no regard for the demands of his nature or the interests of others. This holds even for those who do not believe in God but nevertheless have an intensive sense of some meaning in life. Those who see life as absurd, and only freedom as meaningful, will not, of course, agree with anything we have said.

While a prudential ethic may admit the possibility of theoretical cases where a man can directly take his own life, much of our religious tradition has held to an absolute prohibition of suicide. While we do not wish to go into a discussion of these absolute, religiously founded ethics, we must insist that the ideas we have developed need not conflict with such an ethic. Pure ethics, with its limited resources, can only argue on the basis of reason. Religious ethics has superior resources and can give wiser answers to the problems of life.

The foregoing discussion raises several far-reaching questions. How do you define suicide so that you include all cases and only those cases where self-killing is an ethical evil? The same sort of question can be asked about fornication, lying, and murder, or about any particular act. Do all ethical definitions of acts contain or imply so many circumstances that they are general descriptions rather than absolute normative definitions? To put it another way: Are ethical definitions of particular acts only short-hand formulas designed to handle the general run of cases, so that we can solve the extraordinary cases only by going back to the most basic notions of the ethical and the unethical?

THE LIVES OF OTHERS

Can we ever ethically exercise control over the continued existence of others? May we ever deliberately kill another human being? These are vital questions, for war, abortion, and capital punishment continue even though ordinary murder is not the most common of events.

To a certain extent, we can simply argue that if we may not take our own life deliberately, much less may we take the life of another. It is not really so simple, for men of good will make some important exceptions. One point, however, should be stressed: the deliberate killing of another involves us in actions which at best cast doubt on the dignity of the individual and at worse involve us in playing God.

Most people in our culture consider the *deliberate killing of an innocent person on one's own authority* as unethical. There is nevertheless considerable practical disagreement about who is a person and who is innocent. The individual favors abortion because the unborn child is not, in his opinion, a person. He may object to capital punishment or reject the right of the nation to wage war. A nation which will spend a fortune in saving the life of a single individual trapped in a mine cave-in may also be ready to order its spies to kill themselves when caught. In short, people are not always consistent in this area.

At first glance, the main problem appears to be one of definition, but there are other factors at work. The definitions are not purely descriptive formulas. They are tailored to fit our purposes and even our feelings. We are quite willing to call an unborn child a person until there is some conflict between the interests of the child and those of other persons. We also define innocent in terms of what a given society considers right or wrong and in terms of our own feelings about people in special circumstances as well. As in the case of suicide, we may also absolutize some definitions in order to cut down on the unwarranted exceptions which might result from a more carefully nuanced definition. Those who object to such procedures believe that they avoid problems by avoiding definitions, but this merely leaves us with an ethic so vague that we cannot use it to help us in making decisions about concrete cases.

In point of fact, ethical rules that are applicable to concrete circumstances have to operate on a set of assumptions, since we often lack absolutely certain criteria as to whether or not even the best definitions apply exactly in a given case. In the concrete, of course, we must be on guard against the rationalizations we use in order to escape the less acceptable conclusions that follow from reasonable assumptions. Men try to fool themselves into making other men less than men for a variety of reasons. In some tribes, all outsiders were looked upon as inferior beings who might be killed practically at will. In time of war, as we have said, we find it necessary to convince ourselves that the enemy is a faceless monster who has no humanity in common with us. The person who is going to perform an abortion tries to regard the unborn fetus as a faceless blob which has no humanity, and so no rights. The criminal who is sentenced to death is looked upon as having lost his rights, if not all of his humanity. We must, then, face squarely a problem we raised in the second chapter of this book: How do we recognize a human being?

We would have true and certain signs of humanity if the being before us exhibited signs of both the animal and the rational sides of human nature. If he exhibits these, he is a man, no matter what color, or size, or shape, or nationality, or previous actions. What, however, are we to say, in terms of the definition above, of the lunatic, the tiny child, or the sleeping figure that is shaped like a man but gives no signs of rationality at this moment? May we treat them as if they were not men? What of the man who may have been insane when he committed serious crimes but now exhibits all the signs of being a man?

In all these cases, the men of our civilization would answer that they are men and are to be treated as men. The lunatic, the child, and the sleeping man all came from human parents. The only reasonable assumption is that they are human. All three may show signs of intelligence if we give them time. The sleeping man showed signs of rationality when he was awake, and even the lunatic may have lucid intervals. Moreover, all these have a constitution which is found only in men. Though some might like to quibble about the theory, these are men for all practical purposes. To treat them any other way, would be to disregard reason.

Interestingly enough, the same arguments support the contention that the unborn fetus is to be treated as human. It comes from human parents; it will develop into a human being in time; and it has physical characteristics which are only found in human fetuses. How, then, can some be so ready to allow abortion?

The explanation lies in the fact that the fetus is faceless and yet can make demands on a person. As a result of both these factors, it is both emotionally easy and personally convenient to disregard its humanity. We do not know at what precise moment the human soul is infused into the fetus. It may be at the moment of conception, or at the moment of implantation.[2] It may be after four months of pregnancy. The information we have at the present time does not enable us to settle the question. Future research may give us practical certitude, but we must make decisions here and now.

For all practical purposes, the fetus must be treated as a human being from the moment of implantation or conception. It comes from human beings; it should develop into a human being, and it has specifically human characteristics very early in its development. This evidence is indirect, since we do not see signs of intelligence in the fetus. The evidence is not, however, any more indirect than the proofs we have for the humanity of an infant. If we are free to disregard the indirect evidence for the humanity of the fetus, then, we are free to disregard the humanity of infants.

Despite our practical certitude about the humanity of the fetus, very respectable groups want to permit abortion in specific cases. The model statute of the American Law Institute reads in part as follows:

A licensed physician is justified in terminating a pregnancy if he believes there is substantial risk that continuance of the pregnancy would gravely imperil the physical or mental health of the mother or that the child would be born with grave physical or mental defect, or that the pregnancy resulted from rape, incest, or other felonious intercourse. All illicit intercourse with a girl below the age of sixteen shall be deemed felonious for purposes of this subsection. Justifiable abortions shall be performed only in a licensed hospital except in case of emergency when hospital facilities are unavailable. . . .[3]

In June of 1967, the House of Delegates of the American Medical Association voted almost unanimously to ease their policy on abortions.[4] The causes authorized are the same as those in the model statute. The AMA requires that the necessity of the operation be certified in writing by two physicians other than the one who is to perform the abortion.

Such a position on abortion is the equivalent of Pandora's box. We do not know what evils will come out of it. We can surmise that it will not lead to a decrease of abortions. The mental health of the mother is a vague term. Some doctors, for example, would authorize an abortion in the case of a forty-year-old divorced woman who could not have a child out of wedlock without losing her social status and harming the emotional lives of her two teenage children. Rape is notoriously difficult to prove in court, but the physician would be justified by the statute if he *believed* the pregnancy resulted from rape. It would also appear that fornication with a fifteen-year-old would constitute a grounds for abortion, whether or not she consented to the intercourse. In any event, the rather broad wording of the statute leaves vast possibilities open for those who want an abortion.

Behind these proposals for a change in the law on abortion, we can find some interesting value judgments. The fetus's right to life is subordinated to the physical or mental health of the mother. The good of the physical integrity of the child is made superior to life itself. The right to life is revoked when life was started by the crime of another. The right to life does not exist when the unmarried mother was below sixteen. In short, the right to life is made contingent on some very strange factors. More important, perhaps, is the idea that the right to life is less basic than the right to health.

The strangeness of these value judgments appears even more dramatically if we take a look at some concrete cases. Babies born of a mother who had German measles in the early months of pregnancy may be deformed or crippled. We are not quite sure what the chances of deformity are, but they do exist. Some doctors estimate that the chances of deformity are forty percent if the disease was contracted in the first month of pregnancy, but only ten percent if it was contracted in the third month. To abort such pregnancies on the ground that there is a substantial risk of the child having grave physical abnormalities would seem to be extraordinary, no matter what values one holds. If a person does not believe in the right to life, he ought at least to allow the pregnancies to come to term and then kill off the minority who have grave defects.

Similarly, though many women insist that they will go mad or commit suicide if they have to carry a pregnancy to term, few suffer the threatened breakdowns. What, then, are we to say of the risks involved? Where do you draw the line, once you have denied the fetus a right to live?

If human life is precious and if a fetus has human life, it is difficult to see how one can permit direct abortions. Practically any exceptions proposed are based on extraordinary value judgments and open the door to abuses. If I may will the death of an innocent human being in these cases, I admit that a person can have direct control over the life of another human being. In addition, I have made the right to life extremely relative. For these reasons we do not feel that abortion can be justified until such time as we have evidence which indicates that particular fetuses are not human beings.

In the literature of medical ethics, especially that written by Catholic moral theologians, indirect abortions are permitted.[5] In the indirect abortion, the death of the fetus is not willed as either a means or an end, but occurs as the side effect of some procedure designed to protect the life of the mother. While we do not want to go into all the details involved in the application of this theory, a few points should be made. In the indirect abortion, the fetus is not treated as a means, as a thing which has no right to life. In the indirect abortion, the death of the child is not willed, not made a part of the agenda. The indirect abortion does not assume that anyone has direct and complete control over the life of an innocent human being.

SELF-DEFENSE

Although our society condemns the deliberate killing of innocent human beings, there is considerable dispute about the deliberate killing of those who are guilty of crimes. May one kill in self-defense or in the defense of the nation? Is it ethical to execute persons convicted of crime? Although the conscience of society gives a qualified affirmative answer to these questions, the ethical man will want to examine the question for himself.

Even though we admit the right to use force in self-defense, we insist on certain ethical limitations. In the first place, force may not be ethically used until all peaceful means have been exhausted. Running away and calling the police can be an ethical obligation. In the second place, no more force than necessary may be used. If an attacker can be effectively stopped with the aid of judo, a shotgun may not be ethically used. This is a simple application of the principle of proportionality. Thirdly, and as a general rule, the force should be used only when the attack has begun. The force used may be so great that the defender risks killing the attacker in certain cases. After all, no one has complete control over the effects of a bullet or even a sharp blow. Taking such a risk, however, need not be unethical if such a risk is required by the situation.

The difficult ethical problem does not involve the qualified use of force in self-defense but the right *to will the death of the attacker*. May one ethically use the life of the other as a means? These questions may be purely theoretical at the moment of the attack, when people act under the influence of strong fear and anger, but they are real ethical questions. They bear on the attitude we ought to have towards the life of another even when he is trying to infringe our rights.

While admitting that the question has been and is answered in several different ways, we take the following stand. We may will to stop the attack, but we may not ethically will the death of the attacker. In the first place, the attacker is a human being, even though he is not acting like one. The defender does not have direct control over any human life unless this is given to him by God. Theoretically, it might be argued that God granted the defender such a right in those situations when willing the death of the attacker was a necessary means to defending life. In practice, however, it is difficult to see why it would ever be *necessary to will the death* of the attacker. Granted that the necessary force may lead to death, why is it necessary to will the death if the attack is stopped when the force is applied? Let us be concrete. The only way of stopping a madman who is running berserk is to fire several bullets into his body. Once he is stopped by the bullets, his death is not necessary. Indeed, an ethical defender will make every effort to preserve the life of the wounded attacker at this point.

Some people may argue that this is unnecessary hair-splitting. We feel that the point is important. The temptation to hate and to use others as mere things is so great that every effort should be made to restrain it. If men feel that they can will the death of another in self-defense, they admit an exception which can feed the tendency to go all the way. Perhaps theoretical exceptions are a possibility, but in practice we cannot see either the need or justification for willing the death of another.

CAPITAL PUNISHMENT

The question of capital punishment cannot be properly treated without a consideration of the ethics of the state. However, since the question has a bearing on the right to kill, a few observations may be useful. Capital punishment would be ethical if the state had divine authority to take life. The question cannot be solved by merely appealing to tradition, for custom often justifies barbarity. Even those who hold that the authority of the state comes ultimately from God would admit that it is limited by the common good. Indeed the state would not have a right to inflict capital punishment unless this were a *necessary means* to the maintenance of public order.

We have seen no evidence to indicate that capital punishment is necessary for the attainment of any of the purposes of punishment. It certainly does not reform the convicted person! It does not appear to have any demonstrable effect on the rate of capital crimes. It is not necessary to restore public confidence in the forces of law and order. Indeed there are signs that the existence of capital punishment raises questions about the justice of a society that employs it. Increasingly, the death penalty is not being used, even where it is still legal. Among other reasons for this is an unwillingness to use such a radical punishment when others can serve as well. It is to be hoped that we in the United States have come to realize that brutality brutalizes the user even more than the victim. Since all citizens are the users, we ought to be unwilling to expose ourselves to the charge that we use execution to satisfy our blood lust rather than a well-founded sense of justice.

Perhaps a case can be made for the necessity of capital punishment, and so for a divine grant of authority, in other times or other places, but we have not seen any evidence which would indicate that it is necessary or even very useful in a highly civilized country. Thus we have not seen any evidence that God has given the state in civilized countries the right to exercise the power of life and death over the criminal. Consistently with our own principles, then, we believe that capital punishment is unethical, at least in civilized nations where there is no evidence of a delegation of divine authority over life.

REMARKS ON WAR

The ethics of war cannot be treated in a short book on general ethical theory. Yet the issue of killing in war has a bearing on the ethics of killing in general. The problem is complicated by the fact that we have tended not only to extend the limits of permissible defense but also to invest the warrior with the authority of the nation, so that he is supposed to be killing on higher authority. At the same time, the pacifist seems to feel that he may not only submit to conquest but may also allow his neighbors to fall victim to attackers. This creates a situation where we sacrifice one group of men to another group of men in the name of conscience. This is reasonable if killing in war—or war itself—is to be avoided at all costs. It is not reasonable if we have a right to defend ourselves even to the point of killing.

Because we are blinded by the patriotism that is drilled into us, it is difficult to take a stand on these questions. There is a fear haunting us that we have merely substituted one emotional position for another and not really worked out an ethic of war. As a result, the whole ethics of human life and of killing is left somewhat up in the air.

In the case of war, defense, and punishment, we are dealing with the ethics of the individual or society. We are trying to develop an ethic for a situation which should not, but does, exist. We are attempting to develop reasonable guides for action in what is basically an unreasonable situation. As a result, we twist and turn and find ourselves dissatisfied with nearly every conclusion. Yet we must take a stand. We must decide on priorities. Are there cases where we must permit great evils to ourselves rather than involve ourselves in using the lives of others as means? Are there times when we should renounce our right to self-defense rather than risk the spread of hate? Does the religious injunction to "turn the other cheek" have a place of honor in even a purely philosophic ethic?

Every time we deal with a problem involving life the value of every human life is at stake. For this reason, our concern for that value and for human dignity in general should lead us to be strict rather than lenient.

HEALTH AND THE PRESERVATION
OF LIFE

If life in time is, as far as we are concerned, a necessary means to our perfection, we are obliged to tend and nurture it. The problems arise when we ask about the limitations of this obligation. Are we obliged to use all means to preserve life? Are there circumstances in which we are not obliged to do anything to maintain our existence? Are there cases when for all practical purposes we are forbidden to take steps to preserve our life?

In line with our general principles, we may not use means which involve willing an absolute or quasi-absolute evil. We may not will the death of another as a means to keeping ourself in existence. The rights of others limit our right and our obligation.

Also in line with our general principles, I am free to omit an act necessary for the preservation of my life if the harmful side effects balance out the good. I am not, for example, obliged to save my life if, in the process, others will lose theirs as a side effect.

In line with our general principles, I *may not* use a means when the harmful effects are greater than the good effects. I would say, for example, that I may not drive into a crowd of school children in order to save myself from going over a cliff and to my death. It would of course, be a different case if I were President of the United States and my death would cause disaster for the entire nation. It might be different, too, if I were a married man with ten dependents who would be helpless without me. The problem, as elsewhere, is focused on the difficulty of judging proportionality in the concrete world of complex contingency.

Similar but less dramatic problems arise when we consider my obligation with regard to various medical treatments and regimens. Am I obliged to undergo brain surgery which offers one out of four chances for my survival and one out of ten that I will be more than a cripple? Must I use glucose, intravenous feeding, and the like, when I am a terminal cancer patient? Must I take expensive medicines which will beggar my family and do no more than keep me in existence without the ability to work or support those who depend on me? These are very real and very emotional cases which perplex both doctors and patients and the families of the sick.

The emotions stirred up by these cases cause most of us to look for outside chances or to play the game by the conventional wisdom of the group to which we belong. Yet they are basically cases in proportionality. If the unwilled evil which would be risked or permitted balances out the good, we are not obliged to use the means. If the evil risked or permitted actually outweighs the good, it would appear that we ought to omit the means. If we do not follow these principles, we will end up by making health and life in time into absolute ends which overshadow all other goods and the rights of others.

BY WAY OF SUMMARY

Although there may be room for enlarging the inherent and divinely delegated rights of an individual over his own life, the need to protect the value of life against short-sighted selfishness should make us suspicious of attempts to justify the killing of the unborn, the attacker, or the criminal. Moreover, because we are not obliged to preserve our life in all circumstances, we can ask if it may not be nobler to submit to death, rather than add to the violence and hate in the world?

NOTES

1. Albert Pierce, "The Economic Cycle and the Social Suicide Rate," *American Sociological Review,* 32 (1967), June No. 3, pp. 457–462.
2. *Cf.* Robert H. Springer, "Notes on Moral Theology," *Theological Studies,* 28 (1967), June No. 2, pp. 330–335, for interesting comments on recent medical literature.
3. American Law Institute, *Model Penal Code,* Proposed Official Draft, Sec. 230.3:2 (Philadelphia: American Law Institute, 1962), pp. 189–190. Copyrighted 1962. Printed with the permission of The American Law Institute.
4. "AMA Eases Policy on Abortions to Allow Therapeutic Operations in Specified Cases," *Wall Street Journal,* June 22, 1967.
5. Thomas J. O'Donnell, *Morals in Medicine,* 2nd ed. (Westminster, Md.: Newman Press, 1959), pp. 155–228.

POINTS FOR DISCUSSION

1. Can you imagine a case where it could be argued that God had clearly given an individual a right to kill himself?
2. What sort of evidence would be required to prove that a fetus was not a human person?
3. Discuss the values and priorities of those who want to liberalize the abortion laws.
4. If you admit that the state has a right to execute criminals, why

not admit that it has the right to kill incurable cancer patients, mental defectives, and insane people who are a drain on society?

5. What are the ethics of cigarette smoking? Apply them to individuals with different personalities and smoking habits.

READINGS

Joseph FLETCHER, *Morals and Medicine* (Boston, Mass.: Beacon Press, 1960).

Andrew F. HENRY and James F. SHORT, Jr., *Suicide and Homicide* (Glencoe, Ill: Free Press, 1964). Reprint of 1954 edition.

Edwin M. SCHUR, *Crimes Without Victims* (Englewood Cliffs, N.J.: Prentice-Hall, 1965), pp. 11–66.

Thorsten SELLIN (ed.), *Capital Punishment* (New York: Harper & Row, 1967).

Norman ST. JOHN-STEVAS, *The Right To Life* (New York: Holt, Rinehart & Winston, 1963).

Norman ST. JOHN-STEVAS, *Life, Death and the Law* (Bloomington, Ind.: Indiana University Press, 1961).

11/ THE DIMENSIONS AND MEANING OF SEX

INTRODUCTION

Human sexuality touches nearly all aspects of man's being and activity. It influences not only our bodily structure but psychic life, our approach to life, and our relations with others. As a result of this all-pervasiveness of sex, there can be no simple sexual ethic. There is a constellation of values to be promoted and protected, and this, as we saw in an earlier chapter, is a difficult task, both in theory and in practice. Moreover, because sex is particularly connected with the very emotional areas of love and bodily life, we may be tempted to simplify in order to support a personal whim or a popular myth. Worse yet, we may accept the customs of our society as a norm, and so be caught in either a general laxity or an extreme rigorism, depending on where and when we live. The problem of developing a reasoned sexual ethics is all the more difficult because we have learned sex roles and sexual ideals as children, and so find it difficult to maintain any distance from the problem. To put it another way, the attempt to study sexual ethics is complicated by a personal involvement whose roots are found in childhood, as well as in the stormy period of adolescence, and the day-by-day plodding of adult life. For some of us this means coping with deep-rooted guilt feelings about sex. For others it means looking for the human dimensions of what has been treated as a biological function. In any event, it almost certainly involves an effort to enlarge perspectives and to escape from narrowing views.

The problem of developing a well-rounded and reasoned sexual ethics is particularly difficult for those who have grown up in a religion which once taught a neatly articulated sexual ethic. There are two reasons for this difficulty. In the first place, religious sexual ethics do not always come with reasoned bases. In the second place, even those religiously founded sexual ethics which have reasoned bases are in some sort of transition. The Catholic moral theology of sex, for example, is grappling with problems raised by increasing sensitivity to love and personal values in sex as well as with the issues raised by the population problem, new biological knowledge, and the existence of strongly hedonistic trends in our culture. No matter what the practical consensus among Catholic thinkers (and even this is problematic), there is not a clear-cut consensus as to the exact interrelation between the various values in sex.[1] This is tragic, but it is also a reflection of our general ignorance about sex.

METHODS AND LIMITS

All the difficulties mentioned above are real, but our ignorance of sex is not only real but basic to our problem. Sex, indeed, is like the weather, in that everyone talks about it and is touched by it, while few, if any, know much about it. This may seem strange to those who see the hundreds of books and articles devoted to the subject, but in fact we are not too sure about many crucial questions in this area. On the biological level, we should like to know whether or not certain pills inhibit ovulation or cause abortions or both. On the psychological level, we should like to know whether or not man can establish conscious control over sexual reflexes. How do various sexual activities influence interpersonal relations, the education of children, and the stability of marriages? Is there any relationship between respect for life and various attitudes toward the use of sex? These are annoying questions, yet crucial to the development of a sound sexual ethic.

In the course of the present chapter, we will introduce scraps of evidence which indicate areas of risk but which will not show any necessary connection between sexual practices and evil consequences. We shall also introduce opinions and hypotheses which, while not probative, should make a reasonable man hesitate. In short, we will often be dealing with an ethic of risk and of prudential action. This may not be satisfactory to those who like their ethics neat and clear, but it will at least bring out the issues involved and broaden sensitivities. We trust, too, that it will counter some of the badly oversimplified solutions being offered in the market place.

What follows is not a substitute for a religiously founded ethic of sexuality. Where we are tentative, exploratory, and prudential, some of the great religious teachers are decisive, final, and absolute. Once again, the unsatisfactory nature of purely philosophic ethics will lead many to the teachings of the great religions. At the same time, philosophic ethics may force religious thinkers to distinguish more carefully between the data of divine revelation and the more limited human underpinnings of their teaching. In any event, the present chapter does not pretend to give final answers to some of the most difficult questions in ethics.

At very least, our study should show what sort of factors must be considered by the individual when he is forming his conscience. In line with what has been said about the nature of man in previous chapters, we will be looking for an ethic that considers at least the following interrelated areas of human life: *the biological, the personal, the interpersonal,* and *the social.* We reject absolutely any attempt to treat sex as if it were a purely animal function under the control of some sort of instinct. At the same time, we do not subscribe to a puritan ethic which views all pleasure with suspicion. Human sexuality is not a simple entity.

It has many dimensions, and these must be integrated if man is to grow and attain his perfection.

One additional warning is in order. Many ethicians treat of the morality of sexual acts, to the exclusion of states and processes. In the present treatment we are concerned with acts, states, and processes. We want to know not only how an individual and isolated act affects the four basic dimensions of sex, but how repeated acts influence outlook and growth. Do certain types of activities set up dispositions and attitudes that block the human vision and induce selfishness? Do seemingly harmless activities lead to states of mind which are hostile to the good of other men or of society itself? These questions are important, for a narrow preoccupation with acts in isolation can cause us to overlook many truly significant aspects of the biological, personal, inter-personal, and social dimensions of sex.

THE BIOLOGICAL DIMENSION

On a purely biological level, it is clear that the human sexual organs and their interconnected hormonal supports are designed to make reproduction possible. It is equally obvious that not every union of these organs can or does lead to the formation of new life. One or both parties may be completely sterile. The female is fertile only on certain days during a limited number of years. Any number of factors can make either the male or the female temporarily sterile and incapable of reproduction while they both remain completely capable of sexual union.

These simple facts have some important implications. The sexual organs are reproductive, but nature does not seem to intend that each and every act of sexual union be reproductive. To put it another way, reproduction may be one of the specific purposes of the sexual organs, but not every act of intercourse is designed to produce new life. For this reason, we do not believe that it is accurate to say that an act of birth control by the use of so-called artificial means is necessarily a frustration of the reproductive faculties. The reason is simply that nature itself does not intend each and every act to be reproductive. Indeed, if a couple produces children over a span of time, the reproductive purposes will have been realized, even though most of the individual acts were not reproductive.*

Thinkers who are aware of the fact that nature itself limits reproduction argue that the couple are to decide how many children to have and when to have them in accord with the demands of other dimensions of sex. This need surprise no one, for even older writers insisted that reproduction was not merely for the good of the couple, but for the good of society. This puts the reproductive function into relationship with the social dimension. Furthermore, in man the desire to enter into sexual union is independent of a biological cycle of urgency such as that found in animals in "heat." If nature intended every act of intercourse to be reproductive, it could have limited the desire to those periods when conception was possible.

Nature seems to have left reproduction to the option of couples for a variety of reasons. The need for reproduction in a society is variable. The capacity of various couples to raise and educate children is variable. Finally, as we shall see in the following sections, sexual intercourse can have other purposes.

Although not every act of sexual union is or can be reproductive, the sexual organs are designed for reproduction. Furthermore, every society depends on the reproductive activities of at least some couples. Without rising generations, there would be no one to take care of the old, the sick, and the helpless. If the rising generation is too large, the society may not be able to take care of its young. Reproduction, then, is not a neutral and completely private matter. Couples do not have to make every act of intercourse reproductive, but they are in some way responsible for the

* The author's approach to this question is obviously a philosophical one. For a Catholic, the determining factor remains the teaching of the Church; up to the time of writing, the Pope has given no indication of accepting the argument proposed here.

impact of either reproduction or nonreproduction on the society. The responsibility is somewhat vague, since it rests on all couples as a group and is not nicely pinned down on a quota basis. Indeed, it cannot be pinned down on a quota basis, since considerations from the personal and interpersonal order enter into the question.

Even those who do not reject artificial contraception as intrinsically evil must face the ethical problems that arise from the biological and physiological side effects of various methods. In all honesty we must face the fact that we are not sure of the effects of the various contraceptive measures on the physical health of the couple. The use of oral contraceptives seems counterindicated for some women on purely medical grounds.[2] The interuterine ring may not be invariably without side effects. Only the latest medical literature can give any sort of reasonable answer to the medico-ethical questions connected with contraceptive methods. Even these answers, however, must be somewhat tentative, since medical science is constantly advancing. The ethical man or woman will investigate in order to make sure that he or she is not taking unnecessary risks on the physiological level.

We have not seen any convincing evidence which indicates that abstinence from sexual activity produces physiological damage in human beings. On the other hand, we do know that promiscuous sexual activity creates a danger of certain infections. Although medical science has enabled us to reduce the damage from these infections, the risk of infection is ethically relevant on the biological level.

Autoerotic and homosexual activities disregard the reproductive dimension of sex. As we shall see in the next section, such activity has negative effects on personal development and interpersonal relations. While it also harms society in some cases, we do not have conclusive evidence to show that it is biologically harmful. Prescinding from the religious positions on contraception, autoeroticism and homosexuality, it would appear that from a philosophical point of view the real ethical problems occur in the more properly human dimensions of sex.

THE PERSONAL AND INTERPERSONAL
DIMENSIONS

Human sexuality belongs to a person. It is to be used and cultivated for the good of the entire person and of the society to which
he belongs. Rudolph Allers noted in his *Psychology of Character*
that

. . . sexual behavior must take its stamp not only from the "sex impulse," but also and essentially from the person as a whole. A man's
sexuality is, no less than his conduct at any other level, the expression
of his person and his character.[3]

Our sexuality, then, needs to be integrated into our total
personality and made to serve growth towards an ideal. It must
be made to open us up and not to shut us in. It must be used
with respect for the rights of others, and for the promotion of the
good of others. All this is easier said than done. In the adolescent
years, the growing sexual impulse can be imperious and confusing.
It can cry out for gratification and become so strong that it comes
close to wiping out other values. Indeed it can try to become an
end in itself. When this drive occurs in those who have not yet
achieved identity, worked out their values, defined their roles, and
related themselves to other people, the resulting confusion can be
terrible to behold. At the same time, most people pass through
this stage successfully as they grope for meaning and integration of
the self.

Sexuality relates us to other people in various ways. Ideally,
sexual union is to be both a cause and an effect of deep love and a
lasting human relationship. Sexual relations or abstinence from
sexual relations must be made to serve the exigencies of benevolence as well as of personal development and social need. If sex
is exploited or used as a mere means to pleasure, some of the
richest possibilities in life have been destroyed at the same time
that another person has been used.

Precisely because so much is involved in the uses of our sexuality, every known society has hedged sex with regulations. While many of these regulations aim at maintaining peace and order in the group, others seek to protect the dignity of the individual and to promote his growth. Every society educates its members in sexual behavior because it has to. Not all societies, however, have the same concepts of human dignity. As a result, all do not demand the same degree or type of control. In the present book, our idea of the person and of life will demand greater integration and control than is asked for by groups which do not give as high a position to the person, and especially to the female.

MARRIAGE

Monogamous, stable marriage, based on benevolent love, is an ideal, and an obligatory ideal, for those who wish to give full expression to their sexuality. It is an ideal that cannot be realized in an instant, but requires continual efforts to grow and to serve. No magic formula is available for success in marriage. No automatic mechanisms lead to growth. The same obstacles that block growth in general and growth in love block growth in marriage. Love of the false self, fear, and immaturity can all make marriage difficult. Because marriage is more intimate than any other human relationship, those obstacles can actually be magnified in marriage. The selfishness that is concealed from casual acquaintances can hardly be hidden in marriage. The fears that merely cut us off from selected individuals outside marriage block communication with the most important person inside marriage. For these reasons, a person needs to develop himself and to curb many of his faults before he can responsibly enter into marriage.

The preparation for marriage must include sexual self-control if the partners are to be able to remain faithful. Marriage, after all, does not suddenly make all members of the opposite sex unattractive. In addition, sickness and separation often impose long periods of abstinence during which tenderness cannot be expressed in full sexual intimacy. Finally, even in marriage, respect for the other often demands tender restraint, when the partner's moods and feelings produce a reluctance to enter into intimacies.

Experience has taught us that social peace, reproduction, child care, and personal development are best achieved in a monogamous marriage based on love. Kardiner notes that we do not know of any great civilization which has had a polyandrous pattern of marriage.[4] Some few great civilizations have allowed polygamy, but none of them compares with the cultures based on monogamy. The reasons are manifold. The monogamous family is both compact and plastic. It provides for unremitting care by parents of both sexes and creates stability and growth in emotions and intelligence. The monogamous family protects both society and the individuals involved. For this reason it deserves to be protected.

The monogamous family is a means to the attainment of certain human goals. However, people will tend to reject this form of family life if they do not understand it or if they reject the goals, or change the relative importance attached to the goals. In our own times the monogamous family is under attack for all of these reasons. The stress on personal satisfaction, often measured in terms of sexual pleasure, has caused many people to overlook the social dimensions of marriage. In other cases it has led to ignorance of the fact that more is involved in human relations even on the personal level. Still other groups diminish the importance of the social goals, even though they will admit that they have some importance.

The shifts are not purely and simply accidents. Economic and technological advances have made it possible to give greater stress to personal considerations. The availability of employment for a woman has freed her from economic dependence on the male so that she need no longer fear poverty if the family breaks up. The existence of fairly effective birth control devices has made it possible to enjoy the pleasures of sex without fear of reproduction. The development of antibiotics has reduced the fear of disease which was once a restraint on sexual activity.

Today people feel that they are not irresponsible because they can prevent society from suffering from their personal use of sex.

As we shall see in the next section, they often are wrong, but the fact remains that modern techniques and economic conditions have changed some of the social consequences of sex relations and of marriage. What, however, are we to say of the effects on personal development and interpersonal relations?

Sex on the personal and interpersonal levels is highly ambiguous. We want sex to be tender and loving, an opening on a broader world of human development. Unfortunately, it can be an instrument of aggression and a means of escaping from reality and responsibility. The personal and interpersonal meaning of sex depends on attitudes and intentions as well as on physical union. Attitude and intention, however, are not sufficient to give sex its full meaning. As we have pointed out in our chapter on the expression of love, effective loving demands knowledge of the means. Some activities will not promote the good of another, no matter what our good intention. This is true in the area of sex, as in all else.

THE PROMISCUOUS

The Don Juan who flits from one woman to another is a sick individual. Even if the promiscuous individual speaks of love as well as of sexual gratification, he does not find human completion. He does not meet another person on the deepest level, because the transitory nature of his liaisons does not permit this. Whether he is engaged in a series of "one-night stands" or of short-lived affairs, the time element prevents him from discovering the other and from promoting his full development. The Don Juan is an exploiter, no matter what his explicit intentions. The real tragedy of these people is well put by psychiatrist Edmund Bergler:

The fact remains that clinical experience does prove that running from one woman to another is the typical behavior of neurotic wolves, and running from one man to another, the typical behavior of frigid women. *Under the guise of greater sexual gratification, these neurotics cover up their inability to enjoy sex in the first place.*[5]

Kirkendall notes that sexual intercourse with prostitutes, pick-ups, and casual acquaintances actually forms barriers to attachment.[6] Indeed, it would seem that such a use of sex is chosen in order to avoid any meaningful relationship. In these cases the partner is chosen precisely because involvement, love, and intimacy on the psychic level are ruled out. There is no growth here, but only flight and exploitation.

Premarital intercourse with dating partners to whom there is no strong attachment, with fiancées, and with partners who are the objects of strong attachments do not produce exactly the same results as noted above. Kirkendall, however, makes two very pertinent observations, when summarizing his studies:

This analysis leads the writer to believe that the effect of intercourse, in and of itself, on the strengthening or weakening of a relationship, is indirect and minimal . . .

Also, intercourse is sometimes used as a defense against a deeper involvement, or as an excuse for avoiding commitments.[7]

Other writers have spoken of the inadequacy of simple gratificaton and even romantic sexual passion to serve as a support for either existential communion or fulfillment.[8] Erich Fromm goes so far as to say that the erotic element may even be a barrier to love and human completion.[9] If the erotic is not supported by benevolence, it tends to produce a transitory relationship because it concentrates on the superficial. Such relationships do not cause growth.

We must recall that the young are particularly prone to form superficial relationships, for, as Erikson has noted, a reasonable sense of identity is necessary before real intimacy is possible.[10] The person who is confused about what he is has little to give. He may have a deep need for others, but he is not so fully in control of his own personality that he can enter into mature relationships. Any honest young person will have to admit that he has "fallen in and out of love" several times. If he has not gone through this experience, he is probably not fully capable of distinguishing the authentic relationship of love from one that is exploitive.

Our bodies may be capable of sexual union in the early teens; our emotions and personalities, however, may not have developed sufficiently to make the use of sex truly human and ethical. For this reason, if no other, the young should be suspicious of their own motives and maturity. This is not pure speculation. Teenage marriages break up more often and more rapidly than other marriages, even though the married relationship has the support of society. The reason is not sexual incompatibility but immaturity. The personalities of the young were not capable of creating and sustaining a real, stable love relationship.

Many people who will admit that all of the above is generally true will propose themselves as exceptions. Let me quote you a typical couple. "We really love one another and intend to get married. It is not a question of an affair or of promiscuity, we intend to stay together. Why should we wait for a marriage ceremony? It can't increase our love."

Many couples who talk this way are sincere. They are not giving the speech as a cover-up for lust. Unfortunately, sincerity may not be enough. Any experienced counselor has seen dozens of such couples break up, with severe traumatic effects on both parties, but particularly on the girl. At times, the counselor is hard put to it to fight down a certain cynicism based on experience. He has heard it all before and knows it is not enough. Of course the honest counselor knows that a marriage ceremony is not enough either. A glance at divorce, separation, and desertion statistics will convince anyone that a ceremony does not guarantee stability or enduring love.

No one can offer guarantees of success. We can, however, test the sincerity of love and protect it when love is genuine. If we fail to use the means available, we will have acted unethically. We will have risked the happiness and growth not only of the two people involved but of children yet unborn. What are the tests of love? What are the protections available?

Love should be tested by asking how much the two people really know about each other. Do they have a love based on a sharing of worries, ideals, and a frank recognition of defects, or have they shared no more than embraces, chit-chat, and a few good times? If the relationship is superficial, of short duration, and almost purely physical, any mature person will be suspicious. We can only say: Deepen your human relationship before you think of sexual intimacy. You have not as yet discovered a real basis for an enduring relationship.

Love should also be tested by asking if the two people are willing and able to accept real responsibility for each other. Let us be concrete. One can doubt the readiness and ability of a couple to accept responsibility if they plan on having parents support them. Are the couple ready and willing to take care of each other's health, housing, and food, or are they only prepared to share bed and recreation? More important still, are the couple ready to accept the responsibility for the growth and happiness of each other? This means accepting the possibility of suffering and privation on behalf of one another. It means accepting self-control during long periods of separation. It means a real merging of two lives.

If a couple are sharing more than superficial things and are ready and able to assume real responsibility for each other, they may be ready for marriage. What, however, does marriage add to their present state? What difference will a public ceremony make?

The willingness to enter into marriage is both a test of the couple's sincerity and a protection of love. If either or both do not want to announce their union and to assume the legal responsibilities that go with that announcement, we may rightfully doubt their sincerity. A look at the reasons generally given for not going through with the marriage ceremony confirms this suspicion. "Her parents will be upset." "My parents will cut off the money for my education." "We want to finish our schooling first." In short, the people involved are not willing to pay a price for their love. They are not willing to stand on their own two feet and accept responsibility for their actions.

Marriage offers protection for love, though it cannot guarantee it. Marriage is a public announcement of exclusivity supported by public officials. Not merely the two individuals involved but society as a whole commits itself to protecting this union. In one way or another, society will provide secondary motives for remaining together and fulfilling the responsibilities which have been assumed. This is not surprising, since society has a great stake in marriage. The interests of society and of the couple may not be identical, but they touch at many points, as we shall see in later sections.

All this leads us to say that sexuality cannot lead to the full development of individuals unless it is coupled with real love. Real love in its turn depends on maturity and on the tests and protections offered by society. In the concrete, then, not only promiscuity but also premarital sex is at odds with the full development of the individual. The ethical man, who is concerned with both his own growth and the fulfillment of others, will see that in this area at least the traditional attitudes are well founded in experience. Jean Guitton sums this up beautifully in his *Essay on Human Love:*

Love admits of so many illusions, it is so ambiguous, so inconstant, so near to neurotic, so recalcitrant to all wise counsels, so apt to become inverted or dissociated, so estranged from its normal purpose, so quick to become bestial, absurd, or even demonic, that society must intervene to protect it against itself. And this is the justification of sexual morality and of the social institution of marriage and of monogamy, as well as of the customs which surround them. Far from being obstacles to love, this collection of taboos, interdictions, fashions, usages, human and divine laws, more or less simulated sentiments, which form the humus in which love generates—all this makes it possible for a great number of people, in spite of their self-deception and mediocrity, to experience this improbable yet perpetual state.[11]

Because union in marriage calls for the deepest self-revelation, the preparation for marriage calls for practice in communication. This, in its turn, involves learning to interpret the moods and gestures as well as the words of the beloved. It also demands a continual effort to be honest and frank about one's deepest fears and highest ambitions. Courtship practices which concentrate on superficial chit-chat, or having a good time, may actually be a block to growth. The engaged couple who have seldom shared serious conversation should have doubts about their readiness to enter into a state of life where nearly everything is to be shared.

OTHER SEXUAL PRACTICES

While there is little to be gained by a discussion of all known sexual practices, a few comments on homosexuality and masturbation may help to clarify the problem of sexual development as a part of the growth of the individual.

Despite a great deal of propaganda in favor of the homosexual way of life, the fact remains that most homosexual relations are short-lived, impersonal, and characterized by a great deal of promiscuity.[12] There are some homosexual marriages which may last for years, but they are exceptions. Homosexual relations offer little if anything to human development, not only because such a use of sex is relatively meaningless and unstable but because it reinforces certain basic character traits which are obstacles to development and maturity. Harper, on the basis of his clinical practice, says that the main psychological components of the homosexual are:

(1) A basic antisexuality or puritanism—an early instilled and well reinforced non-acceptance of sexuality in general and heterosexuality in particular; (2) low personal self-esteem and self-confidence—that is, deep-seated feelings of inadequacy—immaturity; and (3) compulsive adherence to the continually reinforced homosexual mode of orgastic satisfaction.[13]

Harper also notes that the homosexual neurosis is like that of the alcoholic or drug addict in that it involves relatively permanent means of attaining short-range alleviation of insecurity and low self-esteem.[14] In the long run, all such means are self-defeating. Kardiner speaks of the homosexual as having a low emotional regard for others[15] and an incapacity for sustained tender relations with others. In short, the homosexual is a stunted individual—a tragedy.

Some societies have tolerated homosexuality because they did not feel it was a real threat to social order.[16] Our own society has often been unnecessarily cruel to the homosexual, and there is serious doubt about the wisdom and justice of laws that make private homosexual behavior between consenting adults a crime. We should not forget, however, that homosexuality is a tragedy and a real block to development.[17] We must, then, be concerned with the proper sexual development of children and young people, lest they be trapped into deviance.

We know that an extremely large number of teenage boys masturbate at some time or other. This does not necessarily produce permanent damage to the personality, but habitual masturbation is not without its psychological dangers. Such masturbation may be a sign of deep-rooted disturbances, but even if it is not it can reinforce a preoccupation with the self and one's own body. For this reason, if for no other, the young man must be encouraged in his efforts to control and integrate his sexuality. But such an effort at control should not be made the center of life, lest the effort itself produce morbid preoccupation. Autoerotic activity can be escapist. Sometimes it is indulged in as a symbolic defiance of authority. Often it is compulsive and largely indeliberate. Unless the underlying causes are faced, the mere elimination of autoerotic activity will not mean a great deal.

The evil of habitual masturbation appears most clearly when it is seen as a block to the development of the interpersonal dimension of sex. Masturbation in fact does not even serve to satisfy the sex drive, which aims at union, at bridging the gap between two human beings. Masturbation which continues into adulthood is an indication and a result of retarded development. Schwartz notes that after puberty it is generally a neurotic symptom requiring treatment.[18] Once again, a sex activity cannot be considered in isolation from the total development of the person.

THE SOCIAL DIMENSION OF SEX

Although we have already mentioned the social dimension of sex in the earlier pages of this chapter, a few points need to be driven home in a culture that tends to exalt the individual and his sexual happiness without much reference to social obligations. This is particularly true because the proliferation of easy birth control methods has created the illusion that free and easy sexual activity does not threaten society with illegitimate children, and illegitimate children with being unwanted human beings.

The strongest advocates of birth control insist that devices work *only if used*. People who act in the heat of passion and with little regard for other people are not likely to worry about using birth control devices, if they think about them at all. As a result, the spread of birth control information and the availability of devices does not seem to have reduced the rate of illegitimacy in our society. There is evidence to indicate that illegitimacy rates increase with increasing sexual permissiveness.[19] The fact that many people use abortion to remove an unwanted pregnancy serves to point up the fallacy of saying that the birth control revolution has removed one of the great arguments against premarital sex. Birth control devices may make the limitation of births a possibility, but it has not made it a universal fact for the simple reason that no device can substitute for self-control and a sense of responsibility.

The illegitimate child placed in the hands of the state is not merely a financial burden on society, he or she is a personal tragedy. Institutionalized children have higher death rates than children in normal homes, even though the institutionalized child may get better medical care. The institutionalized child develops his intelligence, his speech, and his emotions more slowly and with greater difficulty. This should surprise no one, for he does not enjoy the constant loving care of the child who has both parents in a normal family; he has been deprived of one of the most important growth materials: intimate love.[20] Anyone who has ever worked in an orphanage has experienced these children's deep and heart-rending need for affection and attention. It is not merely a question of statistical studies, but of a felt deprivation which is so real that you can almost touch it.

No real substitute for the family exists. No responsible person can risk bringing children into the world if he is then going to deprive them of the home and constant care they need until they are mature. To take such risks in the name of passion or love or anything else is to be supremely irresponsible and unethical. No amount of rationalization can cover over the evil.

Children need not only a home but a stable home. The human child is a dependent for a long period, and no casual liaison of partners can take care of his needs. It is for this reason that society has insisted that marriage must be permanent. Civil law permits the break-up of marriage for a variety of reasons, and it may be that there are cases where the children are better off with one parent than in the midst of constant stress. The need for stability, however, remains, and no ethical man can take this lightly. For this reason, any sexual relationship which will not lead to the foundation of a stable marriage involves the risk of serious harm to human beings yet unborn. Forced marriages—and, as we have seen, teenage marriages—have a bad record on the score of stability, which would seem to indicate a need for tighter, rather than more permissive, rules on sexual conduct.

ARE THERE EXCEPTIONS?

While most people will agree with what we have written so long as it is applied to other people, a great many individuals see themselves as exceptions. They are sure that they will not harm the other person, society, or themselves by the use of sex outside marriage. They will cite instances of acquaintances who are exceptions and argue from such cases that they themselves are not bound by the general rules, no matter how well-founded. These would-be exceptions do not see themselves as taking any risks but envisage all sorts of goods that will come to them. While some of these individuals are insincere and dishonest with both themselves and others, many are speaking in all candor and with the best good will. Unfortunately, they overlook one very important point: the effect of their actions on others.

Even if we grant the possibility of exceptions, the fact remains that every breach of the general norm provides the weak, the insincere, and the irresponsible with living justification for what they want to do, no matter what the consequences. In short, the would-be exception weakens the whole social fabric which should support individuals in their effort to mature and use their sexuality responsibly. The would-be exception thus hurts not only individuals but society, no matter what his good intention may be. So long as we owe support and good example to others, there can really be no exceptions. While this conclusion may seem very strict, it is based on the very sound idea that our love for others often binds us to avoid even the appearance of evil. In an area of human life where so much is at stake this obligation is extremely serious.

Experience in counseling indicates that many of those who sincerely think they are exceptions have not looked at the problem from all angles. Many of these "candidates for exception" break off engagements and leave broken hearts behind them. Still others end up with a forced marriage despite their certitude that this could not happen to them. Many find out that their love was not quite as unselfish as they imagined. They were not really so much giving themselves to each other as running away from home or loneliness or the uncertainties of a world that lives under the cloud of nuclear weapons. In all honesty, counseling experience does not point to the existence of any real exception. We are all human beings who need the support of basic institutions which can stop us from making great mistakes under the veil of good will and half-truths.

OBLIGATIONS OF SOCIETY

Society has a big stake in marriage and the proper use of sex. Educators, clergymen, doctors, and parents are the chief sex educators in society, with the result that they have the obligation of training people to use their sexuality responsibly and in the interests of real growth. Their job is not easy. On the one hand, they must reject the old terroristic methods which made sex an ugly thing surrounded by all sorts of unreasonable taboos. On the other hand, they must fight the propaganda that makes of sex a casual recreational toy, or a purely personal affair. In addition, they must face the fact that social change has influenced the definitions of sex roles and family functions, so that young people are confused about their sex identity.

Society and its adult members must not only provide suitable sex education and a sound definition of sex roles, it must also provide examples. The doubts of the young about the soundness of basic sexual norms do not spring from *Playboy* magazine alone. The young can see that many adults do not live up to the rules. They may hear their fathers talk about the double standard and possibly see them practice it. They know of mothers who think that they have protected their daughters and educated them because they have fitted them out with birth control devices. The young are well aware that many adults escape from the effects of irresponsibility by using abortionists. Worst of all, they see too many marriages in which there is little love and maturity, so that infidelity and divorce follow. It is not easy to stomach the precepts of those whose actions give the lie to the precepts.

THE RELIGIOUS VALUES

A purely philosophic ethic of sex falls far short of the demands of the great religions, because it does not have the breadth and depth of a theology based on revelation and the accumulated experience of the churches. The Christian theologian, for example, sees the ideal of consecrated virginity in which the intimacy of sex is sacrificed so that a man or a woman may be more free to serve others. He sees the body as the temple of the Holy Spirit, and so demands the greatest reverence for it. The Christian, moreover, believes that God will give him the grace needed to make his body serve love rather than merely selfish cravings. The epistles of Saint Paul are clear and forceful in their condemnation of sexual abuses, so that the believer is supported by the word of God and not merely the experience of men. For all these reasons, any ethic of sex needs to be supplemented by a theology of sex.

NOTES

1. *Cf.* "Sexuality and the Modern World: A Symposium," *Cross Currents,* 14 (1964), Spring No. 2, pp. 129–267; *Moral Problems and Christian Personalism* (New York: Paulist Press, 1965); Peter Chirico, "Tension Morality and Birth Control," *Theological Studies,* 28 (1967), June No. 2, pp. 258–285.
2. As I was writing this, the following headline appeared in the *Wall Street Journal* for August 15, 1956: "FDA Orders New Tests of All Contraceptive Pills on the Market." The new tests will involve the use of dogs and primates. Previously, primates, animals in the same class as man, were not used in long-range tests.
3. Rudolph Allers, *The Psychology of Character* (New York: Macmillan, 1931), p. 303.
4. Abram Kardiner, *Sex and Morality* (New York: Charter Books, 1954), p. 194. The entire work of this psychoanalyst and anthropologist can be read with great profit.
5. Edmund Bergler, *Divorce Won't Help* (New York: Harper & Brothers, 1948), p. 228.
6. Lester A. Kirkendall, *Premarital Intercourse and Interpersonal Relationships* (New York: Julian Press, 1961), pp. 185 ff.
7. *Ibid.,* p. 196.
8. Ignace Lepp, *The Psychology of Loving* (Baltimore: Helicon, 1963), pp. 186 ff.
9. Erich Fromm, *The Art of Loving* (New York: Bantam, 1963), pp. 44–48, and especially p. 46.
10. Erik H. Erikson, "Growth and Crises of the Healthy Personality," *Psychological Issues,* 1 (1959), No. 1, p. 95.
11. Jean Guitton, *Essay on Human Love* (Chicago, Ill.: Franciscan Herald Press, 1966), p. 217.
12. Edwin M. Schur, *Crimes Without Victims* (Englewood Cliffs, N.J.: Prentice-Hall, 1965), p. 88.
13. Robert A. Harper, "Psychological Aspects of Homosexuality" in Hugo G. Beigel (ed.), *Advances in Sex Research* (New York: Harper & Row, 1963), p. 187.
14. *Ibid.,* p. 193.
15. Kardiner, *op. cit.,* p. 181.
16. For examples of these societies, *cf.* the index of Clellan S. Ford and Frank A. Beach, *Patterns of Sexual Behavior* (New York: Harper & Brothers, 1951).
17. *Cf.* "Intersexuality" in Peter Flood (ed.), *New Problems in Medical*

Ethics (Westminster, Md.: Newman Press, 1953), Vol. IV, pp. 45–123, and especially pp. 90–123.

18. Oswald Schwartz, *The Psychology of Sex* (Baltimore: Penguin Books, 1949), p. 47.

19. Harold T. Christensen, "Cultural Relativism and Premarital Sex Norms" in Robert W. Roberts, *The Unwed Mother* (New York: Harper & Row, 1966), p. 65.

20. John Bowlby, *Child Care and Growth in Love* (Baltimore: Penguin Books, 1953), and *Deprivation of Maternal Care* (Geneva: World Health Organization, 1962).

POINTS FOR DISCUSSION

1. Discuss the ethical problems of birth control inside marriage: (a) in an overpopulated society, (b) in an underpopulated society, (c) in general.

2. What subsidiary obligations can be derived from the obligation to use sex for growth and with respect for both society and other persons?

3. What would ethics say of necking, petting, and sex play short of intercourse?

4. What social changes would make marriages more stable and contribute to people's observing sexual ethics?

5. Discuss the reasons people give for their unethical sexual conduct.

READINGS*

Robert R. BELL, *Premarital Sex in a Changing Society* (Englewood Cliffs, N.J.: Prentice-Hall, 1966).

William C. BIER (ed.), Marriage: *A Psychological and Moral Approach* (New York: Fordham University Press, 1965).

Richard F. HETTLINGER, *Living with Sex: The Student Dilemma* (New York: Seabury Press, 1966).

"Sexuality and the Modern World: A Symposium," *Cross Currents,* 14 (1964), Spring No. 2, pp. 130–269.

* In addition to the books and articles mentioned in the notes, these should prove useful.

12/ SOCIETY IN GENERAL

INTRODUCTION

The social dimension of man's existence is different from the area of interpersonal relations, though obviously the two are related. Social relations are, in general, more impersonal, although the movement from interpersonal relationships to almost mechanical organizations is so gradual that it is often difficult to see when one is dealing with a society rather than with the interpersonal sphere. The family is almost like a bridge between the two areas, since it is at once highly personal and characterized also by some structures which are group phenomena. In the present chapter we shall not give a great deal of attention to the family and to communities or primary groups. While these groups are of crucial importance, it is the problems of the secondary groups, such as political society, universities, unions, and big business corporations which are the source of the greatest confusion. For this reason, we have contented ourselves with developing general notions which will be useful for discussing problems in secondary groups. While the same notions can sometimes be applied to communities, this should be done with great care, since the differences are as important as the similarities.

NEED FOR THE GROUP

Man cannot exist as man outside human groups. Even the hermit, who might seem to be autonomous, is subject to this necessity. In the first place, he takes with him into solitude all the gifts of all the groups of which he was a part in his early life. In the second place, the vast majority of would-be hermits continue to make at least sporadic raids on the treasures developed by the groups of which they do not want to be a part. As we pointed out in an earlier chapter, the few examples we have of true isolates—the so-called wild children—confirm the thesis, for where these individuals have lived apart from all society they have not developed into what we understand as normal human beings.

The social need of man appears most clearly in the case of the human child. Unlike the young of so many other species, he depends on others for a long period of years. It is not merely a question of the group supplying the child with food, clothing, medicine, and protection, but also of its giving him emotional support and all the knowledge which he needs to survive as an adult. Lacking the instincts and most of the chemically transmitted information which other species have, man is, and remains, dependent on the information and skills gathered and transmitted by groups.

This dependence is almost as true of adults as it is of children. The whole history of civilization has been a history of man's ability to cooperate with others for the attainment, or at least the easy attainment, of those things necessary for humanity but beyond the power of isolated individuals. Nearly all our institutions and instruments of culture are social. Speech, technology, libraries, schools, and churches are the more obvious examples. Where one or more of these products of group life is missing, the individual is stunted, if not destroyed, by a hostile environment.

Man's ability to escape the limits of his environment is also the result of social cooperation. The division of labor has been, and will remain forever, a necessary condition of human progress. Indeed, it is in proportion as economic cooperation has resulted in greater efficiency that man has had a chance to be a man and not merely a gatherer of food, balanced precariously on the edge of mere biological survival.

Even a cup of coffee on the breakfast table is the result of cooperation so far flung and so complex that the imagination cannot comprehend all the threads in the social network involved. The transport systems of two continents, the banks, the chemists, the agronomists, the metallurgists, as well as wholesalers, retailers, processers and salesmen are involved. Each of these individuals in his turn is supported in his work by another network which stretches out beyond the imagination. The same is true of nearly everything we use and of nearly every idea that enters our head.

Man is obliged to take a part in group life, for outside it he cannot be a man. It is not merely a question of the survival of the individual, but also of his obligations to other men. Without group life, our *response* to the needs of humanity must remain either narrow or ineffective. Even if all of us were endowed with perfect good will and infinite knowledge, we would still need group life in order to discharge our responsibilities and to realize our own potential.

Earlier in this book, we called attention to factors which make social life a necessity for men. Without societies, men would resort to force as a means of settling disputes. More important, men need society if they are to express their love to the widest possible group of men. As we have pointed out, there are many obligations that the individual cannot fulfill except by working for the formation of a group which has the collective power to promote the necessary good or eliminate a serious evil. Our remarks on love should also make it clear that we need group life in community if our needs for emotional support, intimacy, and personal recognition are to be met. A rereading of chapters on obligation, rights, love, the expression of love, and sexuality should reinforce the conclusion that groups are necessary for human life.

TYPES OF GROUPS

Man needs group life. Some groups, though not necessary, are extremely useful to the individual. As a result, there is a great variety of societies, some of them unorganized and informal and others organized and highly structured. The informal embraces the ethnic groups, social classes, neighborhood committees and, to a certain extent, what we may call the general society in a nation or area. The organized groups include not only such necessary and natural societies as families and the state but also a large number of associations such as corporations, fraternal groups, labor unions, schools, and religious orders. Some groups, though they are associations from a historical point of view, become so necessary in a given society that they may almost be classified as semi-natural societies. Our public utilities and some of our larger corporations would seem to fall into this classification. Other societies, such as the family, seem to have lost some of their functions over the course of time. The American family is no longer a primary unit of economic production, though it remains the basic unit for economic consumption. As a result, the American family no longer has the same significance as it did a hundred years ago. Points like this must be kept in mind, since such changes can modify the obligations of parents and children.

For the present we shall concentrate largely on the nature of society insofar as it is necessary for human development, leaving to another book the treatment of the problems which arise from the relationship of individuals to associations for merely useful ends, and of such associations to the necessary societies.

NEEDS AND PURPOSES

In the thought of nineteenth-century political liberalism, the attention of thinkers was focused largely on the political society as a protector of individual rights and of internal security. Society was viewed largely as a negative means of advancing public prosperity or the individual welfare. The reason for this was simply that the individual and the public welfare were supposed to result from the free play of competitive forces, so long as the state prevented anyone from getting the upper hand. In fact government was viewed largely as a necessary evil and not as a creative force. This type of thinking tended to obscure the positive function not only of political society but of societies in general. The good of society, for many thinkers, was only the sum of individual goods; and its immediate goal, the protection of the freedom of those who had fixed rights.

Factually, however, societies are necessary not only for the negative function of protection but for the positive function of promotion. Furthermore, both functions require cooperation, since neither the good of the individual nor that of the society is guaranteed by any automatic process. The brief examples given in the introduction to this chapter illustrate this clearly. Any serious attempt to study the actual functioning of existing societies can only confirm the conclusion.

Even a family is more than the sum of the individual goods of its members. There are things which belong to the family as such, no matter where the legal title may reside. The home, its furnishings, its atmosphere, belong to the group, for they have been created by the cooperative efforts of the group. In our political society, the currency system, the fire department, and the educational system are in the possession of the groups as such, and not of individuals. They did not come about as a result of merely searching for one's individual benefit, but by cooperation in view of needs which could not be satisfied by any private individual or a chance combination of private individuals.

The cooperative nature of society distinguishes it from a mob milling in the streets, or from a crowd at a ball game. A society is not a mere aggregate of human beings, it is a group characterized by a willingness to work together. It has a certain unity of action in view of the goal of cooperation. Mere cooperation for a goal does not make a group into a society. A customer freely exchanges his money for the goods offered by a storekeeper. We do not, however, refer to a storekeeper and his customers as a society, since each of them seeks directly only his own personal good. The shopkeeper and his customers do not exhibit a unity of action.

The members of a society cooperate for a common or social good. They unite to produce something which, though it can and should benefit all members in some way, belongs immediately to the group itself. The currency system, the fire department, and the army are not private possessions. They are produced by cooperation, belong to the group, and in some way benefit all members. The same can be said of the family-owned house, the morale of a team, and the reputation of a school.

We may call a society a group of persons working together for a common good. It is more than the sum of its members, but it is not a substance or a being which exists for itself. A society involves a set of relationships between members and a unity of intention, whether implicit or explicit. The common good is not the society, but it does manifest its presence and nature. It is the purpose of the society, but ultimately it is only a means to the perfection of its members. For this reason, as we shall see, the individual is not purely and simply subordinated to the groups of which he is a member.

THE COMMON GOOD

The common good is not a single good but an ordered complexus of particular goods, each one of which bears the three characteristics mentioned above. The police force, the fire department, the road system, the currency system, the legal regulations of a city, all pertain to its common good. What constitutes the concrete common good of a society depends on the needs of the members and on their purposes in organizing the society. There is, in short, no possibility of an exhaustive concrete definition of the common good in general, or even of the common good of a given society. This should surprise no one, for new needs develop in time, and these, too, will pertain to the common good. In times past, we may have considered medical services as something involving only a personal relationship between a doctor and a patient. Today, however, we know that we cannot have good medical services without broader social cooperation. Since the general level of health and hygiene affects every man in a given society, the medical services can be considered as a part of the common good. Today we see the educational system as a vital part of the common good, where once it may have been looked at as a private luxury for a select few.

These warnings are necessary, for many people object to the common good on the ground that it is an empty phrase used to justify every sort of tyranny. Often their charge is justified, but this is so only because men have avoided the hard work necessary to determine what does pertain to the social good of a given society.

The social good is an *ordered* complexus in two ways. First, it is ordered ultimately to the good of all members of a society. Secondly, the ultimate ordination demands that the parts be balanced in view of the true function of a society. A society rich in roads but poor in schools is far from having established a true common good. A society in which it is easy to buy a car and difficult to get adequate medical attention has failed to observe the hierarchy of values and principles of urgency which are as necessary in social as in individual life. It is not an easy task to determine the correct balance, for needs and resources change. What must be avoided is the effort to settle the correct balance once and for all, since this will render society unable to meet the dynamic purposes with which it must deal.

These few paragraphs should make it clear that the purely formal notions developed in this chapter cannot be applied without the most intensive research into needs and into the concrete structures of individual societies. For lack of such research, social ethics can become a sterile, rationalistic, *a priori* exercise, leading to complacency rather than to really practical ethical norms for concrete men and groups.

The nature of the common good of any society imposes obligations on both the individual member and the society itself. The society cannot exist without cooperation and the contributions of its members. The member, then, has an obligation to contribute as long as he remains a member. In those cases where membership is necessary to fulfill basic obligations, the contributory obligation can be considered absolute. The obligation is not, of course, unlimited, even when it is unconditional. A man's rights and talents and the concrete nature of the common good must all be considered in deciding on the exact nature of the obligation. This point will be considered more fully when we discuss the limits of authority in a society.

If the individual must contribute to the society, the society must distribute to its members. A society and its goods are ultimately justified only if all the members benefit from their cooperative efforts. Thus distribution is, in some way, an essential part of the social good. A society which has a huge gross national product while half its people live in poverty has not attained its goal. The wealth of the society has not been so distributed that all men can satisfy their basic needs. To put it another way, the common good has not been so structured that it serves its ultimate goal, the perfection of individuals.

Distribution demands structure and balance, not only at the present moment but with regard to the future. If the present distribution of goods destroys the society or makes it impossible to satisfy the needs of future generations, the common good has not been realized. Any ethic of distribution, then, must be constructed so that it does not lead to "killing the goose that lays the golden eggs." In practice, this means that the society must consider not only the needs of its members but their contributions. If we distribute only on the basis of need, men will feel that their contributions are not recognized and may reduce their contributions. On the other hand, if distribution considers only contributions to the society, many will be left destitute through no fault of their own. In practice, the ethics of distribution must deal with the tension between present and future, as well as the tension between need and contribution.

Because contribution must be considered, the distribution of goods can never be perfectly equal. Yet we must recognize the fact that some goods are so essential that all men have a right to them. Thus, all have a right to equal protection of the laws. All men need food, clothing, and shelter. To deny men access to these basic goods would be unjust, and at odds with the purpose of society. On the other hand, not all individuals need or can profit from a college education or a personal aeroplane. Society can justly distribute such useful goods unequally as a reward for contribution.

In practice, the way in which goods are distributed has important ethical implications. A society which distributed all goods directly to its members might end up by crippling initiative and killing the cooperative spirit. Experience indicates that a society operates best when it provides its members with the opportunity to satisfy their own needs. It is better to create jobs than to hand out alms. It is better to create a climate of order in which men can live securely than to provide every man with a gun. Such indirect distribution not only encourages initiative but creates freedom and encourages men to develop themselves.

We must recognize the fact that not all individuals in a society can take advantage of the opportunities created. A free public college is meaningless to the boy who is so poor that he must work in order to support his mother. The fact that a factory needs workers does not create an opportunity for the man who is badly crippled, or one who lives so far from the factory that he cannot afford the cost of transportation. The aged poor may not be in a position to exercise any initiative. In the case of such individuals, society may have an obligation to distribute directly in order to satisfy basic needs.

In the American society there is a tendency to judge both needs and contribution in monetary terms. This can be extremely unrealistic. People are motivated by status, prestige, pride in workmanship, and a desire to serve as well as by dollars and cents. After a man has reached a certain level of comfort, his primary motives for making greater contributions are often humanistic rather than purely economic. If this fact is recognized, we can increase our sense of social responsibility and humanize our society without fear of destroying the economic underpinnings.

Contribution cannot really be measured in dollars and cents for a variety of reasons. Nearly everything we produce is the result of complicated social cooperation. It is almost impossible to disentangle the contributions of the various agents. Who can say how much of a given student's education is due to a particular teacher? how much of his education was due to fellow students, principals, alumni, parents, or a guidance counselor? We do not really know the exact contribution of each. We cannot measure the contributions, yet we are sure that each of these factors had an important effect on the student.

Even inside a business, with its elaborate methods for assigning costs and productivity increases, who can actually say how much of the product is due to the worker, the accountant, the maintenance man, the washroom attendant, the schools who supplied the workers, and the society which supplied roads, police protection, and a currency system? The more one studies a given group, the more doubtful one becomes about making any real objective assignment of contributions. The very difficulty of making the assignment has often caused many areas of social life to degenerate into power struggles. where the rewards go to the strong and ruthless rather than to the contributors.

Men dream of a day when the problem of distribution will be solved because society has such resources that not only the needs but also the desires of all men can be easily satsified. We shall never see the utopia for several reasons. Need grows with satisfaction. When we have been freed from worry about food and shelter, we allow ourselves to feel the need for beauty and knowledge. No man has ever quenched a fully developed thirst for knowledge. Even on the material level, the revolution of rising expectations shows us how exposure to a higher standard of living stimulates the desire of men. For all practical purposes, then, we shall always have to face the tensions involved in distribution.

AUTHORITY

The necessity of balance and of practical decisions as to the relationship between production and contribution should be obvious. This problem, however, is only one aspect of the more basic social problem. Cooperation, whether in production or in distribution, is not automatic. Even if all men were wise and endowed with great good will, effective cooperation would not be automatic. There is no accurate norm in nature itself which assigns position and decides all disputes. Since society cannot exist without such assignments and decisions, it must have a right to accomplish these tasks. This right grows out of the need of society and ultimately out of the needs of its members.

If we gather nine men together to play baseball and all of them were equally competent and determined to win the ball game, there would still be no automatic way of deciding who should play each position. If the ball game is to start, there must be an exercise of authority either by an individual or a group. In practice, they would probably elect a captain and allow him to assign positions. They might not see any particular virtue in the man they elect, but they would see the need for some method of assigning positions. They might also assign positions by drawing lots or tossing a coin. In any event, they would have to agree on some method of exercising the authority of the group.

Unless one sees clearly that authority springs from a need which does not necessarily have anything to do with the malice or ignorance of the members, there is a temptation to view it as a necessary evil rather than a necessary good. Authority is a substitute for consensus, when there is no clear basis for consensus or no easy way of arriving at universal agreement. Because it enables societies to function and individuals to grow, authority is an instrument of the greatest importance.

In many societies there is a second set of needs which makes authority necessary. Thus, in a family, the fact that children do not know enough to guide their own lives intelligently makes it necessary to have the parents act as authorities and teachers. In several societies the fact that some citizens are malicious and not respectful of the rights of others makes it necessary to have coercive authority which enforces at least a minimum of external conformity. However, neither educational nor coercive authority is of the essence of authority itself. Indeed these two functions of authority aim at their own abolition. The parent who does not educate his child to make intelligent and informed choices fails. So too, civil government fails unless it tries to remedy more than harmful external activities. Because educational and coercive authority are supposed to be temporary, at least with regard to a given individual, they are not the essence of authority, but only substitutes for the wisdom and virtue which some members lack.

When people confuse essential and substitutional authority, real injustices can result. Paternalism, or the exercise of substitutional authority over mature and reasonably virtuous adults, shows a lack of respect for human dignity. University authorities who try to regulate the private lives of students can be guilty of this. Parents who treat grown sons and daughters like children fall into the same error. Unfortunately, the attempt to overextend substitutional authority can lead to contempt for authority in general. Holders of authority should examine the basis and limits of their rights, lest they weaken society's ability to coordinate action in view of the common good.

THE LIMITS OF AUTHORITY

The right of a group to direct its members to the goal is not unlimited. It is conditioned by the purpose of the particular society, the character of its members, and the rights of both members and other societies. In a natural or involuntary society such as the state, the authority may ethically demand only such useful goods and services as are necessary or highly useful for the common good. If the authority seeks to exact more, it will be frustrating the ultimate goal of the society, the perfection of all individuals. It is just to impose food rationing when there is a shortage, since only in this way can all have some assurance of minimum nourishment. It would be wrong to impose rationing when there is plenty of food available. In this second case, the freedom of citizens would be curbed without reason. In some societies, the rights of the authority holder may be either increased or decreased by constitutional provision, or by the agreement of the members. Constitutional limits are extremely important, since they not only make it clear who has what authority, but prevent abuses of authority.

Substitutional authority is limited by the rights of the individual and by his degree of maturity and virtue. A father does not have the same authority over an eighteen-year-old son, as he does over a six-year-old child. In particular, substitutional authority must be exercised reasonably—that is to say, it should not unreasonably interfere with the individual's pursuit of necessary and useful goods. In practice, this reasonableness should be demonstrated rather than assumed, since if the authority appears to be arbitrary, it will not be able to attain its goal.

In our own times, it is often difficult to determine the limits of authority in a given society, since constitutional and contractual provisions modify the authority of even natural societies such as the family and the civil state. Thus, though the state may have the right to censor in certain circumstances, the United States Constitution denies this authority to the Federal Government. Similarly, though ethics would tend to limit authority to what is necessary or highly useful for the common good, many societies appear to have agreed, at least tacitly, to allow the government authority over areas of the merely useful. It is for this reason, among others, that government power grows rapidly and private groups, such as corporations, assume more and more control over the private lives of members. While there is no ethical problem when members freely give a truly voluntary association more authority, the trend can be dangerous when the society is one to which a man has to belong whether he likes it or not. For this reason, more careful thinking about the limits of natural and semivoluntary or involuntary associations is very necessary.

The basic abuse of authority involves the use of the power destined to support the common good for purely personal goals, or for the purely private benefit of private groups. For example, a tariff which protects violin makers at the expense of American consumers is abusive, since violin makers are in no way necessary for the common good. On the other hand, a tariff which protects an industry vital to the defense of the nation is quite justified, even though consumers may have to pay higher prices for the products of this industry. So, too, in a family, the parent who arranges things for his own convenience rather than for the good of the entire group is really abusing his authority.

THE LOCATION OF AUTHORITY

Because authority arises from the need of the group, it belongs to the group. At the same time, it cannot generally be exercised effectively by the group. As a result, society has found it necessary to designate certain individuals as holders of authority. The authority, however, does not belong originally to the king, the president, the father; *it belongs to the group.* The need which gave rise to the authority was the need of the society. As a result, the right which is authority springs from and belongs to the group. We are not concerned with the origin of authority, but with determining who legitimately exercises authority in the name of the group. This is extremely important, since when there is doubt about who holds the authority, the authority itself cannot direct citizens effectively to the common good.

In the history of the West, various theories have been proposed to explain how legitimate rulers are designated. Some believed that God himself designated the ruler. This, however, is rather an impractical theory, since there have been no signs since early biblical times that God has designated anyone. Even the Roman Catholic Church has always used human instruments for the selection of a pope, though his authority come from God once he is elected.

Others have appealed to the patriarchal theory and held that nature itself designates the ruler in virtue of his outstanding qualifications for the job. Such a theory might be tenable in a small society. In a family it is obvious that only the father and the mother are capable of ruling, at least while the children are minors. In larger societies, nature does not seem to give any clear superiority to any one individual. As a result, the patriarchal theory is of little use in these cases. In between the large and the small societies, there occur groups in which the exercise of authority is so hooked up with special competence that the authority would appear to belong necessarily to those who have the special knowledge and skills required. In college, for example, only a person competent in French literature can properly decide what should go into a course in French literature. Moreover, since no one man is generally a master of an entire field, such decisions probably belong to the competent members of the French department. In such situations, the patriarchal theory seems to have application, though in a modified form.

The most common theory holds that the consent of the governed, whether explicit or implicit, legitimizes the holder of authority in a civil society. This theory has the advantage of being flexible enough to cover all forms of government from a hereditary monarchy to a democracy. In addition, it can explain the legitimacy of authority which was actually usurped in time past. Finally, it provides a means of determining the conditions for the just withdrawal of authority on the part of the society.

The theory of popular consent has some interesting implications. If a society can withdraw authority from an individual completely, it can certainly withdraw it in part. Thus, if some of the authority in a corporation comes from the consent of the workers, the workers may modify the authority and the rights of management. To the extent that the authority of a university president is legitimized by the consent of student and faculty, as well as by the vote of the trustees, professors and students can, under certain conditions, withdraw or modify the authority that they have consented to.

MULTIPLE SOURCES OF AUTHORITY

At the present time, there is considerable confusion about the nature and limits of authority in what we may call complex societies. For example, a school is first an instrument of the larger society, an instrument of the parents, and, in some cases, an instrument of the church, but secondly it is also a society. As a result, some of the authority in the school is authority delegated by the parents, the church, or the civil society, while some arises from the very needs of society itself. While it may be neat and simple to act as if all authority in the school had come from on high— that is, from the delegating groups—this disregards the actual situation. Not all authority is in the hands of the school administration, for not everything is within their competence.

In addition, the school is not even a single society, for it is composed of sub-societies; the student body, the teaching faculty, and the administration. Each of these groups has a common good which, while subordinated to the overall good of the school, is not identical with it. As a result, when students and faculty speak of their right to have a say in the running of the school, they are not leading a revolt, but asserting that there is some authority, arising from the existence of the sub-society, which they have not delegated to the administration.

In the past, professors and students were not sufficiently organized, and so had little to say about school affairs. Increasing organization has made it possible for these subgroups to exercise their authority, and to make clear whether or not they consent to the holder of authority in the university as a whole. As subgroups come to have a greater sense of identity and improved instruments of organization, we can probably expect new shifts in the location and exercise of authority.

Something similar is found in the case of corporations, which, like the school, are composed of sub-societies. The management certainly have the authority to administer the material goods entrusted to them by owners and stockholders. In addition, the wage contract certainly grants them a definite amount of authority over the workers. Since the management is not a father who has authority over all aspects of the workers' life, the sub-society of workers retains authority over many aspects of their work life. Unless this complicated situation is recognized, authority can be abused by being overextended. This results not only in contempt for authority but in a failure of cooperative action and injury to the overall common good.

Although little has been written about the problem, difficulties also arise when one individual holds authority from two or more sources. Here, there is a danger of confusion and abuse, since the holder of authority may use power which he has in virtue of one office to enforce decisions in another area. Thus a religious superior who is also head of the school must be careful, lest he use his right to command religious obedience in one area to give illegitimate commands in another. So too, the teacher must remember that he cannot legitimately use his authority in the classroom to get action in an extracurricular activity in his care.

THE RELATIONSHIPS OF SOCIETIES

The existence of sub-societies on a large scale makes necessary the development of a theory covering the relationship of these groups. Unfortunately, our theory in this area is as yet quite crude.

What we may call the classic theory relies on the principle of subsidiarity. This principle states that a higher society should not do what a lower society can do as well or better. It implies, obviously, that a society should not do what an individual can do as well or better. It is an attempt to delimit the areas of authority in accord with need and competence. It has two faces. It implies an obligation not to interfere with individuals and lower groups unless this is necessary. But it also implies an obligation to coordinate the efforts of individuals and groups when this is necessary for the purposes of the larger society.

Subsidiarity assumes that, all other things being equal, those who are closest to a problem have the greatest interest in solving it. It also acknowledges the value of freedom and the need to protect it by having many relatively autonomous centers of initiative and power. Because subsidiarity leaves room for initiative and the exercise of responsibility it can promote the growth of leaders and so contribute to the overall movement of society. This principle is very useful. However, unless we work out more exact criteria for its application, it can merely obscure the problems or turn into a slogan used indiscriminately by all parties.

Those who developed the principle assumed that the higher society had the power as well as the right to coordinate the efforts of others. In fact this assumption is not always verified. Local communities are often less powerful than corporations located within them. Managers and administrators often find that they lack the power to enforce their legitimate commands. The existence of such factual situations serves to confuse the areas of legitimacy. Often the situation leads to substitution of might for right. For these reasons, the development of criteria is imperative.

In practice, the sub-criteria are often written into constitutions which attempt to specify areas of competence and to distribute power so that no subgroup may have the upper hand and so that the higher society has enough power for its legitimate purposes, but not enough for tyranny. Constitutionalism, though widespread in the political order, has not been fully developed in other areas, with the result that the relationships between many societies are still matters of power.

Many of the most crucial social problems are not concerned with the relations of higher and lower societies, but with the horizontal relationships of groups having approximately the same functions. The relationships between corporations, unions, universities, and interest groups pose difficult ethical problems. As particular groups grow more powerful, the problems grow more acute, for power can be substituted for principle. Should one corporation be allowed so much power that it can swallow up all its competitors? Should a single university in a state be given so much financial assistance that it can monopolize the best professors and students? These questions touch not only on the rights of groups but on the relation of private power centers to the common good. While we cannot attempt to answer them here and now, the reader should be aware that we have not evolved any completely satisfactory answer to questions of this sort.

AUTHORITY AND UNITY

Authority is supposed to insure necessary coordination and unity of action. Its ability to do so, however, depends on the existence of certain attitudes and institutions. This is true in families as well as in international organizations. If authority lacks the proper human foundation, its moral and juridical roots will soon decay.

In the first place, there must be at least a minimal agreement about the goals and values. Though a society can tolerate, and should tolerate, discussion and dispute about means, it will be paralyzed, if not destroyed, if there is widespread disagreement about ends. This means that both society and its authorities must be vitally concerned with some minimum of ultimate values which are, at least in the short run, held by the vast majority. In addition, no society can function unless the members have a fairly high degree of confidence that authority will act for the common good. Furthermore, members must feel that their fellows will cooperate in attaining their common goals. Thus, the regularization of expectations and the enforcement of controls and agreements become vitally important for the society as a whole.

Cooperation depends on communication, with the result that societies have a large stake in protecting the channels of both information and value formation. Without an adequate communication structure, either chaos or distrust will result.

For all these reasons, modern societies are rightfully concerned not only with traditional problems such as lying, breach of contract, and fidelity to promises but with the maintenance of discussion and the increased flow of ideas. It is no accident, then, that we hear increasing demands for discussion, dialogue, and communication, both up and down in the hierarchy of authority. The demands spring from the increasing realization that a society cannot operate, and much less operate justly, without these mechanisms.

THE GIANT TASK OF ETHICS

Since increasing areas of human life are bound up with societies and faced with new needs that the individual cannot meet in isolation, social ethics becomes increasingly important. At the same time, it becomes increasingly difficult. Not only are the societies more complex, but the data which must be used are more numerous. Economics, business, sociology, political science, psychology, history, geography, and even linguistics are necessary tools if the ethician is to tackle real problems with real competence. Unless the thinker knows the reality to which his principles must apply, he can miss the mark and find his work regarded as a mere curiosity.

Like everything in this book, the last sentence assumes that ethics is not only practical but creative—and as a result, supplies us with more questions than answers. Some may want to quibble with this. Let them. If these assumptions are not true, then ethics is the only science which is free of the demands of rapidly changing reality and of man's greater consciousness of his need for new adjustments and new rational guidance.

POINTS FOR DISCUSSION

1. Describe and analyze the common good of a particular university, a fraternal order, and a large business corporation.
2. What contributions are demanded by each group in number one? What distributions are made and how?
3. What are the ethical limits on the authority of each group?
4. Whence does a university or a corporation get its authority?
5. Analyze the relations between federal, state, and local governments in terms of subsidiarity.

READINGS

Robert N. BECK (ed.), *Perspectives in Social Philosophy: Readings in Philosophic Sources of Social Thought* (New York: Holt, Rinehart & Winston, 1967).

Whitaker T. DEININGER, *Problems in Social and Political Thought* (New York: Macmillan, 1965).

YVES R. SIMON, *Philosophy of Democratic Government* (Chicago: University of Chicago Press, Phoenix Books, 1951).

Joseph TUSSMAN, *Obligations and the Body Politic* [New York: Oxford University Press, 1960).

Robert Paul WOLFF (ed.), *Political Man and Social Man: Readings in Political Philosophy* (New York: Random House, 1960).

INDEX

Abernathy, Glenn, 129
Abortion, 209–213, 238
  direct, 214
  indirect, 214
Abstinence from sexual activity, 227
Adler, Mortimer, 96, 104
Affectivity, *see* emotion
Allers, Rudolph, 228, 242
Allport, Gordon W., 135, 155
Alternates, 68, 75, 99, 114, 152
American Law Institute, 212, 220
American Medical Association, 212, 220
Aristotle, 22, 37, 43, 45, 47, 58
Associations, 247, 256
Atheists, 11, 37
Authority, 116, 124, 254–260
  abuse, 257
  coercive, 255
  essential, 255
  holders of, 257, 259–260
  limits of, 255–257

  location, 257–260
  multiple sources of, 259–260
  substitutional, 256
Autoerotic, 227, 237
Ayer, Alfred Jules, 59

Bad example, 188–190, 207, 239–240
Baker, Herschel, 39
Beck, Robert N., 263
Bell, Robert R., 243
Bergler, Edmund, 231, 242
Bertocci, Peter A., 85, 105
Bier, William C., 243
Birth control, 225, 230, 238, 241
Body, 26–27, 200–221
  and soul, 202
Bowlby, 158, 177, 243
Brinkley, Luther J., 14
Brown, Roger W., 155

Capital punishment, 108, 205, 209–210, 216–217

Casey, David J., 84
Causal influence, 69, 75, 81
Chirico, Peter, 242
Choice, 61–81, 98, 151
Christensen, Harold T., 243
Circumstances, 82
Civil rights, 122
Code ethics, 11, 38, 79
Cognitivists, 10
Commitment, 53, 99, 160, 167–168, 184
Common good, 153, 216, 249–253, 257, 259, 262
Communication, 159, 180, 235, 262
Community, 164
    categories, 143
    norms, 142
Conflict of interest, 123
Conformity, 140–141
Conscience, 130–155, 193, 224
    selective, 131
Conscientious objector, 154
Consensus, 254
Consent, 258
Constitutions, 256, 261
Contraception, 227; *see* Birth control
Contracts, 187, 256
Contribution, 253–254
Cooperation in evil, 188, 190–193
Criteria, 43, 61
Cross Currents, 242
Cultural, universal, 16–18
Culture, influence of, 1, 17–19, 22, 25, 29, 32–33, 35, 57, 72, 75, 92, 102, 116–117, 130, 140, 160, 209, 245

Custom, *see* Law, 111, 113, 120, 125, 222

D'Arcy, Eric, 156
Davitt, Thomas E., 60, 104–105
Death, 27, 200, 202
De Entreves, A. P., 60
De Finance, Joseph, 85
Definition in ethics, 33–34, 209–210
Deininger, Whitaker, T., 264
De Jouvenel, Bertrand, 129
Distribution, 251, 254
    indirect, 252
Doubt, 130, 147–149

Edel, Abraham, 40
Edel, May, 40
Emotion, 98, 134–137, 151, 160, 181–184, 222
Emotional blackmail, 195
End, 67
End of man, 76
Epicureans, 58
Equality, 117–118, 122
Erikson, Erik H., 133, 155, 158, 177, 232, 242
Ethical categories, 141–142, 202
    evil (moral), 70
    good, 78
    judgments, 33
    man, 79
    obligation, 91
    without qualification, 78
    restricted sense, 76
    scepticism, 4–6
    systems, 9, 11, 33, 37–38, 55–58, 82–83, 100–104, 200

Ethics, 1–9
  applied, 3
  and law, 3–4
  special, 109
Evil
  cooperation, 190–193
  lesser, 122
  major, 71, 80
  minor, 71
  quasi-absolute, 218
Exceptions to general rules, 206–207, 210, 239
Existence in time, 52

Fagothey, Austin, 84
Family, 238, 244, 247–248
  monogamous, 230
First amendment, 117
Fletcher, Joseph, 60, 174, 178, 221
Flood, Peter, 242
Force, *see* Power, 103, 120–122, 215, 246, 261
Ford, Clellan S., 242
Frankena, William K., 14
Freedom, 25, 27, 35, 55, 65, 83, 87, 91, 95–101, 122, 124, 256
  circumstantial, 96–100
  collective, 96, 99
  limited, 25
  political, 96, 99–100, 126
  self-determination, 96, 98
  self-perfection, 96, 98, 100
  self-realization, 101
Fromm, Erich, 158, 177, 232, 242
Fuchs, Josef S.U., 60

Full-development of man, 56, 173–174
Functions, 119

Garrett, Thomas M., 84
Gelhorn, Walter, 129
Girvetz, Harry K., 156
God, 21–22, 24, 47–53, 55–57, 62, 82–83, 89–90, 101–103, 157, 169, 173–176, 201, 203, 205–206, 216–217
Good, 41–60, 62, 86, 91
  befitting, 82
  as end, 43–46, 57–58
  existence, 45, 49
  extrinsic, 82
  as function, 43
  instrumental, 82
  intrinsic, 59, 82
  means, 43–44, 51–52
  necessary, 72, 74
  pleasurable, 82
  useful, 72–74, 82
  value, 58
Grotius, 102
Group morality, 138, 141
Growth, 19, 21, 26, 62–63, 72, 74, 79, 97, 99, 132–134, 152, 168, 173, 182, 202, 225, 235
  in love, 168
Guitton, Jean, 178, 235, 242

Habit, 101
Happiness, 58
Hare, R. M., 59
Harper, 236, 242
Henry, Andrew F., 221
Hettlinger, Richard F., 243

Hierarchy, *see* Priorities, 42, 46, 49, 55, 69–70, 73, 75, 142
and constellation of rights, 109
of goods, 91
Higgins, Thomas J., 85
Hobbes, 102
Homosexual, 227, 236–237
Hudson, Edward G., 128

Ideal, 16, 21–25, 46, 52, 63–64, 73, 93, 99, 118, 145, 172, 177, 228
Ignorance, 54, 68, 144–147, 189
culpable, 146
indeliberate, 144
Illegitimacy, 238
Immortality, 27–28
Impersonality, 170
Instincts, 61
Institutionalized children, 238
Intellect, 130–155
Interpersonal relations, 157–179, 224, 231, 244
Interuterine ring, 227
Involvement in evil, 190

Johann, Robert, 178
Johnson, F. Ernest, 14
Jones, Howard Mumford, 129
Jones, W. T., 14
Justice, 166, 175, 185–188, 194, 198

Kant, 11, 57–58, 102–103
Kardiner, Abram, 236, 242
Kiley, W. Paul, 40
Killing, 17
Kirkendall, Lester A., 232, 242
Kluckhohn, Clyde, 39

Knowledge, 45, 83, 130, 144, 157, 181, 184
ethical, 6–8, 31–38, 53, 132–135
subjective side, 35–36

Law, 3, 103, 111, 113, 115, 120, 123, 132, 142, 148, 237, 252
Leclercq, Jacques, 14, 84
Lee, Dorothy, 40
Lehmann, Paul, 60
Lepp, Ignace, 242
Lie, 142
Life in time, 200–221
value of, 202–204
Liking, 165
Lillie, William, 14
Linguistic analysts, 42, 59
Locke, 102
Loneliness, 158–160, 169
Love, 113, 157–179, 204, 233, 238
altruistic, 160
benevolent, 161–163, 166, 168–169, 174, 232
of desire, 160–161
expression of, 180–199
and justice, 185
mutual, 163
obligation, 174
paradox of, 161, 173
of self, 170–171
of self-donation, 175–177
selfish, 160
service, 166–167, 176
to be tested, 233–234
unselfish, 160, 165
Luijpen, William A., 40, 178

Man, nature of, 15–31
  creature to be made, 21
  as end, 48, 52, 57
  individual, 19–20, 29
  normal, 16–18, 30
  paradoxes, 20–31
  social nature, 30–31, 49
  species, 16–18
  theological concept, 21–22
Maritain, 14, 102, 104
Marriage, 224, 229–235, 240
  stable, 239
  teenage, 233
Maslow, Abraham H., 46, 54, 58, 85, 134, 155, 158, 177
Masturbation, 236–237
Means, 67
Menninger, Karl, 158, 177
Mercy killing, 207
Mersch, Emil, 105
Messner, Johannes, 84
Metaphysical transcendentalists, 10
Milhaven, John G., 84
Monden, Louis, S.J., 156
Moral object, 82–83
Moral sceptism, 145
Moral training, 130
Motive, 82
Mouroux, Jean, 40
Murder, 209
Mutual exploitation, 164, 174, 196

Natural law, 57, 102
Natural rights, 106–107
  types, 109
Naturalism, 10, 47, 83
Nature of man, *see* Man

Nedoncelle, Maurice, 178
Needs, 46, 55, 73–74, 118, 143, 195, 198, 250–251, 253
Non-cognitivists, 10, 42
Norm, 33

Obligation, 86–101, 198
  absolute, 90
  conflicts of, 142
  to contribute, 251
  to distribute, 252
  doubtful, 148
  general, 92
  hypothetical, 87–88
  positive, 92
  prima facie, 92
O'Donnell, Thomas J., 220
Omission, 188, 193
Ought, *see* Obligation, 36, 86

Patriarchal theory, 258
"Perfectionism," 93
Permitting of evils, *see* Risk, 70, 72
Person, 26, 29, 31–32, 35, 48–49, 53, 56–58, 82, 90, 108, 114, 116, 163, 169, 171, 173, 175, 210–211, 228
Personalism, 57
Physical evil, 70
Piaget, 139, 155
Pieper, Joseph, 129
Pierce, Albert, 220
Plato, 58
Pleasure, 61, 82
Political liberalism, 247
Political society, 247
Popular Consent, 258

Power *see* Force, 106, 108, 119–127, 153–154
Premarital intercourse, 142
Preserving life, 205, 218
Primary groups, 244
Priorities, *see* Hierarchy, 22–23, 47, 58, 62–64
Promiscuity, 227, 231, 236
Proportionality, 69–71, 74–75, 77, 81, 113, 115, 120, 144, 146, 148, 153, 161, 204–205, 215, 219
Prudential ethic, 208

Race, 108, 138, 186–187, 193–194
Reasonableness, *see* Proportionality
Respect for men, 166, 169, 175, 186
Responsibility, 25, 62, 64, 71, 75, 122, 145–146, 172, 191
Revolutions, 127
Rights, 71, 72, 80–83, 97, 106–127, 158, 175, 187, 228, 255
    conflicts of, 113
    of conscience, 151–154
    exercise of, 110, 112, 115, 121
    are inherent, 10
    to life, 110, 213
    limits of, 112
    and power, 119
    quasi-absolute, 110, 112–114, 122
    relative, 110, 115–116
Risk, 62, 65, 68–70, 74, 76, 112, 115, 119, 121, 126, 147–148, 152, 189, 191, 204, 224

Saint Augustine, 24
St. John-Stevas, Norman, 221
Saint Paul, 241
Saint Thomas, 102
Sanctions, 125
Schnackenburg, Rudolph, 178
Schneiders, Alexander A., 182, 199
Scholastic philosophers, 48
Schur, Edwin M., 221, 242
Schwartz, Oswald, 237, 243
Secondary groups, 244
Self
    false, 171–172
    ideal, 171
    true, 171
Self-actualization, 46, 55
Self-defense, 120-121, 215–216, 218
Self-developers, 54
Self-donation, 166–167
Self-interest, 109, 162
Selfishness, 170, 187
Sellin, Thorsten, 221
Seskonske, Alexander, 105
Sex, 17, 160, 168, 222–243
    biological, 225–227
    interpersonal, 228–241
    and love, 168
    social dimension, 226, 229–235, 237
Shoben, Edward Joseph, Jr., 39
Sidgwick, Henry, 14, 22, 39
Simon, Yves R., 60, 264
Situation ethics, 11, 57, 60
Sloyan, Gerard S., 156
Smith, P. H. Nowell, 59
Social responsibilities, 142

Society, 18, 30, 72–74, 109, 112, 114–116, 120–121, 123, 126–127, 131, 138, 150, 154, 173, 185, 192–193, 210, 226, 228–230, 240, 244–264
  complex, 259
  involuntary, 255
  relationships between, 260–262
  ultimate goal, 255
Soloviev, Vladimir, S., 179
Sorokin, Pitirim A., 178
Springer, Robert H., 220
State, 216
Status, 119
Stevenson, Charles L., 59
Stoics, 58
Student rights, 123, 125–126, 255, 259
Subjective, 35–36, 75, 78
Subsidiarity, 260–261
Suffering, 204
Suicide, 204–209, 213
  direct, 205
  indirect, 205
Superego, 131
Swabey, William Curtis, 14

Teleological, 56
Theology, 3, 5, 22, 24, 27, 47, 51, 57, 64, 83, 201, 204–205, 214, 223–224, 241
Thompson, Clara, 131, 155
Title, 111
Toleration of evil, 77
Toulmin, Stephen, 59
Tribal morality, 108
Tussman, Joseph, 264

Unethical, 75–76, 78
Urgency, 69, 74, 198
Utilitarians, 11, 56, 58

Values, 23, 25, 33, 41, 63
  intrinsic, 56

War, 108, 121, 140, 148, 153–154, 191, 209–210, 217
Warnock, Mary, 14
Werkmeister, William H., 85
Wheelis, Allen, 156
Wild, John, 35, 39
Wisdom ethic, 11
Wolff, Robert Paul, 264

Zink, Sidney, 85